Caricatures of Americans on the English Stage Prior to 1870

Colonel Hiram Pegler.   *Monsieur Capot.*   *Agamemnon.*

Jonathan W. Doubikin: I guess!!!   *Miss Mangelwurzel.*   *Mr O' Sullivan.*

The Characters of *Mathews in America*, 1824.
(From *The London Mathews*, Hodgson & Co., London, 1824.)
By courtesy of the British Museum.

Caricatures of Americans on the English Stage Prior to 1870

by

NILS ERIK ENKVIST

KENNIKAT PRESS, INC./PORT WASHINGTON, N. Y.

CARICATURES OF AMERICANS ON THE
ENGLISH STAGE PRIOR TO 1870

First published 1951
Reissued 1968 by Kennikat Press

Library of Congress Catalog Card No: 68-26273
Manufactured in the United States of America

CONTENTS

PREFACE 5
ACKNOWLEDGEMENTS 6

CHAPTER I. INTRODUCTION

1. Caricature in Early American Drama 9
2. Theatrical Conditions in England 16
3. American Themes on the English Stage, 1760—1824 22

CHAPTER II. THE INTRODUCTION OF HUMOROUS AMERICANS ON THE ENGLISH STAGE

1. Charles Mathews and His American Tour 27
2. »Mathews in America,» 1824 33
3. The Twenties: Echoes of Mathews. The First Frontiersman 42

CHAPTER III. SOME MINOR CHARACTERIZATIONS PRIOR TO 1833 47

CHAPTER IV. RIP VAN WINKLE 52

CHAPTER V. 1833—1839: THE ESTABLISHMENT OF A TRADITION

1. Nimrod Wildfire in England 60
2. George Handel Hill as the Yankee Peddler 66
3. Jonathans, Dutchmen, and Negroes 71

CHAPTER VI. NEGRO MINSTRELSY IN ENGLAND, 1836—1870

1. The Birth of Minstrelsy 76
2. Thomas Dartmouth Rice in England 78
3. American Character and Humour in Minstrelsy 82
4. Minstrelsy in England after Rice 87
5. Contemporary Comments 90

CHAPTER VII. THE FORTIES 94

CHAPTER VIII. THE FIFTIES

    1. Caricature in Social Comedy: *Fashion* 101
    2. Josh Silsbee as the Yankee Ploughboy 106
    3. *Uncle Tom's Cabin* 111
    4. A New Attraction: the Yankee Gal 118

CHAPTER IX. THE SIXTIES

    1. *Our American Cousin* 124
    2. Traditions Continued 131

CHAPTER X. SUMMARY AND CONCLUSIONS

    1. Summary 139
    2. Conclusions 142

APPENDIX: PLAY LIST 156

BIBLIOGRAPHY 159

INDEX 163

PREFACE

I originally conceived this study as a chapter of a work on American humour in England before Mark Twain. It attempts to cover the history of humorous American characters on the English stage between 1824 and 1870. Further, it illustrates English reactions to American humour, a field which some Victorian critics thought the only original transatlantic[1] contribution to literature, and provides examples of the contacts between the theatrical worlds of England and America during the period in question. It also sheds some light on popular taste in nineteenth-century England. From our perspective most of the materials dealt with are of low aesthetic value. It is, however, my belief that in our day, when both the beginnings of an independent American literary tradition and Anglo-American cultural contacts are topics of importance, a treatment of the present subject will not be void of interest.

The period before 1870 covers the heyday of the early type of American humour which was based on caricature rather than social problems. 1824 was the year of Charles Mathews' American entertainment, when the British general public could first get acquainted with a humorous treatment of transatlantic character. The year 1870 marks the beginning of the decade when Mark Twain's works became popular in England, and may also serve to indicate the approximate time when American social comedy eclipsed the early types of caricature humour on the stage.

It has been my aim to document my work with primary sources. This often necessitated a long and arduous search for materials.

---

[1] Throughout the present work the word »transatlantic» should be taken to mean »American.»

ACKNOWLEDGEMENTS

This study was made possible by a British Council scholarship, which enabled me to collect the material for a work on American humour in nineteenth-century England in the academic year 1949—50. The kindness and hospitality of the British Council Staff greatly contributed to make my stay in England both pleasant and profitable.

The debt of gratitude I owe Professor Ole Reuter of Helsinki University can never be adequately expressed. During the many years I have enjoyed the privilege of working under Professor Reuter's guidance as a student and a member of his Staff I have greatly profited from his friendly and kind encouragement and his unfailing interest. For the numerous helpful suggestions that had to do with the present work I offer my heartfelt thanks.

I am under an obligation to Professor C. J. Sisson of University College, London, who supervised my work in 1949—50 and gave me valuable advice. Professor Daniel Aaron, Visiting Professor of American Literature at Helsinki University in 1951—52, and Professor William P. Randel of the University of Florida, former Visiting Professor of American Literature at Helsinki University, were kind enough to go through my manuscript and suggest several improvements. Thanks are also due to Mr. Terence Spencer, B. A., of University College, London; and to my senior colleagues at Helsinki University, Mrs. Joan Rossell, M. A. (Oxon.), and Mr. James Bramwell, B. A. (Oxon.), for reading my manuscript at various stages of its development and expressing both friendly and fruitful criticisms. Miss Gloria Mandeville, M. A., of Barnard College, Columbia University, saved me valuable time by her expert knowledge of the availability of background materials and by sending me some data from London after my return to Finland.

I am indebted to Professors Gunnar Castrén, S. B. Liljegren, and Rafael Koskimies, who read my typescript after completion.

To the courtesy of the Lord Chamberlain I am indebted for access to the Lord Chamberlain's Collection of Play Manuscripts at St. James's Palace.

I should like to express my gratitude to the authorities and staffs of the libraries and collections where I gathered my material. These were: the British Museum (Main Library, Manuscript Department, Prints Department, and Newspaper Library); the University of London Senate House Library; University College Library, London; the Enthoven Collection, Victoria and Albert Museum; the Lord Chamberlain's Office; the Bodleian, Oxford; the University Library, Cambridge; the University Library, Oslo; *Carolina Rediviva*, Uppsala; *Svenska Akademins Nobelbibliotek*, Stockholm; the University Library, Helsinki; the American Institute Library of Helsinki University; the British Council Libraries in London and Helsinki; and the United States Information Service Libraries in London and Helsinki.

I am grateful to *Presses Universitaires de France* for permission to quote from Henri Bergson's *Le rire*.

I am sensible of the honour of having the present work included in the publications of the *Societas Scientiarum Fennica*.

Helsinki, Finland
September, 1951

N. E. E.

Caricatures of Americans on the English Stage Prior to 1870

CHAPTER I

INTRODUCTION

1. Caricature in Early American Drama.

Of all major forms of literature, the drama was the slowest to attain maturity in the United States. A number of causes made the worship of Thalia a comparatively late feature of American civilization. The serious religious and moral atmosphere of the intellectually dominant New-England colonies was not conducive to the encouragement of dramatic art. Direct laws and vigorous opposition from the clergy and from church-minded citizens prevented the theatre from taking its place in the community: histrionic art was condemned together with such idle pursuits as the writing and reading of fiction. Even in the Southern colonies, frequent emergencies and constant governmental problems absorbed much of the attention of the ablest thinkers and writers. Epidemics further restricted the intercourse between different communities. Later, lax copyright regulations made it easier to take over or adapt European plays than to bother about royalties and fees to indigenous authors. This did not encourage prospective or potential American playwrights. Even when, towards the end of the eighteenth century, the theatre began to be accepted as a permanent institution, there were still no signs of any original American contributions to dramatic art.[1]

---

[1] Thus, Thomas Godfrey's *The Prince of Parthia*, the first American play (written before 1763), was »Elizabethan in pattern and Oriental in subject matter» (R. E. Spiller, W. Thorp, Th. H. Johnson and H. S. Canby, eds., *Literary History of the United States* [New York, 1948], I, 185). For a general introduction to American drama, see Arthur Hobson Quinn, *A History of the American Drama from the Beginning to the Civil War* (New York, 1943), particularly Chapter XI, »American Comedy Types, 1825—60»; and Quinn, *A History of American Drama from the Civil War to the Present Day* (New York, 1936).

In his series of articles on American literature published in *Blackwood's* in 1824—25, John Neal gave the following crushing characterizations of transatlantic comedy and farce:

COMEDIES — see DRAMA. No such thing in America. One Mr. White has written two or three; but we have never seen or read them. They are spoken well of — in America.
DRAMA... Mr. Noah has written some tolerable farces, and some intolerable popular entertainments...
FARCES. About a dozen or twenty sober, childish, or disagreeable »entertainments» have been produced, in the United States of America, — by the natives — within the memory of man, we believe — under this title...[1]

The author then proceeded to say that the audience never knew »whether to laugh or cry.» Although Neal's intense preoccupation with his ego makes a present-day reader suspicious of the validity of his dicta, these passages provide an example of a literary expert's opinion of American light drama at the end of the first quarter of the nineteenth century.

But even if the literary manifestations of any original traits in American drama were slow to appear, in the field of oral folklore there were elements that were to become the basis of new stage treatments. By 1825, American folk humour was well under way to crystallizing into the patterns that are traditionally said to have assumed literary forms around 1830.[2] The reasons preventing a wholesale adoption of humorous stage Americans were now external. Such characters had sporadically been used by patriotic playwrights, but had not gained the popular appreciation which is necessary for the establishment of stock characters. It was not until after the Civil War that American comedy began to replace the early caricatures of folk types with individualized characterizations of more up-to-date representatives of the

---

[1] »American Writers,» XVI, 427 (October, 1824); XVI, 567 (November, 1824); XVII, 48 (January, 1825).

[2] »During the years between 1825 and 1831» is the statement given by Walter Blair in *Native American Humor* (New York, 1937), pp. 38—39. The almanacs, *e.g. Poor Richard's Almanac* (1732—58), greatly furthered the crystallization of the Yankee as a humorous type. The Revolutionary War precipitated the awareness of American peculiarities; the very term »Yankee» dates from this period. (*Ibid.*, pp. 17—37.) For a general introduction to American humour the reader should consult the works of Walter Blair, Constance Rourke, and Jennette Tandy listed in the bibliography of the present study. Further, see Will D. Howe, »Early Humorists» in William P. Trent *et al.* (eds.), *Cambridge History of American*

United States.¹ From the point of view of the development of American humour, the characters discussed in the present work could thus be classified as descendants of folk humour displayed through a literary medium.²

Royall Tyler's famous play *The Contrast* of 1787 was the first to employ native characters and compare them with European ones.³ The central theme of the play is the contrast between Colonel Manly, a simple, honest, straightforward American, and Dimple, a deceitful English fop. Both gentlemen are competing for the hand of an American belle. The patriotic playwright used this framework to air his ideas on the superiority of new-world virtue. Tyler clearly intended his hero to personify American national character. And for comic relief he inserted the first stage Jonathan, the prototype of the comic American, whose common sense, self-reliance, strange mixture of morals and materialism, and native humour established a new dramatic tradition.⁴

The entrance of native American humour into drama can conveniently be discussed in terms of the most important comic characters. Perley Isaac Reed, a student of the realistic presentation of American character in native American plays, summarized the development of the stage Yankee as follows:

Before 1774, there is no suggestion of the Yankee type. »There are

---

Literature, II, 148—159. An interesting account of the media that helped to spread transatlantic fun and make it popular is given in Blair, »The Popularity of Nineteenth-Century American Humorists,» *American Literature*, III, 175—194 (1931). An excellent selected bibliography is available in Blair's *Native American Humor*, pp. 163—196. Robert E. Spiller *et al.* (eds.), *The Literary History of the United States*, Vol. III (Bibliography), also contains pertinent bibliographical information.

¹ John G. Hartman, *The Development of American Social Comedy from 1787 to 1936* (Philadelphia, 1939).

² The products of the »literary humorists» of the United States, *e.g.* Artemus Ward, signify one further step away from folk traditions; they used materials and techniques borrowed from the latter, but their fun was essentially an urbane product of the artistic imagination of an individual.

³ Reprinted in Arthur Hobson Quinn's *Representative American Plays* (New York, 1917).

⁴ The fact that *The Contrast* was never performed in England may have been due to its actively anti-British tenor, which would have been strongly offensive to English audiences having the American Revolution and other Anglo-American conflicts in recent memory.

perhaps to be discovered remote hints of some of the distinctive elements which distinguish American nationality.» Before 1787, there are no satisfactory Yankee characters. Tyler's Jonathan was to some extent anticipated by Simple in *The Block-Heads* of 1776, which formed an American answer to Burgoyne's violently pro-British *The Blockade*.

The Contrast seems to have evoked some response, since Yankee characters can be found in four or more different plays between 1787 and 1789. However, there were very few characters of this type in the American drama of the next eighteen years.

Between 1805 and 1815, the Yankee can be found in at least seven plays. During this period he seems to have developed into a stage clown, and is generally less natural than in the early presentations.

From 1815 to 1829, we find the Yankee assuming his role of an accepted stock character of American comedy and farce. Although he impressed some contemporary critics as being true to life, a modern commentator would tend to call him overdrawn. From 1829 to 1845, one can find a large number of broadly caricatured Yankees. In spite of the tendency towards exaggeration, they »seem to reproduce existing persons with essential verity.»

Between 1845 and 1860, the Yankee type still preserved his popular appeal. Although »fundamentally the portrayed strongly suggests the real,» there is little change in characterization from the previous 25 years.[1] These »Yankee plays» were of great importance in the history of American drama, partly because they attracted attention outside the United States.[2]

The concept of another prominent stock character, the frontiersman, was first shaped by oral tradition. In 1822 Noah Ludlow, a comedian, sang a song called »The Hunters of Kentucky» to an audience of Mississippi flatboatmen in a New Orleans theatre.[3] Davy Crockett, that extravagant being of the Jacksonian era, became the personification of the frontier in humorous literature.[4] In the field of drama, the

---

[1] Perley Isaac Reed, *The Realistic Presentation of American Characters in Native American Plays Prior to Eighteen Seventy* (Columbus, 1918), *passim*. This study contains reference lists of Yankee and other native American characters on the American stage.

[2] Quinn, *American Drama to the Civil War*, pp. 302—3.

[3] Robert E. Spiller *et al.* (eds.), *Literary History of the United States*, II, 719.

[4] The Crockett legends grew up around the character of David Crockett, a frontier representative in Congress. See Constance Rourke, *Davy Crockett* (New York, 1934).

ferocious »half-horse, half-alligator» type, who could »whip his weight in wild-cats,» is usually said to have emerged from the legendary status of Crockett and Mike Fink[1] into the clear glare of the footlights in James Kirke Paulding's *The Lion of the West* of 1830.[2] The main character, Colonel Nimrod Wildfire, was the epitome of frontier behaviour, and the audiences generally believed him to be another of the many incarnations of Davy Crockett.[3] After 1830, we may consider the backwoodsman one of the established comic characters of nineteenth-century transatlantic drama.

Ralph L. Rusk and others have summed up the dominating character traits of typical regional representatives. Thus, frontier oratory was characterized by a specific style: the speakers defied criticism and felt free to say whatever they felt like saying; there were »unrestrained superlatives and extravagantly florid diction.» The Western frontiersman was akin to the Southerner: both were self-confident and demonstrative, and loved a florid style.[4]

Although the characters of the calculating, shrewd, noncommittal Yankee, and the impetuous, bragging, exaggerating Southern or Western hero have little in common, even purely American letters did not always keep the twain apart. The backwoodsman assumed many Yankee characteristics. Even Nimrod Wildfire's uncle was a Yankee, and Down-East shrewdness became a quality of the frontiersman as well. Similarly the Yankee often received a transfusion of Western qualities: Sam Slick could brag about his dancing and about his jumping over three horses standing side by side, and once he even confessed to be »a ring-tailed roarer.»[5] Thus, the American folk character tended to be built up as a synthesis of the two important types of the Yankee and the frontiersman.

The humorous characterization of American women closely followed that of the American male. The women could be gentle, virtuous counterparts of Colonel Manly, like the heroine of *The Contrast;* they also could be sturdy female Jonathans or Nimrod Wildfires. Thus Sally

---

[1] Mike Fink was the hero of the Mississippi flatboatmen.
[2] Quinn, *American Drama to the Civil War*, pp. 293—294.
[3] Constance Rourke, *American Humor* (New York, 1931), p. 71.
[4] *Literature of the Middle-Western Frontier* (New York, 1925), I, 204 ff.
[5] Rourke, *American Humor*, pp. 72—76.

Ann Thunder Ann Whirlwind Crockett was well versed in frontier arts, and demonstrated her muscular femininity by wearing a hornet's nest for a bonnet, adding a few wolf-tails for trimmings. For audiences conditioned to the surface decorum and etiquette of the mid-nineteenth century it was incongruous to think of women who were just as active in their love-making and bold in their approaches as their most enterprising male counterparts. This source of fun was also utilized on the stage.

The Negro had made his debut on the American stage at a far earlier period.[1] The *Robinson Crusoe* theme was used for dramatic presentations in New York in 1786 and 1817. Negro characters occurred in Murdock's *The Triumphs of Love*, which was acted in Philadelphia in 1795 (here the name of the coloured man was the standard Sambo), in *A New Way to Win Hearts*, 1802, and in *The Battle of Lake Champlain*, 1815. *Obi; or, Three-Finger'd Jack* was performed in New York about 1820 by »The African Company,» possibly a group of coloured amateur actors. A contributing factor to the vogue of the comic Negro came from a field outside legitimate drama: Negro minstrelsy. »Coon songs» had been performed on the stage as early as 1799, when Gottlieb Graupner sang »The Gay Negro Boy» at the end of the second act of *Oroonoko's* Boston performance. In 1823 Edwin Forrest sang and danced at the Globe Theatre, Cincinnati, while impersonating a Negro in Sol Smith's farce *The Tailor in Distress*.[2] In the early eighteen-thirties Thomas Dartmouth Rice, the originator of Negro minstrelsy, conceived the genre which was to provide so much entertainment on both sides of the Atlantic in years to come.[3]

Hence, the traditional concept of Negro character developed away from the noble-savage ideal towards a more humorous presentation. The coloured people were later pictured as lazy, but very excitable men and women, who spoke a peculiar dialect, were often fond of long words and malapropisms, loved gaudy dress and had their large mouths twisted

---

[1] In England, after *Othello* and Thomas Sotherne's *Oroonoko* of 1696, the latter essentially a noble-savage characterization, Isaac Bickerstaffe included a Negro called Mungo in *The Padlock*, a comic opera presented at Drury Lane in 1768. A pantomime on the *Robinson Crusoe* theme at Drury Lane, 1781, included Negro characters.

[2] Laurence Hutton, *Curiosities of the American Stage* (New York, 1891), pp. 89 ff.; Carl F. Wittke, *Tambo and Bones* (Chapel Hill, N.C., 1930), *passim*.

[3] See *infra*, pp. 76—93.

in a constant broad grin. After the topical problems of slavery directed serious idealistic attention to the status of the coloured man, Negro character regains some of its previous noble dignity in the dramatizations of *Uncle Tom's Cabin*. This did not, however, exclude the humorous aspects of the stage Negro.

The American Indian never provided equally important materials for humorous treatment. The stage versions of Cooper's novels followed the author's romantic characterizations, which followed the noble-savage ideal. Burlesques might use Indians for humorous effect, but the red man never became a stock comedian at par with the Yankee, the frontiersman, or the Negro.

Representatives of various groups of European immigrants were also included in plays to provide laughter. Washington Irving's New-York Dutchmen gained the status of minor stock characters after the dramatizations of *Rip van Winkle*. They were described as easy-going, indolent, beer-loving Teutons, and their vogue lasted for some time even after the initial interest in Irving's work had subsided. The French-American was a character of the English rather than the American stage. The later immigrants, Caucasian or Oriental, were not important enough prior to 1870 to provide prominent stock characters.

Before 1870, the American Irishman cannot be considered a native American character. He was a lineal descendant of the Teague or Larry of English comedy, and acquired no prominent new-world characteristics.

These, the Yankee, the frontiersman, the Negro, and the immigrant, were the main comic representatives of America before 1870. The American theatre of that time was an amorphous provider of entertainment undergoing a period of rapid growth. The more sophisticated audiences of the eastern centres of culture looked towards Europe with much nostalgia. Foreign themes, the more romantic the better, were more important than native ones. There was a conflict between the crudeness of native characters and the nobility and elegance of old-world people. Play titles like *The Gunmaker of Moscow*, *The Idiot of Normandy*, *The Blacksmith of Ghent*, and *The Shoemaker of Toulouse* testify to the yearning of New-York audiences for the distant in time and place. Sometimes alien themes were changed into native ones: the English play *The Purse; or, the Benevolent Tar* became *The Purse: or, the American*

Tar by the substitution of an American sailor for the British Jolly Jack.[1]

Even to the audiences in frontier areas, realistic plays on life in the West and characterizations of native character types had little appeal. Comparatively few such plays were staged, and they often failed. A number of titles of dramatic presentations of native themes have been listed,[2] but there still was a preponderance of classical and European topics on the frontier stage. Spectacle and melodrama were conditions *sine qua non* in the developing Middle West. However, the barnstormer troupes that moved freely in the frontier areas enjoying much adventure seem to have developed some independent traditions that influenced the concept of native American character.[3]

2. *Theatrical Conditions in England.*

Between 1824 and 1870 the English theatre suffered from serious maladies.[4] In the late eighteenth century commercial considerations led the proprietors of important playhouses like the Theatres Royal, Covent Garden and Drury Lane, to enlarge the sizes of their halls. Coarse, rough acting had to be substituted for the subtler techniques of the more intimate small houses. Action became more important than

---

[1] Maurice W. Disher, *Blood and Thunder* (London, 1949), p. 247.

[2] In *Literature of the Middle-Western Frontier*, I, 420—428, Rusk lists titles like the following: *Lion of the West; The Kentuckian; Nick of the Woods*, an adaptation of Bird's novel; *Daniel Boone*, performed in Cincinnati in 1824; *The Kentucky Rifle*, Louisville, 1830; *Huzzah for the Boys of the West*, Louisville, 1832; *Main Street, Louisville*, and *Life in Cincinnati*, 1836—7; *The Hoosier; or, the Yankee Outwitted*, St. Louis, 1836; *The Hunter of the West*, Cincinnati, 1837; and *The Pedlar* by Alphonso Westmore, a three-act farce, St. Louis, 1821. See also William G. B. Carson, *The Theatre on the Frontier* (Chicago, 1932).

[3] Rourke, *American Humor*, Chapter IV: »Strollers.»

[4] For more extensive background information, *e.g.* the following works should be consulted: Allardyce Nicoll, *British Drama* (London, 1949); Nicoll, *A History of Early Nineteenth Century Drama* (Cambridge, 1930); Nicoll, *A History of Late Nineteenth Century Drama* (Cambridge, 1946); Ernest Reynolds, *Early Victorian Drama* (Cambridge, 1936); H. B. Baker, *The London Stage* (London, 1886); Winton Tolles, *Tom Taylor and Victorian Drama* (New York, 1940), pp. 1—25; Errol Sherson, *London's Lost Theatres* (London, 1926); Bradlee Watson, *Sheridan to Robertson* (London, 1926); Donald Brook, *The Romance of the English Theatre* (London, 1945); and the numerous histories of individual theatres like H. Saxe-

dialogue, spectacle more attractive than art. Foreign influences stimulated the trend towards melodrama.¹

The quality of the audience had changed, too. In the first half of the century the upper and middle classes tended to avoid the theatres, which were left to noisy mobs and an added sprinkling of aristocrats of dubious morals. Howls and catcalls could disturb the progress of the plays, while throngs of prostitutes carried on their approaches in the foyers. »Penny gaffs» flourished in the East End.² The church once again condemned the theatre as a haunt of sin. It was not until after the middle of the century that the theatre regained its respectability among the middle class, which was partly due to Queen Victoria's patronage.

These circumstances and the low remuneration of playwrights caused a serious decline of dramatic standards, and kept the most prominent authors of the time from developing their playwriting talents. In a period when »Shakespeare spelt ruin, Byron bankruptcy»³ the stage was mostly left to melodrama, burlesque, and farce. Judged according to the critical standards of dramatic art, the attempts at comedy and tragedy were awkward and lifeless. The period contributed little of permanent value to the history of English drama. In the history of the English theatre, the year 1870 may serve to mark the beginning of »a truly extraordinary alteration in attitude and accomplishment,» and the end of the low period of dramatic art.⁴

In spite of the ephemeral character of most of the plays performed on the English stage between 1824 and 1870, the theatre as an institution developed much. In 1800, there were nine playhouses in London; in 1837, eighteen; in 1899, sixty-one.⁵ Along with increasing upper and

---

Wyndham, *The Annals of Covent Garden* (London, 1906); Lilian Bayliss, *The Old Vic* (London, 1925); Nigel Playfair, *The Lyric, Hammersmith* (London, 1925); W. Macqueen Pope, *Theatre Royal Drury Lane* (London, 1945); and Desmond Shawe-Taylor, *Covent Garden* (London and New York, 1948).

¹ The influences of Kotzebue, Schiller, Goethe, and Pixérecourt should be mentioned. See Nicoll, *Early Nineteenth Century Drama*, I, 78—88; and Alexander Lacey, *Pixérecourt and the French Romantic Drama* (Toronto, 1928).

² Henry Mayhew, *London Labour and the London Poor* (London, 1851).

³ Chatterton's words during his attempt to revive old glories at Drury Lane in the sixties.

⁴ Nicoll, *Late Nineteenth Century Drama*, I, 4.

⁵ For lists of theatres, see Nicoll, *Early Nineteenth Century Drama* and *Late Nineteenth Century Drama*, appendices in vols. I. The following, as of 1837, are

middle-class patronage, the expansion of the important population centres, and the improvement in communications, the number of theatres grew spectacularly in the latter half of the century. Other factors like the monopoly system dating from the reign of Charles II tended to check the free development of playhouses. The Theatres Royal, Drury Lane, Covent Garden, and the Haymarket (the latter operating under limited rights) jealously protected their old rights and won a crucial lawsuit by default. Not until 1843 did the Patent Theatres Act give the »minor theatres» a standing on equal terms with the Theatres Royal; till that time the majority of playhouses had to camouflage their plays to conform with permitted categories like that of »burletta,» mostly by adding music and a few songs.

Melodrama and farce were the types of plays *par excellence*. Lengthy stage-directions and the division of acts into numerous short scenes testify to the love of vigorous action and gaudy spectacle. German romance and the Gothic tradition gave ample materials to adapters and playwrights; where the original story did not contain sufficient quantities of blood and thunder, it was easy to change the plot or add scenes to meet the requirements. In the absence of definite regulations concerning dramatic copyright practically any source could be used as a basis of dramatization. English, French, German, and American drama was heavily drawn upon, and popular works of fiction usually found their way to the stage in suitably garbled and mutilated form. Playwriting became a craft instead of an art. Man-hunts, murders, lost documents, last-minute escapes, dark machinations of even darker villains, and other standard elements of melodrama could be added to almost any story and surrounded with appropriately eerie Gothic scenery and accompanied by suitable sound effects, preferably piercing yells and volleys of thunder. If the writer or producer was bent on a farcical effect, it was equally easy to provide the play with a few of the comic stock characters, and to bring about the necessary twists of the plot and disguises leading up to the final *dénouement*. No wonder a competent critic, George Henry Lewes, complained: »Instead of asking, 'Does the new drama brighten majestic truths in the steady

---

listed in Walter Besant (ed.), *London in the Nineteenth Century* (London, 1909), p. 17: Her Majesty's, Drury Lane, Covent Garden, Haymarket, Lyceum, Prince's (later St. James's), Adelphi, City of London (Norton Folgate), Surrey, Astley's, Queen's (later Prince of Wales's), Olympic, Strand, Coburg (Victoria), Sadler's Wells, Royal Pavilion, Garrick, and Clarence.

light of noble poetry? does it exhibit character and elemental passions?' people ask, 'Is it splendidly »got up»? are its situations striking?'»[1] English drama of the mid-nineteenth century was thus standardized to fit one or another of the popular patterns. The period was a golden age of stock characters.

Among the leading London theatres a certain specialization took place. Directors tended to develop their own specialties and stick to certain recognizable patterns that had proved safe and successful. Thus »Adelphi drama,» named after the Adelphi Theatre, became synonymous with vigorous melodrama that relied on forceful action and was presented with a lavish use of spectacular stage effects. Madame Vestris, the attractive and popular actress who became one of the outstanding managers of the period, was known for more sophisticated entertainment at her theatre, the Olympic; her settings were frequently artistic and her stagecraft polished. At the Haymarket, which was run by such experienced actor-managers as Webster and Buckstone, the emphasis tended to be placed on the performances of individual actors. At Drury Lane Chatterton braved the preferences of the public of the sixties by an attempt to make his theatre live up to its great traditions: the classics, however, led to a rapid decline of cash income, and had to be given up for more popular and lucrative plays. As long as the fashionable West-End playhouses had to cater for low popular taste it is understandable that the theatres of the drearier parts of the metropolis, like the Surrey and the Victoria, became homes of staple melodrama and farce. The portrayal of comic stage Americans did not remain the prerogative of any one theatre; their vogue spread, and the names of the whole range of London playhouses from the Theatres Royal down can be found in a list of presentations of transatlantic character.[2] The availability of specialist actors and the demands of the moment seem to have been the most important factors in determining what theatres were to take up plays relying upon the appeal of the caricatured American. It can also be surmised that the English traditions of comic acting had little influence on the presentation of American parts; caricatures of Americans were introduced in England by star

---

[1] »Art or Amusement,» *Dramatic Essays* (London, 1876), p. 153. See also *ibid.*, pp. 155 and 160.

[2] See Appendix, pp. 156—158.

actors, and their methods rather than the principles of various London managers can be expected to have governed the performance.

By the second quarter of the nineteenth century English play censorship no longer prevented American materials from being utilized. Although censors could be very officious, the Lord Chamberlain's censorship policy was now mostly directed against plays that were in bad taste morally.[1] Although Anglo-American political relations continued strained, the licensers allowed both English and American humorous characters to extol the virtues of their native lands and to depreciate their Anglo-Saxon cousins with considerable vigour. Occasional passages were deleted, but they seem to have been considered in bad taste rather than politically dangerous.[2] In later plays, perhaps because of periods of less acute political conflicts, perhaps due to the personal attitudes of the licensers, deletions become increasingly rare.[3]

The conditions on the English stage between 1824 and 1870 seem to have been auspicious to the introduction of humorous American characters. Farcical presentations were in great vogue. Stock characters were abundant, and the audiences did not object to stereotypes. Last but not least, in England there was a great interest in the New World and its life. The large and constantly increasing number of travel-books bears witness to the zeal of the English public for reading about conditions in the United States. The liberal-minded were hoping to get an example of the practicability of their democratic theories, while the Tories wanted to give their countrymen a warning example of what dismal abysses awaited those who strayed from the virtuous path of aristocratic rule.

---

[1] On play censorship, see Nicoll, *Early Nineteenth Century Drama*, I, 17 ff.

[2] Thus, in *The Kentuckian; or, a Trip to New York*, performed in London in 1833 (*British Museum Add. MS 42920.* pp. 651—674), the American Mrs. Freeman delivered hectic speeches against hereditary titles etc., of which parts were deleted by the licenser Colman. But the same fate awaited the ultra-British Mrs. Luminary's statement: »... my experiment to ameliorate the barbarism of manner in America has been the ruling wish of my life, my husband the only obstacle to its fulfilment, by his death has provided me with the means ...» The play ends in a highly conciliatory note stressing Anglo-American affinity.

[3] It was only in the Civil-War period that an English censor again felt called for to exercise his authority and ban a play on American themes. This was H. R. Beverly's *The Last Slave*, license refused on August 16, 1865, and granted on July 18, 1867, because of the change in American affairs. The play contained a scene on Lincoln's assassination and another, a very melodramatic one, on Booth's death. (*Lord Chamberlain MSS 6/1865*, i.e., vol. 6 of 1865).

Wars and commercial conflicts intensified the curiosity of the Britons. The market for travel-books on America was unlimited. We may be certain that this interest greatly added to the popularity of plays containing American elements on the English stage.[1]

A practical impetus to the introduction of humorous treatments of American character on the English stage came from the close relations between the theatrical worlds of the United States and England. At the present, when Anglo-American relations in the field of drama still remain uncharted, one can only guess at the extent of influences in both directions. Many, perhaps most of the important playwrights, directors, and actors of the mid-nineteenth century had personal experiences of work on the other side of the ocean. Some of them crossed the Atlantic so frequently or were so extensively active in both countries that it is difficult for a present-day student to decide whether to consider them English or American. The American audience was well able to appreciate English drama; although British actors could complain about missing the usual laughter and applause when they performed in the United States, even the most critical ones had to admit that »the audience was usually attentive and intelligent.»[2] The absence of international copyright further facilitated these activities. English producers could easily take over plays from across the sea.

Because of all these factors it is inconceivable that any important developments could take place in the American theatre without being observed in England, or vice versa. If certain stock characters were successes in one country, the other was likely to adopt them and try them on its own stage.[3]

---

[1] For background, see Jane Louise Mesick, *The English Traveller in America, 1785—1835* (New York, 1922). Many travel-books, *e.g.* Mrs Trollope's *Domestic Manners of the Americans*, now available in a well-indexed edition by Donald Smalley (New York, 1949), contain general observations on drama and the theatre.

[2] John Bernard, *Retrospections of America, 1797—1811* (New York, 1887), p. 50. See also Tyrone Power, *Impressions of America during the Years 1833, 1834, and 1835* (London, 1836), I, 63, 88, 123 ff., 210, and Mesick, *Op.cit.*, p. 233.

[3] Although not dealing directly with the present topic, the comments of one mid-nineteenth-century theatregoer of unusual perspicacity, Henry James, provide some background for a comparison of the American and the English theatre. See Leon Edel's introductory essay »Henry James: The Dramatic Years» in Edel (ed.), *The Complete Plays of Henry James* (Philadelphia and New York, 1949), pp. 19—69; Henry James, *A Small Boy and Others* (London and New York, 1913), and James, *Notes of a Son and Brother* (London and New York, 1914).

3. American Themes on the English Stage. 1760—1824.

Before 1824, no humorous American characters have been found on the English stage.[1] The references to the New World still revolved around two distinct themes: the noble savage, and patriotic motives depicting Englishmen in the serious and noble business of enlarging and enriching the British Empire.

The noble savage had an honourable ancestry.[2] Having become a conventional literary type long before Rousseau he continued to haunt the stage until the latter half of the nineteenth century. He could be black, like Mrs Aphra Behn's Oroonoko; he could be an American Indian, like Cooper's Uncas. Born and conceived in Europe, far from the areas where actual savages could be found, this character type lacked all trace of realism. A romantic stock character of tragedy, he could not serve as a stage medium for the presentation of racy American humour. When the Yankee, the frontiersman, and the comic Negro became established types of the English stage, the noble savage seemed doomed. External events brought back the idealized treatment of the unsophisticated Negro: the extreme popularity of *Uncle Tom's Cabin*, which began in 1862, led to numerous dramatic exaltations of

---

The fact that most of the famous nineteenth-century actors of both England and the United States travelled across the Atlantic is well known. A student will find many more indications of the scope of Anglo-American dramatic contacts. A few instances:

American city humour in drama, as exemplified in the New York plays celebrating Mose, the fireman, was first inspired by Moncrieff's *Life in London* of 1821. (Quinn, *American Drama to the Civil War*, pp. 303 ff.)

The pioneer of burlesque in America was a man named William Mitchell, a strolling actor who had started out displaying his talents at fairs in England. (Rourke, *American Humor*, pp. 120—121.)

A Cockney, Stephen Massett, spent many years entertaining American audiences, including those of the West and the Far West. (Stephen C. Massett, *Drifting About* [New York, 1863].)

An Irish temperance apostle known as Father Mathew went to America in 1849 to play Sir John Barleycorn. He also posed as an Irish patriot and soon received a public subscription in New York City. (»Our Weekly Gossip,» *Athenaeum*, July 28, 1849, 768.)

[1] Cf. Clarence Gohdes, *American Literature in Nineteenth-Century England* (New York, 1944), pp. 73—74.

[2] One of the comprehensive studies of the noble savage is Hoxie Neale Fairchild's *The Noble Savage* (New York, 1928). For another very stimulating study, see Yrjö Hirn, *Goda vildar och ädla rövare* (Helsingfors, 1941).

Uncle Tom's and his fellow-sufferers' inherent nobility. In the same decade, however, there appeared broad burlesques of both Uncle Tom and Pocahontas. The noble savage had disappeared from the English stage in the last quarter of the nineteenth century.

The patriotic play displayed the glories of the British Empire by contrasting the gallant behaviour of English empire-builders or empire-preservers with that of representatives of other nations. Historical or topical themes formed the favourite subject matter. Here dashing heroes in scarlet and blue rescued fair damsels from rascally enemies. Here a jolly Jack Tar with a heart of gold performed great feats on His Majesty's service. Here loyal subjects kept in the path of virtue by observing at least passive hostility towards the enemies of England. The high pitch of noble fervour prevented these plays from becoming markedly humorous, and where amusing passages were inserted, the laugh was on the enemy. Therefore the patriotic drama could not become a medium of native American humour on the English stage.[1]

A short scrutiny of some plays having to do with America which were acted or printed in England from 1760 to 1824 will give an idea of their quality.

Thus, in 1760, Covent Garden presented a drollery named *The English Sailors in America*. The same play seems to have been acted at Bartholomew Fair in 1767 under the title *The French Flogged*.[2] No copy has survived. Robert Rogers's noble-savage presentation *Ponteach; or, the Savages of America* was never performed on the English stage. It received a notice from John Genest: »This is a strange Tragedy, but

---

[1] A good example of a patriotic melodrama on American themes is Dibdin's *Paul Jones* (Sadler's Wells, September, 1827). The playbill gives us an idea of the quality of the play. The first scene of Act III was described as follows: »Romantically Picturesque View on the Banks of an American Lake, Stupendous Bridge, Cataract and Indian Ceremony of Commencing War, Reconciliation of the Tribes by Female Influence, GRAND INDIAN BALLET DANCE. The Neutrality of the Tribes solicited by the Anglo-Americans and English Party. Entry of the American Sharp Shooters or Riflemen, Distant Appearance of the British Infantry, with REAL CAVALRY. In the foreground, GENERAL SKIRMISH Between the Americans, the British, and War Manoeuvres of the Indians. SINGLE COMBATS &c.» After »A GRAND SEA FIGHT» this melodrama ended with a »TREMENDOUS EXPLOSION.» No wonder *Paul Jones* became a success with the public. It can be seen that American-type humour had little place in plays of this calibre.

[2] Allardyce Nicoll, *A History of Late Eighteenth Century Drama* (Cambridge, 1927), play list. The play lists in Nicoll's works will hence be referred to as *Nicoll*.

not altogether without merit.»[1] George Cockins's *The Conquest of Canada; or, the Siege of Quebeck* was a historical tragedy in five acts. It was performed in Philadelphia in 1773, and printed in London in 1776. There are no native American themes in the play.[2] Mrs. Carr's comic opera *The Fair American* was performed in Crow-Street Theatre, Dublin, on May 18, 1771.[3] General Burgoyne's *The Blockade of Boston* was probably played in America only. Royall Tyler's *The Contrast* was never staged in England.

Genest mentions an American play called *Father of an Only Child*, acted in New York in 1788, which is perhaps identical with William Dunlap's *The Father; or, American Shandyism*. It was never acted in England, yet Genest found it deserving.[4]

Four plays entitled *The American Heroine*, among them one translated from the French, were performed in London between 1790 and 1796. One was a pantomime, the others come under the heading of »entertainment.»[5] A comic opera entitled *American Slaves; or, Love and Liberty* was performed at Dumfries in 1792. A three-act play named *The American Indian; or, Virtues of Nature*, by Jas. Bacon, was printed in London in 1795.[6]

On October 18, 1790, Charles Dibdin (1745—1814) staged a one-man show at the Lyceum, »written, composed, spoken, sung and accompanied» by himself. It was advertised as »an entirely new, and perfectly original Entertainment, in Three Parts, with an Exordium,» and its

---

[1] John Genest, *Some Account of the English Stage* (Bath, 1832), X, 184. (This work will hence be referred to as *Genest*.) See also Reed, *The Realistic Presentation of American Characters in Native American Plays prior to 1870* (Columbus, Ohio, 1918), p. 144. (The latter work will be referred to as *Reed*.)

[2] *Nicoll, Reed.*   [3] *Nicoll.*

[4] Summary: Colonel Campbell, an American, had been sent to Edinburgh to study. While in Scotland he married. After the premature death of his wife he left his little son with friends and returned to America. After a number of years he was led to believe that his son was one of the British gallants killed in the battle of Bunker Hill. But the son was still alive, and the Colonel established his identity by means of a ring. The comic underplot employs a character called Tattle, who, however, shows none of the characteristics of the later stage American. (*Genest*, X, 196—197.)

[5] Royal Circus, June 30, 1790; King's Theatre, Haymarket, March 19, 1792; Astley's, May 9, 1797 (from the French); Sadler's Wells, April 18, 1796. (*Nicoll.*) The Haymarket version was a farce built on Colman's noble-savage play *Incle and Jarico*. (Reginald Clarence, *The Stage Cyclopaedia* [London, 1909].)

[6] Clarence, *Op.cit.*

title was *The Wags: or, the Camp of Pleasure*. The motley group of characters included »A Half-Pay Brigadier, a Yellow Admiral, a Shatterbrain Irishman, a Traveller, a Musical Amateur, a Dealer in Mysteries, a Physiognomist, a Jester, a Boxer, a Dustman, and a Negro.» Among the songs some anticipated the later vogue of minstrel themes: »An Indian Death Song,» »A Savage Love Song,» and »The Negro and His Banjer.»[1]

Dunlap's *Leicester* and *The American Indian* were never acted in England; Genest calls the latter »dull,» and complains about the language not being »sufficiently simple.»[2] *André*, Dunlap's version of the famous Revolutionary episode, was published in London in 1799, but not performed on the stage.[3]

A burletta on the *Oroonoko* theme by Murdock was performed at the Surrey on May 11, 1813.[4] A revival of this old favourite had taken place at Covent Garden in March, 1806, and it was also performed at Bath in April, 1815.[5] Another version of the same theme named *The Slave* was staged on November 12, 1816, at Covent Garden.[6]

J. H. Barber's farce *America* was printed in London in 1805.[7] Similarly, Charles Breck's *The Trust*, which contains a native American character named Robert and which, according to Reed, »significantly reflects American life,» was published in London in 1808.[8] There is no evidence that either was ever performed on the English stage.

James Nelson Barker's American comedy in five acts, *Tears and Smiles*, contains a native American character called Nathan Yank.[9] According to Nicoll it was performed at the Lyceum on May 8, 1809. However, *The Times* of May 8, 1809, announces other plays at the Lyceum. The Larpent Collection has the manuscript of a musical romance in two acts by Edmund John Eyre named *Tears and Smiles*, which was licensed in May, 1809, and produced at the Haymarket on August 1 as *The Vintagers*.[10] It is probable that this item is responsible for the confusion; neither Genest nor Clarence's *Stage Cyclopaedia* mention any

---

[1] Austin Brereton, *The Lyceum and Henry Irving* (London and New York, 1903), pp. 21—23.
[2] *Genest*, X, 201, 203.   [3] *Ibid* 212—4.   [4] *Nicoll.*   [5] *Genest*, VIII, 2.
[6] *Genest*, VII, 603.   [7] *Nicoll.*   [8] *Reed*, p. 151; *Nicoll.*
[9] Reprinted in Paul H. Musser, *James Nelson Barker, 1784—1858* (Philadelphia, 1929). Nathan Yank was a minor character.
[10] Dougald MacMillan, *Catalogue of the Larpent Plays in the Huntington Library* (San Marino, Calif., 1939), number 1576.

performances of Barker's comedy in England.[1] Moncrieff's *Smiles and Tears; or, the Widow's Stratagem*, another play with a confusingly similar title, was a social comedy without any American elements. The latter was staged at Covent Garden on December 12, 1815.[2]

On March 27, 1811, London saw the first performance of a new comic opera called *The Americans* at the Lyceum Theatre. It was written by Samuel James Arnold under the original title of *The War-Whoop*,[3] and contained sizable choruses of American Indians, Britons, and Africans.[4] The music was composed by M. P. King and Braham. It was not very popular, its run being restricted to about five performances. The Drury Lane Company revived it at a benefit at the Lyceum in May, 1812.[5]

Thomas John Dibdin's musical drama *America; or, the Colonists* was put up by the Surrey on March 30, 1812.[6]

In June, 1818, the Lyceum staged a wild-west show with a troupe of »Native American Indian Warriors lately arrived in England.» Their authentic war-whoops excited English audiences as much as their *pièce de résistance*, »Surprise and Attack of the Planter's Cottage.» This troupe lasted for sixty performances, but finally had to yield to an Automatic Trumpeter from Vienna.[7]

James Nelson Barker's *Pocahontas; or, the Indian Princess* was simply a revision of *The Indian Princess; or, La Belle Sauvage*. The latter had been performed in Philadelphia on April 6, 1808; Barker's version appeared at Drury Lane on December 15, 1820.[8] A notice in *The Times* admired the harmonious blank verse and the interest in »intercourse of civilized life with savage habits and manners.» However, this commentator was particularly disturbed by the entire absence of humour in the play: this »communicates a leaden dullness which must prove a formidable barrier to a long and brilliant career.» When it was announced that the performance was to be repeated, the announcement »was not received with much ardour.»[9] Genest blamed the playwright on the same grounds.[10]

The same year, 1820, saw another Indian theme at Covent Garden.

---

[1] *Genest*, II, 531. [2] *Ibid.*
[3] MacMillan, *Catalogue of the Larpent Plays*, number 1669.
[4] Lyceum Theatre playbill of May 18, 1811, at the British Museum.
[5] *Nicoll; Genest*, VII, 217; *Morning Post*, May 11, 1811, 2.
[6] *Nicoll.* [7] Brereton, *Op.cit.*, pp. 51—52. [8] *Nicoll.*
[9] *Times*, December 16, 1820, 3. [10] IX, 83—84.

It was a revised version of O'Keeffe's *Basket Maker*, a musical tale. By the simple addition of Indian elements it underwent the transmutation to *Iroquois; or, the Canadian Basket Maker*.[1]

To conclude the list, a typical title combining both the patriotic and the noble-savage themes: *The British Captain and the Indian Chief* by Simpson, acted at the Royalty Theatre, November 4, 1822.[2]

Clearly, then, the American themes that have been found on the English stage before 1824 contain no humorous treatments of American character. Jonathan and Nimrod Wildfire were still busy Down East or Out West, and had not had time enough to step before English footlights. The above play titles bear a marked contrast to those that dealt with American themes during the following half century, when Jonathan's name on a playbill had proved an additional attraction. It should also be borne in mind that native American humour did not assume its definitive literary shapes until around 1830.

CHAPTER II

THE INTRODUCTION OF HUMOROUS AMERICAN CHARACTERS ON THE ENGLISH STAGE

1. Charles Mathews and His American Tour.

Charles Mathews the Elder was born in London in 1776 as the seventh son of a bookseller.[3] A family legend informs posterity how the Great Garrick once dandled little Charles. Whether this contact with the celebrated actor injected him with histrionic inspiration or not, Mathews showed an early interest in the theatre. At St. Martin's, Merchant Taylors', and Madame Cottrell's French school off the Strand he was known for his talents in mimicry and acting. After various youthful undertakings in the fields of the theatre and journalism, he got the long-expected chance to become a professional actor in Dublin in 1794.

---

[1] *Genest*, IX, 100—101. [2] *Nicoll*.
[3] For a biography, see Joseph Knight, »Charles Mathews,» *Dictionary of National Biography*.

Adverse circumstances soon reduced the youngster to a walking gentleman on one guinea a week. After various badly-paid engagements his miserable *Wanderjahre* ended in a comic triumph at the Haymarket in 1803. After this, his popularity and fame were assured. As a mimic his skill was phenomenal, and his acting in comic parts excellent. This »wizen, dark man, with one high shoulder, a distorted mouth, a lame leg, and an irritable manner»[1] possessed the rare talent of improvising imitations of people he knew, and could completely subjugate his own personality to his concept of the person he was imitating for a whole hour.

Between 1803 and the end of his active career in 1834 (he died at the age of 59 in 1835), Mathews acted most of the famous comic parts in English drama. But his undertakings were not restricted to conventional plays alone. Because of his outstanding virtuosity in mimicry, a series of »At Homes» were written for him with the express purpose of allowing him to display his greatest talent. In these entertainments, Mathews put on a one-man show by assuming one part after another. These different impersonations were worked into a connected story, and the shows usually finished with a »monopolylogue» where Mathews alone presented a conversation between the characters.[2] Even if he himself preferred to be known as an actor rather than a popular entertainer or showman, the »At Homes» formed the basis of his wide popularity. Mathews was the idol of London; from Byron, Macaulay, and Dickens to the East End Cockney all enjoyed his performances.[3]

Like many of his colleagues before and after his day, Charles Mathews showed a peculiar lack of acumen in business matters. Pecuniary considerations certainly were among the reasons that induced him to visit America in 1822—3.[4] He was also short of subject matter for fur-

---

[1] Brander Matthews and Lawrence Hutton, *Actors and Actresses of Great Britain and the United States* (New York, 1886), II, 216.

[2] The first »At Home» was *Mail-Coach Adventures* of 1818. Then followed *The Trip to Paris* (1819); *Country Cousins* (1820); *Adventures in Air, Earth, and Water* (1821); and *The Youthful Days of Mr. Mathews* (1822). (Matthews and Hutton, *Op.cit.*, II, 198, 216; Brereton, *The Lyceum and Henry Irving pp.* 45—51.)

[3] *Ibid.*

[4] Mrs. A. Mathews, *Memoirs of Charles Mathews, Comedian* (London, 1839), III, 286 ff. (*Infra* referred to as *Memoirs*.) S. J. Arnold published a rebuttal titled *Forgotten Facts in the Memoirs of Charles Mathews, Comedian* (London, 1839), which also contains relevant material.

ther »At Homes,» and hoped to collect a good crop of new materials west of the Atlantic.[1] Thus Mathews left England with the express purpose of making observations of American character and behaviour, observations he could use for future entertainments.

The external events of Mathews' American tour are recorded in his letters.[2] When the comedian arrived outside New York after a 35-day voyage, the city was suffering from a yellow-fever epidemic. The fishermen who first informed the passengers of the dreaded malady did so with »the most ignorant and shameful exaggerations,»[3] perhaps enjoying the scared expressions of the European visitors when faced with their American way of phrasing facts. The over-careful Mathews was laughed at when he steadfastly refused to enter New York City before the epidemic had been completely conquered, but he persisted in his decision.

This resolution compelled him to alter his schedule. He went to Philadelphia, where he made the acquaintance of a real American heatwave. In the same September he found time to visit Baltimore, where he made his debut on the American stage in his old show *Trip to Paris*. This took place on September 23, 1822. After short stays in Philadelphia and Washington Mathews moved to New York City at the beginning of November. Here his shows made »a prodigious hit,»[4] and achieved great popularity among everybody except the Rev. Paschal Strong of the Middle Dutch Church.[5]

The last days of December saw Mathews in Boston, where the notoriously cool audience huzzaed when the curtain fell after his first performance of *Goldfinch* and *Tonson*. Early in February he was back in New York, still complaining about the severity of the winter cold. After further visits to Philadelphia (February—March) and New York (April—May) he sailed for Liverpool in the latter half of May, 1823, and arrived safe in England after a 30-day passage.

---

[1] *Memoirs*, III, 287. [2] A selection is available in *Memoirs*, vol. III.
[3] *Ibid.*, 304. [4] *Ibid.*, 326.
[5] On November 17, 1822, the Reverend preached a sulphur-and-brimstone sermon, the gist of which was that the yellow fever was God's punishment of the sins of mankind. The theatre and Charles Mathews were prominent in the latter category. Just before his departure for England, Mathews wrote an equally acrimonious epistle to Strong, which he signed: »I have, sir, the honour to be, most gratefully your obliged, angelic, yellow-fever-producing friend, C. Mathews.» (*Memoirs*, III, 340—345.)

Mathews had thoroughly won the admiration of the American public. Even financially, the trip was a success. The transatlantic mail carried thousands of pounds sterling to England for him. High box-office intakes were commonplace.[1] Yet, for Mathews personally there were no large gains. S. J. Arnold, his English manager, had to be paid compensation for the lost London season. The severe winter was a comparatively bad time for entertainments in the United States. The epidemic made him lose valuable time. Thus, even if the tour was a financial success *per se*, the situation from the comedian's own point of view was less favourable.[2]

Inside this framework of events during the American tour from August, 1822, to May, 1823, Mathews succeeded in acquiring a good insight into American life and manners. Although fundamentally a good-natured person, he was not always a good mixer; among people he disliked he could be sullen and quiet, and abstain from entertaining the company with his usual imitations. This critical bent of his did not make him enthusiastically pro-American; neither was he hostile by principle. He was capable of using his spectacular talent of observation and analysis in an objective way, and this is what the art of imitation and caricature requires. A keen perception of the essential characteristics of the subject is necessary before the caricaturist can begin the creative task of exaggerating certain aspects and synthetize a comic entity out of them. As both contemporary and modern observers have repeatedly remarked, the ordinary English travel-book on America could not be credited with an objective approach. Therefore Mathews had to rely upon fresh observations.

The sources of Mathews' knowledge of American humour and character were of three kinds. Firstly, he was bound to meet a number of actors, artists, and literati, who could, wittingly or unwittingly, supply him with native American materials. Secondly, there were ample opportunities for him to observe the behaviour of the people he met. Thirdly, he may have found humorous items in American newspapers. There is no evidence that Mathews ever saw Yankee parts acted on the American stage.

In spite of the scanty information available on the English actor's American contacts, scholars have succeeded in tracing some of his

---

[1] In Baltimore, *e.g.*, one benefit grossed $ 1000; in New York, one night's show brought $ 1800. (*Ibid.*, 327.)

[2] The tour is called a financial failure in Matthews and Hutton, *Op.cit.*, II, 203.

American jokes to their source. Three of the prominent jests of Mathews' American entertainment, staged in London in 1824, have been identified as having been told by the American artist, wit, and storyteller John Wesley Jarvis. The latter, one of the most jovial members of the Bread and Cheese Club of New York, was generally known as a »master of anecdote.» Jarvis's extensive contacts with the theatrical circles during the very years when Mathews visited the United States leave little doubt about the fact that the two gentlemen were acquainted. Perhaps a gay nightly session took place in New York, and Jarvis and Mathews entertained their friends with stories and imitations. Jarvis is likely to have been an inspiring source.[1]

Inspiration was indeed necessary for Mathews if he wanted to put up a London show illustrating American character. A keen observer would not have been satisfied with the humorous stage Yankee as the only representative of the New World. But it was not easy for Mathews to make direct observations. In February, 1823, he sent a lament to his wife:

> It will require all your ingenuity, all your fancy (and more than *I* ever possessed), to find real materials in this country for a humorous entertainment. There is such a universal sameness of manner and character, so uniform a style of walking and looking, of dressing and thinking, that I really think I knew as much of them in October as I know of them now in February.[2]

The problem was to select such types as were representative of certain segments of the American population, and then to develop them into comic characters by suitable caricature. Some types suggested themselves: the Yankee was the most prominent native American humorist of the twenties. The French immigrant was a recognizable figure in the United States after the American and French Revolutions; besides, Mathews excelled in imitating Frenchmen, who had been among his standard imitations ever since the »At Home» of 1819. The Irishman was another obvious subject. The American Negro could not be pressed into the traditional mold of the noble savage; a new concept was necessary. In his letters Mathews mentioned some of his contacts

---

[1] H. E. Dickson, »A Note on Charles Mathews's Use of American Humor,» *American Literature*, XII, 78—83 (March, 1940).

[2] *Memoirs*, III, 381. Even Hugh H. Brackenridge, the American author of *Modern Chivalry* (1792—1815), had to content himself with the Irishman as the main comic representative of America.

with the coloured American. In Boston, he was present at a Negro religious ceremony: »I have heard a black preacher, who was rather amusing. The pranks that are played in the 'nigger meetings,' as they are called, are beyond belief — yelling, screeching, and groaning, resembling a fox-chase much more than a place of worship.»[1] Another episode is suggestive of the traveller's personal experiences: »A very fat negro, with whom I met, driving a stage-coach (which are almost as peculiar as the French), and urging his horses by different tunes on a fiddle, while he ingeniously fastened the reins around his neck. This would give an opportunity for the only costume which differs from that of our own country, the summer dress.»[2] The character of Agamemnon in the »At Home» of 1824 is reminiscent of this description.[3]

Mathews' letters from the American tour contain numerous comments on American English. He found that in America there were »no phrases, intonations, instances of bad pronunciation or false grammar . . . that I cannot trace to be of English origin.» These peculiarities he thought derivable from the dialects of Yorkshire, Somersetshire, and London.[4] In Boston Mathews found English generally better spoken than anywhere in England.[5] As to vocabulary, he comments on the excessive use of military titles west of the Atlantic, and the humorous effect ensuing from this usage: »Colonel Hunter, your bread is by no means so good as that you baked at the beginning of the year.»[6] Other passages in the letters contain further remarks on American English, including Negro dialect.[7]

Mathews liked American audiences. He thought they had a »quick and nice perception of character,» and noticed that they »seize instantaneously on a little natural touch of look and manner, quite unconnected with an intended point.»[8] On the individual level, the comedian showed a distinct preference for »the upper orders of people.» He thought them »well informed, polite, hospitable, unaffected,»[9] this in spite of the fact that the American upper classes had »less fun than the grave English; not a very quick perception of humour, and [were] appar-

---

[1] *Memoirs*, III, 350.   [2] *Ibid.*, 384—385.

[3] Agamemnon was a fat Negro, constantly brandishing a fiddle and dancing grotesquely to his own playing. Cf. ». . . on the road they meet with a fiddling Negro, who causes them a little amusement.» (*The London Mathews*, Hodgson & Co., [London, 1824], p. 17.)

[4] *Memoirs*, III, 383.   [5] *Ibid.*, III, 384.   [6] *Ibid.*, 323, 385.

[7] *Ibid.*, 385—392, *passim*.   [8] *Ibid.*, II, 314.   [9] *Ibid.*, III, 382.

ently dead to the fascinations of punning.»[1] The most objectionable aspect of transatlantic society was the dominance of »the middling and lower orders.» In America the upper ten were slaves of the lower strata, he thought.[2] At this point his comments coincide with those of the majority of English visitors to America.

2. »Mathews in America,» 1824.

Bearing in mind Mathews' great popularity with the British public it is not surprising that his return from America was awaited with considerable suspense. *Blackwood's* expressed its anticipation as follows:

> Matthews [sic], the pleasantest of all laughers at the laughable parts and persons of society, threatens a prodigious influx of merriment for his forthcoming season. His American tour must have shewn human nature, to his curious eye, in colours sufficiently new for »excellent mirth.» But his pictures will be far from assisting those ungenerous prejudices which have bred ill blood between the mother country and the *daughter* country. The peculiarities of the fanatics, that burlesque religion in America; the habits of life in the interior; the style of narrative and dialogue among the haranguers in steam-boats, stages, and inns, will probably make up the largest portion of his humorous gleanings in a country in which he almost uniformly met kindness and consideration.[3]

The Londoners did not have to wait long. On March 25, 1824, Mathews gave his new entertainment at the English Opera House.

The show began with a few puns in Mathews' usual vein.[4] He got the first laugh of the audience by stating that since he had last been *At Home*, he had been *Abroad*, and having been *Abroad* he was happy to be *At Home* again. After listing some of the dangers of the West, where one might be »eat up by the Scalps, the Mammoths, and Tomahawks,» he sang a song called »Travellers All.» The next series of jokes consisted of a dialogue between a French and an American boat. The French accent of the *capitaine* »in the key of low D» and the American

---

[1] *Ibid.*, 354. [2] *Ibid.*, 382—383.

[3] »London Oddities and Outlines, V,» XV, 194 (February, 1824).

[4] The British Museum has three printed versions of the show. The present account follows *The London Mathews* of Hodgson & Co. (London, 1824.) Details are also accessible in Francis Hodge's recent article »Charles Mathews Reports on America,» *Quarterly Journal of Speech*, XXXVI, 429—499 (1950).

3 — *Soc. Scient. Fenn., Comm. Hum. Litt. XVIII. 1.*

»up at F alt,»[1] the American's constant answer »William Thompson» to all questions, and the gradual hoarsening of the frantic Frenchman proved irresistible, and the titters of the gallery broke out in roaring laughter.

A few remarks on the American use of »I guess,» »I reckon,» and »I calculate» gave a suitable transition to the description of Mathews' shipmates. Then we arrive in America and get the traditional travel-book comparison between hotels in the Old and the New World. A description of Mathews' travels and entertainments west of the ocean is interspersed with the necessary amount of jokes and descriptions of life in the United States. The showman comments on Mr. Raventop, the American humorist at Mrs. Bradish's boarding house in New York (perhaps a parody on Jarvis). After further jokes, a song, and a passage on Anglo-American amity and understanding, Mathews came to his famous passage which contained the Opossum song.

Allegedly our narrator went to the »Niggers Theatre,» where a jet-black tragedian was performing his version of *Hamlet*. The soliloquy went like this:

    To be or not to be?
    that is the question — whether it is nobler in the mind
    to suffer — or tak' up arms against a sea of
    Troubles, and, by Opossum, end 'em.[2]

At the word »Opossum» the coloured audience »burst forth in one general cry — Opossum! Opossum! Opossum!», until the dark tragedian stepped in front of the footlights and told his admirers that he would sing their favourite tune, »Opossum up a Gum Tree.» This simple »coon song» with its very catchy tune proved one of the musical hits of nineteenth-century England.[3]

---

[1] »Mathews in America,» *Blackwood's*, XV, 425 (April, 1824).
[2] *London Mathews*, p. 10.
[3] The British Museum Music Library has a copy of the sheet-music arranged by T. Philipps. The words, however, differ from those of *The London Mathews*. The following version was printed in the latter:

    Opossum up a gum tree,
    On de branch him lie;
    Opossum up a gum tree,
    Him tinks no one is by;

The American militia was an easy laughing-stock for those used to the smart and well-disciplined appearance of English troops. Mathews made capital of this fact by including a description and song on the Militia Muster. Here a group of American citizens solemnly practised military arts using umbrellas for guns, led by a confused, but meek Captain, who read the commands from a book.[1]

The second part of *Mathews in America* begins by introducing the audience to an American named Daniel Doolittle. The latter's most prominent characteristic is his truly American independence. Daniel refuses to become anybody's servant, and even declines the more polite offer to take him on as »a help.» After an etymology of the word *Yankee* (derived from *l'anglais* via *inglée*) and some doggerel on the Bunker Hill monument we are told about a real Yankee, Jonathan

Opossum up a gum tree,
Nigger him much bewail;
Opossum up a gum tree,
He pulls him down by de tail.
    Opossum, &c.

Opossum up a gum tree,
Him knows not vat to follow;
Opossum up a gum tree,
With Nigger in de hollow;
Opossum up a gum tree,
Him know not what him ail;
But Nigger go up de gum tree,
And pull him down by de tail.
    Opossum, &c.

Opossum up a gum tree,
Have no fear at all;
Opossum up a gum tree,
Him never tink to fall;
Opossum up a gum tree,
Him hop, and skip, and rail;
But Nigger, him too cunning,
So he pull him down by de tail.
    Opossum, &c.

[1] The Militia Muster theme was used by Oliver H. Prince, an American humorist, in an item published in *The Monitor*, a small Georgia newspaper, as early as 1813. It was often reprinted and found its way to Longstreet's *Georgia Scenes* of 1835. (Blair, *Native American Humor*, p. 26.)

W. Doubikin,[1] and his equally Yankee Uncle Ben. This episode was based on one of Jarvis's stories. The two gentlemen are shooting. Uncle Ben promises Jonathan a shilling for climbing a tree and bringing down a dead squirrel which he, Uncle Ben, had shot. When Jonathan gets the animal, Uncle Ben in true Yankee fashion conveniently forgets all about the shilling. This, of course, causes Jonathan great grief. Follows a linguistic joke about Jonathan's conversation with an Englishman:

Jonathan: There's a sleight *I guess.*
John: You shouldn't say *I guess, you know.*
Jonathan: But you should say *I guess.*
John: But if I say *you know,* you say, *I guess you know;* but I don't say *you know, you know.*[2]

Then comes another popular story: that of M. Mallét, the Frenchman, at the Boston Post Office. Mallét is eagerly expecting a letter, which the ignorant clerk withholds not understanding that »Mallay» and Mallét are the same person. In his rage the Frenchman finally tears up the precious message, and the episode ends with his efforts to put the pieces together again. This incident gave Mathews a chance to show his skill in imitating a French accent and the Gallic temperament, and provided materials for a later play.[3]

After some punning on the name of Providence, R. I., we depart for Worcester. On the road we meet the fiddling Negro, the counterpart of the coloured man of Mathews' letters. The next event is a dinner in honour of General Jackson; this was based on one of Jarvis's anecdotes. A little Frenchman gets up in spite of Jackson's express wish to avoid all politics during the meal, and compares the General to Hannibal, »because he shoot all the English, and can shoot anybody, and kill them all to death with his own grand sabre.» Follows »An Ode to General Jackson.» After this episode we get acquainted with an American Court of Justice, presided upon by a German-American Judge.[4] Before the finale of the second part of the show there is an account of how Mathews confused Maximilian, a Negro waiter, with his ventriloquism: when the poor servant heard »Mr. Mathews' child cry in

---

[1] In some versions, Doubikins.
[2] *London Mathews,* pp. 13—14. [3] See *infra,* pp. 44—47.
[4] The ultimate source of this story has been identified as Hugh Henry Brackenridge. (Blair, *Native American Humor,* p. 27.)

de box» he poured the soup down an elderly gentleman's back, and laughed »most immoderately.»

The third part of the entertainment was devoted to the »monopolylogue.» Its title was »All Well at Nachitoches,» and its dramatis personae were Colonel Hiram Pegler, a Kentucky Shoemaker; Agamemnon, a poor runaway Negro; Jonathan W. Doubikin, a »real Yankee,» Agamemnon's owner [*sic!*]; Monsieur Capote, a French emigrant tailor; Mr. O'Sullivan, an Irish improver of his fortune; and Miss Mangel Wurzel, a Dutch heiress. The setting was simply »an American town in winter,» with Pegler's shop on the ground floor of a house, Capote's on the first floor. Opposite was Miss Wurzel's dwelling, and close to the Pegler workshop was a well.

The London Mathews describes the ensuing action at some length:

The cobbler is a thirsty soul, and not only thirsts after liquor, but for the money of Miss Wurzel; and indulges at the same moment in the pleasures of the bottle, and the anticipation of marrying the Dutch heiress; he is a major in the army, and talks of mending boots, and soling shoes, and circumventing the French tailor, who is likewise a suitor for the hand and fortune of the fair Dutch lady. Colonel Hiram Pegler resolves to teaze the Frenchman to death, or come off triumphant.

Monsieur Capot, the French emigrant tailor, detests his military rival, and swears to subdue him; still he endeavours to tantalize the cobbler, and uses every method in his power to annoy him; sometimes he will cry, »Monsieur Peglare how do you do? — how you do, Monsieur Peglare?» and in the same breath will call him a d-d vagabone, and roar out, »Monsieur Peglare, you are *von* rascal! I have found out your *histoire*, your grand grand *pere* was *von transporte.*»

Miss Mangel Wurzel, the Dutch heiress, seems to view their discord without regret, and is only waiting for the right man to take possession of herself and fortune.

Agamemnon, the runaway Negro, is a fat unwieldy fellow, and has been sold by my uncle Ben to his nephew Jonathan, Mr. Doubikin; he enters, pursued by his master, and conceals himself in the bottom of the well.

Jonathan W. Doubikin, the real Yankee, enters with a gun in pursuit of his runaway Negro, and tells a long story about his uncle Ben, who sells Agamemnon to him for sixty dollars and twenty-five cents; and Jonathan finds he has got a bad bargain, for Agamemnon possesses many bad qualities, and is not only very fat, but addicted to laziness. However, Jonathan makes up his mind to tell Uncle Ben of it the next time he meets him, and means likewise to mention the other small trifle, meaning the shilling for getting the grey squirrel out of the tree. Having made up his mind to this, he next declares that if he once sees Agamemnon he is determined to wing him; and gives a ludicrous account of the manner in which he bought the Nigger of his uncle, and speaks nearly to the following effect: — »Well, uncle Ben, I calculate you have a Nigger to sell?» »Yes, I have a Nigger, I guess. Will you buy the Nigger.» »Oh, yes! If he is a good Nigger, I will, I reckon; but this is a land of liberty and freedom, and as every man has a right to buy a Nigger, what do you want for your Nigger?» »Why, as you say, Jonathan,» says Uncle Ben, »this is a land of freedom and independence, and as every man has a right to sell his Niggers, I want sixty dollars and twenty-five cents. Will you give it?» . . .[1]

Whenever Mathews had to dash backstage to change his attire, he filled the gaps with various sound effects illustrating the controversy between Pegler and the Frenchman, or with Pegler's favourite songs in praise of General Jackson. The last character to enter is O'Sullivan, who sings an Irish song, releases Agamemnon from the well, swears by St. Patrick that he will carry off the Dutch heiress, and proceeds to do so.

Thus ended Mathews' American entertainment, a performance that took a total of three and one-half hours.

From the quality of the show it is easy to see that Mathews' primary purpose was to amuse the audience and display his imitative talents; the question of the verisimilitude of his descriptions of American society and character was secondary. Thus there is an undue proportion of French immigrants in the entertainment. Colonel Pegler's main frontier quality is his constant admiration of Jackson; otherwise he fails to show the bragging impetuosity which later became the main characteristic of his breed. Jonathan is made a slave-owner, which is certainly not typical. No contrast is worked out between the frontiersman and the shrewd, taciturn Yankee. In the Negro characterizations, an attempt was made at systematic use of a coloured dialect; otherwise the lazy Agamemnon and the irrepressible Negro Roscius have little in common. In short, Mathews fails to give us a systematic analysis of life west of the Atlantic. His show displays a few caricatured Americans in a series of separate incidents kept together by a most slender thread of plot.

Yet the selection of characters was representative. Mathews chose the Yankee, the Kentuckian, the foreign immigrant, the Negro, and the American Irishman for main heroes, and by so doing anticipated such celebrated ambassadors of American fun as Sam Slick, Nimrod Wildfire, Hans Breitmann, Uncle Remus, and Mr. Dooley.

---

[1] *London Mathews*, pp. 19—22.

Mathews was keenly aware of the delicate character of his undertaking. The Americans of 1824 were quite as touchy about their national honour and quite as unable to take English criticism as the Americans of 1842, who were furious with Dickens's *American Notes*. Being aware of this sensitivity the comedian wrote James Smith asking his opinion. The reply was reassuring: Smith advised Mathews to emphasize the comic aspects without dread, but to insert a complimentary passage on Anglo-American friendship in the end.[1] There were some American reactions to the London show,[2] but Mathews defended his performance by stating that Jonathan's character was planned to represent »what in America is considered a fair subject of laughter and ridicule, like the *gascon* of France, and the Cockney of England, which are quoted by the natives themselves as a fair specimen of ignorance, conceit, and boasting.»[3] In Mathews' mind, the Yankee still was the number one comic representative of the United States.

Mathews in America proved spectacularly popular with the London audience. »Opossum up a Gum Tree» instigated a vogue of the coon song. Large numbers of pirated editions of the entertainment appeared in both Britain and America. One of the English publishers ran up to thirty editions in a short time.[4] The reviews in periodicals and newspapers reflect the success.

In the daily press Mathew's reception was very favourable. *The Morning Post* stressed his excellence as an acute observer and passed comments which reflect on the average travel-book author:

---

[1] *Memoirs*, III, 428.

[2] In the first London performance there was a passage where a British Negress told an American Negro that he would be free the moment he stepped on British soil. The latter answered: »Free! What is that? I have heard a great deal about *him*, in America; but never knew what *he* meant.» At this reply there was some »shuffling in the pit,» and the passage was promptly omitted from the following performances. (John Neal, »American Writers,» *Blackwood's*, XVI, 418 [October, 1824].) An anonymous letter, signed »A Native Yankee,» was sent to the Editor of *The European Magazine*, objecting to the obvious *faux pas* and inaccuracies of the entertainment. It was noted that Jonathan could not be a slaveholder, that the clothes of the characters were all wrong, etc. (*Memoirs*, III, 516 ff.).

[3] *Memoirs*, III, 517.

[4] Gohdes, *American Literature in Nineteenth-Century England*, p. 74. No bibliography is known of these literary curiosities. The British Museum has three different issues; Gohdes calls the Harvard collection »splendid.»

> In his late trip to America, Mr. MATTHEWS [sic] has not failed to catch many of the leading characteristics of *Jonathan*, for the amusement of his friend *John*. He is not one of those torpid and incurious travellers who can allow all the heterogeneous scenes of the universal Drama to flit before his eyes, without having a clear perception of anything, — who can travel from »Dan to Beersheba, and cry 'tis all barren.» He has cultivated the fruit presented to him in a strange country, and brought it back in a high stage of preservation... In the course of the entertainment we were furnished with many highly amusing sketches of American character and independence. Mr. MATTHEWS, however, never deals harshly either with the national manners, or individual peculiarities, and takes every opportunity of doing justice to the good fellowship with which he was treated... The house was full to an overflow.[1]

The Times noted the warm applause of the audience and considered the final »monopolylogue» the best part of the show. The only criticism was that the script was not so well written as Mathews' best performances had been, although there was »novelty in the subject.»[2] The commentator of *The Sun* emphasized the inexhaustible supply of comic characterization of which the actor was capable, and thought he had been very kind to the Americans and exercised great restraint because of the hospitality he had enjoyed in the United States.[3] *The Sunday Times* praised the parts of the tailor, the cobbler, and the Irishman.[4] *The Examiner* »had expected a greater diversity of American portraiture, and a few attempts at the delineation of nationality of a higher class of society — the *elite* of the larger towns.»[5] *The Observer* commented at some length on the correctness of the analysis of America and her citizens in a review which is significant because it reveals the Englishman's knowledge of his transatlantic brethren in 1824:

> Almost all the views of America that have been published in this country, appear to have been taken by Travellers, through the medium of gross ignorance, or a most distorted vision; and they have been served up again by the *Quarterly Review* and other similar political publications, with a delighted love of misrepresentation, and an utter disregard of any gratification, but that of the basest passions, the narrowest principles, and the vilest taste... Mr. MATHEWS, though profound in no science but physiology, may be said to have produced the most liberal, as well as the most entertaining and correct picture of the habits, manners, and characteristics of the Americans that ever was presented to Englishmen — exaggerated, occasionally, for effect — but never so caricatured as to leave any doubt of the truth of the portrait... Mr Mathews' return from transportation seemed to have the effect of transporting the audience, for his reception was of

---

[1] March 26, 1824, 3. [2] March 26, 1824, 3. [3] March 26, 1824, 3.
[4] March 28, 1824, 3. [5] March 28, 1824, 200.

the most rapturous description; and the Americans having deprived us of mirth for one season, ought not to begrudge their assistance or be sulky at being *helps* in the present, to compensate for our loss. Mr. Mathews, indeed, pays the highest compliment to that country, and places the natives in a very valuable point of view, when he *makes so much of them*, not only there, but here.[1]

In September, 1824, *The Observer* re-stressed the originality and novelty of Mathews' characterizations:

If Mr. Mathews be not the very first, he is the first and only performer of the present day, who has introduced upon the stage of this country the peculiarities of manner and accent, which characterize that remote, but important nation. The novelty of the undertaking affords a strong excitement to the spirit of curiosity, but it is not easy to pronounce upon its merits after all . . .[2]

However, there were English periodicals whose policy was to condemn both low entertainment and American letters. The *Blackwood's* review may serve as an example of the more critical comments:

[The] »Trip to America» is not so smart as most of [Mathews'] summer chit-chat has been; it is rather indeed very feeble, cockney kind of stuff; and, for all the information that it gives about the country in which he has been travelling, it might pretty nearly have been written without stirring out of Kentish Town . . . There is little or nothing in fact at all strikingly American in his Entertainment. Your review of Faux's Confessions, and a score of New-York papers, would have furnished out materials for ten volumes of better tales; then the flavour of what there is, is all softened down with caution and melted butter . . . It is all nonsense, being so over civil with people when we want to be amused with them![3]

Even this reviewer felt compelled to praise Mathews' acting, however.

In general, then, the reviewers were aware of the fact that humorous presentation of American character on the English stage was a novelty introduced by Charles Mathews. They tended to think that »Mathews in America» contained »much accurate delineation of national manner, and many happy descriptions of individual character.»[4] They often believed that Jonathan and his countrymen were essentially true to life, and the show was given a place among the sources of information on the United States that were available in England at the time. In

---

[1] March 28, 1824, 2.
[2] September 5, 1824, 3.
[3] XV, 424 (April, 1824).
[4] An unidentified, possibly rigged review, quoted in *Memoirs*, III, 443 ff.

mock horror, a commentator could even say: »We 'guess' that we may 'calculate' on a 'pretty considerable' intermingling in our conversations of the American colloquialisms and idioms.»[1] The popularity of the entertainment is also indicated by the fact that it was revived on June 18, 1827.[2] Before this London revival it had been taken to the provinces, having *e.g.* been performed at Bath on November 7, 1825.[3]

In 1834—5 Mathews made a second American tour accompanied by his wife. His health could no more stand the strain of an American winter, the exhausting travels and constant performances, but he felt compelled to carry on because of an impairment of his financial position. To reassure his American critics he performed the 1824 »At Home» in New York, while a rival theatre displayed hostile notices, and at the end of the show asked the public whether they thought him guilty or not guilty »of having libelled or ridiculed» them. »Not guilty,» shouted the house amidst cheers.[4]

After his return to England he was too ill to act. His health declined rapidly, and he died a few months later.

3. *The Twenties: Echoes of Mathews. The First Frontiersman.*

Charles Mathews' influence on the history of humorous Americans on the English stage was not restricted to his »At Home.» The entertainment of 1824 was so successful that it soon induced playwrights to adapt ideas from it to legitimate drama. The show contained many episodes and characters that could easily be elaborated; it remained for the dramatizers to concoct a plot, however slender, to present them in a dramatic sequence. Of all the different characters of the original entertainment, the adapters chose two for elaboration. The first was Jonathan W. Doubikin the Yankee, the second Monsieur Mallét with his French *esprit* and temperament.

Thus, Jonathan appeared in *Jonathan in England*, an operatic farce

---

[1] *Ibid.*
[2] Playbill of the English Opera House, *Enthoven Collection.*
[3] *Genest*, IX, 357.
[4] An account of Mathews' second American tour is given in *Memoirs*, IV, 297 ff.

by Richard Brinsley Peake, the English playwright who collaborated with Mathews in the composition of the »At Homes.» It was first performed at the English Opera House on September 3, 1824, before the initial vogue of *Mathews in America* had grown stale.[1]

Jonathan, »the real Yankee» from Vermont was acted by Mathews himself. Agamemnon, »his Nigger,» was also present. The other humorous Americans were Mr. Delapierre, an American citizen settled in London, and Blanche, »a Negro female.» The rest of the dramatis personae were English. The humour depended heavily on the »At Home» of 1824: Jonathan's language; the good ship William Thompson; American names like Josiah, Deborah, Jemima, Aminadab; and other recognizable elements form the fun of the play. The plot was slender and farcical, containing an accidental exchange of two letters of recommendation, so that Jonathan during his visit to England went to see Alderman Grossfeeder as a candidate for a post-boy's job. It was devised to contrast Jonathan with the English characters; Delapierre was not a Yankee, and behaved in a cosmopolitan manner. Some musical entertainment was included as well: Jonathan sang a version of Yankee Doodle, while Agamemnon performed the great hit »Possum up de Gum Tree.»

George Colman, the Licenser of Plays, thought some passages of *Jonathan in England* objectionable, probably because they might incite the anti-American feelings of an English audience, and were otherwise in bad taste. In 1824, the last campaign of the last Anglo-American war was only ten years distant, and the relations between the two countries were not the best. Among the deleted passages was an English lady's remark: » . . . tho' I dislike Americans yet we must for Mr. Ledger's sake be civil.» When Delapierre said: »Sir Leatherlip told me he would not listen to my offers as he detested the very name of an American,» the last words were corrected to the less provocative »as he detested my name.» This dialogue was also deleted:

---

[1] *Jonathan in England* was essentially an adaptation of David Humphreys' *The Yankey in England*, a comedy in five acts published in Connecticut, 1815. The latter was the first play to take a Yankee to England. It was produced by amateurs in the United States in 1814. (Arthur Hobson Quinn [ed.], *Literature of the American People* [New York, 1951], p. 204.) William Dunlap wanted to have it performed on the stage, but failed. (Cf. Gohdes, *Op.cit.*, p. 74; Reed.) *Jonathan in England* is available in *British Museum Add. MS 42868*. pp. 18—57, and in *Dicks' Standard Plays* (589), where it is called *Americans Abroad*.

> *Butler:* But what has a Liverpool postilion to do with American politics?
> *Jonathan:* I guess, that all the Liverpool folk get something by the Americans — Mr. Butler.[1]

These minor changes did not alter the tenor of the play, and it cannot be said that the censor's objections were directed against the presentation of American themes or the praise of the United States.

The Sunday Times criticized the play as follows:

> It is meant to describe the talkative, inquisitive, and blundering qualities of a thorough-bred Virginian [*sic!*], but, in the course of the piece, the manners and notions of Jonathan are very sadly caricatured, and there are some illiberal sneers at his hobby for independence. Neither the wit of the dialogue nor the situations in the piece can compensate for this aberration of good taste; for, although harmless satires upon national peculiarities are quite allowable, yet those which go to impeach the real stuff of their character ought to be discouraged. Of plot there was none; yet, by the aid of Mathews' powers, and those of the other public favourites, the farce went off well; for, somehow or other, John Bull, in spite of his love of justice, relishes a hearty laugh at the expense of his Trans-Atlantic brethren.[2]

The European Magazine noted that the aim of the farce was to »raise a laugh at the strange phraseology of our trans-Atlantic brethren. So long as this object was fairly kept in view, the audience were unanimous in their approbation.» But when the play began to reproach things American, the audience was reported to have given a »strong expression of disgust.» This statement seems to have been written in a pro-American mood. Otherwise this critic liked Mathews' acting and disliked the products of »Peake's pun-manufactory.»[3] In the *Memoirs*, Mrs. Mathews characterizes the play as »eminently successful.»[4]

The theme of Monsieur Mallét and his troubles at the Boston post office was written up by William Thomas Moncrieff.[5] The title was

---

[1] *British Museum Add. MS 42868.* pp. 18. ff.
[2] September 5, 1824, 1.
[3] »English Opera House,» LXXXVI, 272—273 (September, 1824).
[4] III, 516—517.
[5] Moncrieff's career was typical of a nineteenth-century concocter of plays. At first a lawyer's clerk interested in the writing of song lyrics, he became manager of the Regency Theatre, and wrote his first play in 1810. Continuing to work at the bar, he managed various theatres and wrote over 170 dramatic pieces of the most varying content and quality. (G. C. Boase, »William Thomas Moncrieff,» *Dictionary of National Biography.*)

Monsieur Mallét; or, My Daughter's Letter, first presented at the Adelphi on January 22, 1829.[1] This play was Moncrieff's first venture in the field of humorous presentation of American character; in 1838 he followed up his initial success with another piece called *Tarnation Strange*.[2]

Monsieur Mallét, this »Gallo-American Drama of National Manners and Peculiarities»[3] or »Entirely New Burletta Drama, of National Manners and Peculiarities»[4] is remarkable for its comprehensive list of humorous Americans, including the first definite frontiersman:

Patterson, a money-minded Yankee businessman, who always talks in terms of book-keeping and business, and is unaware of the humour of his statements.[5]

Oroonoko, a Negro. Loves acting and misquotes Shakespeare in the vein of Mathews' Negro tragedian, all in Negro dialect.

Jeremiah Kentuck, a bragging, self-confident, versatile, and vigorous frontiersman from Otsego County near Cherry Valley. Congressman, attorney-at-law, dealer in log-wood, orator, and »half-horse, half-alligator, with a touch of the steamboat, and a small taste of the snapping turtle.»

Brandywine, Colonel and innkeeper. Shows true American independence and self-reliance in the tradition of the travel-book innkeepers.

Uncle Ben, or Mr. Commissary Benjamin Brom Van Gunnery, from the Knickenbocker Settlement in the Blue Mountain, a long mile behind Albany. An Irvingesque Dutch-American.

Penweazle, the Postmaster. An elaboration of Mathews' postmaster of 1824.

Oroonoko, Brandywine, Uncle Ben, and Penweazle are clearly traceable to their sources. The Yankee has become a businessman. More interesting is the fact that we find a frontiersman like Jeremiah Kentuck on the English stage as early as January, 1829. He is a typical frontiersman, the first representative of his class on the English, and perhaps on any stage. Even if the Kentuckians, usually hunters

---

[1] Published as an octavo volume in 1851, and included in *Dicks' Standard Plays* (936). The music was composed by J. Barnett. (*Nicoll*.)

[2] See *infra*, p. 73 ff. [3] *Dicks'* caption.

[4] Caption in playbill, *Enthoven Collection*.

[5] Stephen Leacock would call him »super-comic.»

and the prototypes of all frontiersmen, were well-known tall-tale characters in America during the first decades of the nineteenth century, the fixation of the type on the stage did not follow immediately. Eastern newspapers in the United States could refer to Mississippi rivermen as »half-horse half-alligator creatures» without explaining the term as early as 1813. Still, Paulding's *Lion of the West*, quoted as the first play based on frontier character, was not acted in America until 1830.[1] It seems likely that Moncrieff wrote a pioneer dramatization of a character he had read about in transatlantic newspapers or books, or perhaps heard about; maybe the attractions of Mike Fink or Davy Crockett had proved strong enough to warrant more extensive research in frontier character.[2] In any case the dramatic presentation of a humorous American backwoodsman was new on the English stage in 1829.

Another source of fun was the representation of several different forms of spoken English. In this play we meet British English; Yankee, frontier, and Negro dialects, and the speech of Irving's New-York Dutchmen. In addition there is the French accent of M. Mallét.

The plot was based on the Boston Post-Office episode of Mathews' 1824 »At Home.» Here a dramatic framework was added. Mallét, an *ancien régime* aristocrat, sought refuge in America. He had temporarily lost contact with his daughter, and was eagerly expecting news from her. The beautiful Mademoiselle Adelaide arrived in Boston simultaneously with the eventual delivery of the letter to her father. This, and the ensuing complications involving a search and several mistaken identities, form the basis of the plot.

Monsieur Mallét proved a great success. It ran from January 22 to October 3, 1829, to full audiences, and achieved a total of at least 54 performances.[3] The acting was good: Yates played Oroonoko, T. P. Cooke Uncle Ben, and the youthful and unknown Buckstone Jeremiah Kentuck.[4] The reviewers praised the play as »eminently successful»

---

[1] Blair, *Native American Humor*, p. 30; Rourke, *American Humor*, p. 71; Nelson F. Adkins, »James K. Paulding's 'Lion of the West,'» *American Literature*, III, 249 (1931).

[2] Jeremiah Kentuck was a Congressman, which suggests Crockett as a source. The first known instance when Mike Fink stories were published in England was in Mary Russell Mitford's anthology *Stories of American Life by American Writers*, 3 vols. (London, 1830).

[3] Playbills in *Enthoven Collection*.

[4] *Ibid*. It should be noted that the part of Kentuck formed a stepping-stone in Buckstone's eminent career; he was still unknown to the *Times* critic, although

and »the best scenic effort Moncrieff ever made.»[1] Their criticisms show that although the play contained the first frontier character ever presented on the English stage, they failed to grasp the novelty of Jeremiah Kentuck's traits.[2]

To sum up, Charles Mathews' achievement in the history of humorous presentations of American character on the English stage consisted of introducing the Yankee, the Negro, and the immigrant in the »At Home» of 1824, and following up his success by acting the main part of *Jonathan in England* in the same year. He convinced British playwrights, managers, directors, actors, and audiences of the entertainment value and interest of comic Americans.[3] In *Monsieur Mallét*, a play based on an episode of Mathews' 1824 entertainment, Moncrieff introduced the character of the frontiersman in the shape of Jeremiah Kentuck. This took place in 1829, which is a remarkably early date for such a presentation.

1824 remains one of the important years in the entire history of American humour in England. It was then that this genre was brought into the consciousness of many sections of the English population.

CHAPTER III

SOME MINOR CHARACTERIZATIONS PRIOR TO 1833

On September 24, 1827, Sadler's Wells staged a first performance of a play by an unknown author, *Uncle Jonathan; or, Independence*. It was classified as an operatic farce[4] and probably was an English crea-

---

he had acted with the Coburg company since 1823.

[1] *Times*, January 23, 1829, 2.

[2] *Morning Post*, January 23, 1829, 3; »Theatrical Intelligence,» *Atlas*, XIII, 502 (August 11, 1838).

[3] An interesting question is that of Mathews' influence on the history of American humour and on comic characters on the American stage. J. H. Hackett, the famous American comedian who later became famous in England as well (see *infra*), thus copied Mathews by introducing the story of Jonathan and Uncle Ben in America. A scrutiny of this aspect falls outside the scope of the present study.

[4] *Nicoll*.

tion.¹ It ran until October 12, 1827,² as a trailer farce to *Paul Jones*, and the latter received most of the publicity in the newspaper advertisements, which did not mention American themes at all.³

In 1829 Thomas Dibdin, a member of the well-known English family of theatrical people, wrote a play entitled *The Banks of the Hudson; or the Congress Trooper*.⁴ The first performance took place at the Coburg Theatre on December 26, 1829.

This romance forms part of the patriotic tradition in English playwriting. The setting is America during the Revolution. Buckskin, a Yankee lad, tries to be »neutral» in the War. He and two English officers go through various melodramatic adventures. Captain Jonathan Dobson, the vulgar and detestable commander of a ferocious band of American soldiers, is just about to execute one of the gallant Britons by burning him alive with an innocent American family, when the other English officer enters with a detail of heroes in scarlet and blue. After this miraculous escape the play ends on a note of general glee and happiness.

The patriotic and melodramatic action largely obscured the presentation of American character. One of the scenes depicted an American farm. Here the inevitable Negro slave was called Pompey; he had a weakness for more drink than he could stand, and spoke the usual Negro dialect. A slave song was included.⁵ Abundance Allright, a Quaker maid,⁶ can be considered a humorous character because of her use of the language thought typical of people of her faith:

When I, Abundance Allright of Misseewisse, and one of the Society of Friends, agreed to become a domestic help, or maiden of the Chamber, to Cecily, profanely

---

¹ Not listed by *Reed*. ² Advertisements in *Times*.

³ Thus, the first notice: »To conclude with (never acted) an entirely new dramatic improbability called *Uncle Jonathan*.» (*Times*, September 24, 1827, 2.)

⁴ Printed in G. H. Davidson's *Minor Theatres*, vol. II, under the caption »Transatlantic Romance in Three Acts.»

⁵ »We worky for massa.
   Hurry worry, whoo, hoo!
   We worky for massa's son —
   We worky for pretty little young missee, too.
   From rising de sun
   Till daylight be done,
   Den him dance, all fun!
   Hurry worry, hurry worry,
   Hurry worry, hoo, whoo, hoo!» (Act I, Scene 3.)

⁶ Acted by Mrs. Davidge (Playbill in *Enthoven Collection*).

called Miss Morgan, of this farm, homestead, and mansion. I did not agree to be, as it were, solicited by sable slaves, or, to speak more plainly, bothered with the Blacky Moors, or, in the vulgar tongue, annoyed by the Niggers ... [1]

The other characters belong to the sphere of melodrama rather than to that of comedy.

A dramatization of James Fenimore Cooper's *The Pioneers* was staged at Covent Garden in April, 1830. It was a »melodramatic entertainment,» and probably contained no humorous treatments of American character.[2]

In April, 1827, Covent Garden was first visited by James H. Hackett, an American actor who excelled in imitating dialect and regional character.[3] The first night was on the 5th, when Hackett played *Sylvester Daggerwood*, »As Altered from 'NEW HAY AT THE OLD MARKET,' and adapted to the introduction of Sketches of American Character and IMITATIONS.»[4] Further, Hackett took up his adaptations of Mathews' 1824 show and introduced his »Original Yankee Stories of Jonathan and Uncle Ben, And the History of Hans Knickerbocker, (the American Dutchman), together with other IMITATIONS.»[5] The performance was a complete failure:

... Unfortunately for Mr. Hackett his stories of Jonathan and Uncle Ben, and the history of Hans Knickerbocker, had been previously given by Mathews, and though probably not so correctly; yet, being then new, told with greater animation. Mr. Hackett appeared to the audience somewhat tedious, and at length they showed strong feelings of disapprobation; these stories were certainly too long, and though told with a great deal of humour, which we think promises much, were not at all relished by the house ... [6]

No wonder that Hackett's London show of 1827 ran for just one performance.

The persistent American actor had not abandoned the thought of taking his humorous American characterizations to England after his

---

[1] Act I, Scene 3.

[2] *Genest*, IX, 518—519. The dramatization has not survived. Its title was *Wigwam; or, the Men of the Wilderness*.

[3] Hackett was born in New York in 1800. He had been very successful in the United States with the Mathews-inspired Jonathan and Uncle Ben episode. (Matthews and Hutton, *Op.cit.*, III, 160—161.)

[4] Playbill in *Enthoven Collection*. [5] *Ibid*.

[6] One of the unidentified clippings in *Enthoven Collection*. Here the reviewer was in error: Mathews never performed Knickerbocker. Another clipping reveals the reaction of the audience to have consisted of cries: »Off, off!»

first failure. In 1832 he set out to present *Jonathan in England* in London. This play was an alteration of George Colman's comedy *Who Wants a Guinea?* of 1805, where the original Solomon Gundy had been metamorphosed into Solomon Swap, a Yankee.[1] It is not to be confused with Peake's dramatization of Mathews' Jonathan W. Doubikin.[2] Although Swap was a humorous character, the play was not entirely based on American humour; Gundy was originally a very secondary person in the play, and Swap's repliques are but slightly longer. Solomon Swap, a self-styled »merchant» from New Hampshire was employed as a servant in England, and the ensuing complications had provided Hackett with the materials for a New-York success.

The London first performance of *Jonathan in England* took place at Drury Lane on November 17, 1832. It was repeated on November 23. The playbills frankly admitted that it was a »revival» of Colman's original with added American elements.[3] The playwright, who was then Licenser of Plays, was duly shocked at seeing the changes his manuscript had been subjected to.[4]

Although Hackett at this time was an actor of some renown in the United States, he did not achieve the success he was looking for. The fact that Hackett had coupled *Jonathan* to a feeble rehash and echo of Mathews' old *Militia Muster*,[5] did not prove popular with the audience. This was partly due to the imperfect acting of Messrs. Dowton and Power, who did not feel called for to exert their utmost. The public was disgusted and hissed at the performance, which was not repeated. The reviewers tended to praise Hackett as a good actor, but stated several objections to the plays.

---

[1] Printed in *French's Standard Drama*, CCCXX.

[2] See Quinn, *Representative American Plays*, p. 45. Cf. *supra*, pp. 42—44.

[3] *Enthoven Collection*.

[4] When Colman had waded through the manuscript *ex officio*, he sent a note to a friend: »I have received the alterations made by Mr. *Hackett* (a very appropriate name for the purpose) and shall request the Lord Chamberlain to license the rubbish.» (*Sunday Times*, November 18, 1832, 3.)

[5] In April, 1830, Hackett had played Joe Bunker in *Down East; or, the Militia Training* at Park Theatre, New York. (Quinn, *American Drama to the Civil War*, p. 297.) The London playbill (*Enthoven Collection*) called *The Militia Muster* »A New Comic Entertainment . . . written expressly for Mr. HACKETT's celebrated delineation of the American Character.» According to the Drury Lane Account Book of 1832 (*Enthoven Collection*) this sketch was written by Beazley.

The most interesting of these has to do with the intelligibility of American humour and dialect to an English public: »Many of the barbarisms introduced to tickle the ears of Jonathan, were perfectly unintelligible to an English audience, and fell still-born.»[1]

One reviewer thought that Hackett »certainly might be more worthily employed than in exhibiting an extravagant caricature of his fellow-countrymen's peculiarities.»[2] Another called the characterizations »a little exaggerated» and too close to the West-Indian Negro.[3] *The Examiner* condemned the play because of »the grossest allusions, and the most obscene jests.»[4] The reviewer of *The Athenaeum* intimated that he, having visited the United States in his youth, could testify to the genuineness of Hackett's portraitures.[5]

The second part of the show, *The Militia Muster*, was condemned by all reviewers as »exceedingly stupid» and »a gross piece of impertinence.»[6]

It is evident that Hackett's second appearance on the English stage in the role of an ambassador of American humour was a comparative failure. His own acting was relished in *Jonathan in England*, but the plays, particularly *The Militia Muster*, did not prove popular with the audience. His representation of humorous American English and the transatlantic jokes was not always understood by the Londoners; the actor had failed to adapt his technique to the demands of the English stage.

In spite of these objections Hackett was the second important comedian to cross the Atlantic and present comic Americans on the English stage. Mathews had been an Englishman, and although his exceptional talents had enabled him to imitate transatlantic character and speech, his show did not illustrate American society and people with verisimilitude. Hackett again was a native American and knew his country as well as anybody. But he did not possess Mathews' intimate knowledge of the tastes of the British public; neither did he possess Mathews' fame, which in itself was a guarantee of success. The conclusion remains that in the early eighteen-thirties it was still important

---

[1] Unidentified clipping, *Enthoven Collection*.
[2] *Times*, November 19, 1832, 2.
[3] Unidentified clipping, *Enthoven Collection*. [4] November 25, 1832, 756.
[5] *Athenaeum*, November 24, 1832, 764.
[6] *Ibid.*; *Times*, November 19, 1832, 2; three unidentified clippings in *Enthoven Collection*.

to adapt American humour to the English stage. Londoners could not be successfully entertained by the same Jonathan who convulsed the New-York audiences; either Jonathan had to be changed or the British public taught to appreciate him before success was assured.

CHAPTER IV

RIP VAN WINKLE

In 1832 Washington Irving's *Rip Van Winkle* became a medium of humorous American characterizations on the English stage.[1]

Of all the work of Irving, only the stories centering around the Knickerbocker theme and the New-York Dutch were felt by the English to be native American humour. Irving's works were well known in Britain, and the general consensus remained that Irving was a writer in the European rather than American tradition.[2] For some critics this was a point in his favour; to others it meant lack of originality. But in the New-York stories the local colour could not be mistaken; here the author had built up a whole world of characters and incidents that were peculiar to one segment of the United States at a certain historical period. Not knowing America it was easy for Britons to forget that Irving's characters were essentially romantic creations of a past age. When they read Geoffrey Crayon or saw his works acted on the stage, they thought Rip, van Twiller, and the others representative specimens of an actual living class of individuals. Hence, Irvingesque characters are to be found in some of the plays that contain humorous analyses of the United States, and they developed into a minor stock type.[3] Because of this process, the Rip-Van-Winkle theme deserves

---

[1] At Drury Lane, a farce on the Rip-Van-Winkle theme entitled *The Spectre Bridegroom; or, a Ghost in Spite of Himself*, was performed in the summer of 1821. Reviews do not mention humorous treatments of American character. (E.g. »Theatrical Journal,» *European Magazine*, LXXX, 81 [July, 1821].) See William B. Cairns, *British Criticisms of American Writings, 1783—1815* (Madison, Wis., 1918), p. 70.

[2] Cairns, *Op.cit.*, includes an account of Irving's reception in England.

[3] *E.g.*, Benjamin Brom Van Gunnery of Moncrieff's *Monsieur Mallet*. See *supra*, p. 45.

some attention in the present discussion, whatever the opinion of Irving's place in the American tradition. Other American stock characters were also freely inserted into English dramatizations of the story.

William Bayle Bernard, one of the nineteenth-century playwrights who wrote copiously both for the English and the American stage,[1] was the author of the two-act burletta *Rip Van Winkle: or, the Helmsman of the Spirit Crew*. It was first performed at the Adelphi on October 1, 1832.

This dramatization used both the melodramatic effects offered by Henry Hudson's spirit crew and the humorous subjects afforded by the American setting.[2] It is notable that Bernard inserted a considerable quantity of Yankee characterization, humour, and dialect into his version. Ebenezer Twang was the name of his typical Yankee. In 1763, in Colonial days, Twang was a modest politician, peddler, squatter, and vagrant; after Rip's return from the mountains in 1783 his Yankee shrewdness and enterprise had transformed him into Mr. Brigadier Twang, attorney-at-law, and candidate for Congress. He had lost some of his Yankee speech in the process, although the idiom tended to reappear at critical moments. Among Twang's virtues was a war record from the Revolution.[3]

Twang's Yankee qualities are displayed from the very beginning of the play. In his store he monologizes:

Times are nation bad now, I reckon — only one customer today in my variety Store, and a ryal good store I've got sure alive and slick assortment of priorime [?] articles Picle Pork — apple Brandy, — Yankee rum, Ingyn Corn — wooden Bowls — taller Candles — varmint baker — dumbfish taters and lasses dullish life I lead here — mongst the ten breeches tough breeches — short pipes and long pipes — no squatting or swapping of bundling or husking don't even talk — do

---

[1] Bernard was born in Boston in 1807 of English parents, but the entire family returned to the mother country in 1820. He became a professional dramatist in 1830, and wrote some 114 plays before his death in 1875. Many of these were written for America. Bernard was acquainted with American literature; one of the stage versions of Cooper's *The Pilot* bears his name. *Rip Van Winkle* was among his best-known plays. (Richard Garnett, »William Bayle Bernard,» *Dictionary of National Biography*.)

[2] The playbill has the words »SPIRIT SHIP!» in large capitals next to the title, which shows the emphasis on melodrama. (*Enthoven Collection*.)

[3] The present account is based on *British Museum Add. MS 42918*. pp. 230—278.

nothing but smoke all day like a brick kiln — I'm the only Englisher at Kaatskill — the only one that's got a royalistical feeling for our Young King George the 3rd there he swings (*looks at the sign*) heaven bless him he looks like a King with his crown and skipter a priorime King (*goes in again*).[1]

Twang's opportunistic bent made him a strong royalist in 1763, when he exercised his Yankee virtues among the more phlegmatic Dutchmen of the village. »George the 3rd tarnal good King — consarn his inemies,» and »I'm a lyal colonist and can look his majesty in the face at any time» were among his favourite expressions. He was impressed by his own versatility: »I've a notion I can cut wood — feed Pork — dig pounds — dry fruit — mow hay and sticthed [*sic*] shoes . . .»[2] He bragged about his previous career, too; his courtship had been carried out with characteristic gusto: he sat up courting for one night, and got married in the morning.

The most interesting of Twang's statements is an explanation of the typical qualities of different regional representatives of the United States. These passages prove that Bernard was aware of the distinctions between Americans from various parts of the country. Of the Yankees Twang said:

> I calculate they're a riglar squattin swappin, guessin grindin, freakish-waspish-sharpish-cutish-cleverish-pumpkin Eating, lasses-loving, shingle-splitting, cider-drinking, new-notioned — vagabonds.

The New York Dutch were

> Tarnal snarl of barbarians — the whole tote nation true Cap:n I shet my clam at home, but I'm not afeered to tell you that they're a set of sleepy — smoky stuffy, stumpy — stubby, dreamy — drowsy, drudgy, dumpy, bonish, brutish, biggish individuals . . . smoke — nothing but smoke — darn me up a tree.

Of the Southerners, he continued:

> Can't say much of them Cap:n — no great shakes fathers and mothers you know all of the old Bailey breed — brought over the »Birmingham jewels» collars and bracelets in the iron and steelway while they live upon hoe cakes and bacon — mull'd madeiry eggnogg — and appletoddy — specially spry they are — sure alive — oh boxing and gouging, gaming, betting, and wenching and sure like experimental discursions — but they know nothing of the fine arts, and manufactures — nothing of Red'n and writin and figuring — they're a rigler — dram drinking, cock fighting, horse racing — Tavern hunting Sabbath breaking Slave driving, nigger breeding upstarts.[3]

---

[1] *Ibid.*, pp. 242—3. [2] *Ibid.*, p. 245. [3] *Ibid.*, pp. 245—6.

In addition to the eminent Ebenezer Twang, Bernard introduced Samuel Spry, another Yankee and keeper of The Washington Hotel, in the second act. The prominence of American innkeepers in the early presentations of transatlantic character in England owes much to travel-book accounts. Dionysius, »the Brigadier's Nigger,» represents coloured America, and prominent among his utterances is the usual »Iss, massa.» Bernard did not hesitate to make his Yankee a slave-owner.

The Dutch-American humour of Rip and his friends was not equally prominent. Here the fun consisted of more universal topics like Rip's domestic problems and his indolence.

Bernard's *Rip Van Winkle* ran at least until November 17, 1832, while a playbill of October 22 announced it for the »nineteenth time.»[1] It should be called a minor success. The actors were good: Yates's Rip and Buckstone's Twang were praised by the reviewers. A scene where the two Yankees, Twang and Sly, act as rival election candidates at the Kaatskill village, was the favourite. Yet, many objections were made. *The Morning Post* thought »a skilful hand might have produced a far superior drama out of the materials afforded . . .»[2] *The Times* complained about the fact that Irving's original style had been lost in the process of dramatization. It went on to opine that more humour would have helped the play.[3] *The Spectator* commented upon Rip, who was »exceedingly well acted.»[4] *The Sunday Times* review moved in the territory between moderate praise and moderate blame.[5] *The Examiner* had no difficulty in making up its mind. It called the play »a failure; the humour is strained, the plot meagre, the piece tedious.»[6] *The Athenaeum* stated that it »laboured under disadvantage from the confusion of a first performance,» but Bernard »need not be ashamed of his present production.»[7] *The Observer* simply noted that the strength of the Adelphi company was used, »and their exertions were awarded with success.»[8]

By elaborating on Irving's original short story, Bernard thus made *Rip Van Winkle* a medium not only of the genteel fun of the original, but also of humorous presentations of Yankee character. These elements were mixed with melodrama in the Adelphi tradition; Hend-

---

[1] Advertisements in *Times;* playbill in *Enthoven Collection*.
[2] October 2, 1832, 3. [3] October 2, 1832, 2.
[4] October 6, 1832, 946. [5] October 7, 1832, 3. [6] October 7, 1832, 647.
[7] October 13, 1832, 669. [8] October 7, 1832, 3.

rick Hudson's spirit crew provided ample materials for blood-and-thunder treatment. It has not been possible to ascertain to what extent Bernard's version used the two previous American dramatizations for sources.[1]

The next version of *Rip Van Winkle* on the English stage came from the pen of Charles Burke, the American actor and playwright, half-brother of Joseph Jefferson.[2] It was staged at the Theatre Royal, Haymarket, on May 3, 1833, under the title of *Rip Van Winkle; or, a Legend of the Kaatskill Mountains*.[3]

In Burke's play the plot is clearly melodramatic: Rip signs a contract with van Tassel to marry his daughter to young van Tassel. Van Tassel senior knows that Rip has just inherited a fortune from Holland; the heir has not been informed. Rip disappears for his twenty years of sleep, and when he comes back, the court is just about to pass a decision in the matter. By means of a copy of the marriage contract that he finds in his moldy pocket, soiled and yellow with age, he proves his identity.

Both Irvingesque Dutch and Yankee humour can be found. Rip speaks a peculiar Teutonic brand of English:

> Where te tiafle is dat dog — well here's another pad job — hont and hont and hont and hont and nothing cotch'd. I had some fon tho' for all dat for I stopp'd at Winchy von Bummels and dere we raised de diavel, mit play hussel cap and nine bins and mint slings drinking dill all dings was blue 'cobe was so drunk when he went to throw de roller at de nine bins — he fell down and den swore dat de ground had jump'd up and hit him a lickon.[4]

Rip's matrimonial problems add to the humour; when the irate and domineering »Frow» appears, he expostulates: »Vedder hadn't I petter wait a pit till de plast has blown over.»[5]

---

[1] The first of these was named *Rip Van Winkle; or, the Spirits of the Catskill Mountains*. It was played in Albany in May, 1828. The author is unknown. The second version, *Rip Van Winkle; or, the Demons of the Catskill Mountains*, was a »national drama» in two acts by John Kerr, and was first performed at Park Theatre, New York, in 1829, with the celebrated Hackett in the main part. (*Reed*, pp. 155—156.) In any case Bernard probably added the dialect; Kerr's version used the King's English. (Quinn, *American Drama to the Civil War*, pp. 328—329.)

[2] Quinn, *Op.cit.*, pp. 328—9.

[3] Printed in *Dicks' Standard Plays* (340) in the eighties. The following account is based on *British Museum Add. MS 42921*. pp. 451—494.

[4] Act I, Scene 1.   [5] *Ibid.*

In the second act, there is a contrast between »quiet Dutchmen and locomotive Yankees in Nankeen Jackets and Straw Hats.» There are marked similarities between Bernard's and Burke's adaptations at this point. In the latter version, the post-revolutionary changes in the life of the Dutch village also consist of increased Yankee influence. This time the inevitable Yankee hotelkeeper's name is Peashell, and he speaks of the »sleepy, smoky, stringy Dutchmen» much the same as Ebenezer Twang. Constant inconsistencies in the spelling of Rip's dialect suggest that Burke was not on sure ground when composing his manuscript.

But he did not have to be over-careful in filling out the details. As usual, the Haymarket performance relied upon expert acting. Hackett himself had crossed the Atlantic in order to play Rip, a part with which he was familiar from the United States.[1] Buckstone impersonated the talkative Yankee landlord, Webster the village dominie, Mrs. Tayleure the garrulous Mrs. Van Winkle.

The play ran for less than three weeks.[2] It was revived in October, 1839.[3] Reviews called Hackett's Rip »a capital personation,»[4] and the play was said to have »a very agreeable dramatic shape.»[5] The audience reacted with »very lively demonstrations of applause.»[6]

Decades passed, and the English interest in Rip Van Winkle seemed gone and forgotten. Then, in 1865, a combination of circumstances brought the theme back into limelight, and made a play on Rip's adventures one of the great successes of the century.

Joseph Jefferson, the celebrated American actor, paid his second visit to England in June, 1865.[7] When he arrived, he met Dion Boucicault, another of the prominent men of the theatrical world who had worked extensively on both sides of the Atlantic. The latter suggested that a revised dramatic adaptation of *Rip Van Winkle* be put on the stage for Jefferson. Webster, the manager of the Adelphi, was not on the most cordial of terms with Boucicault.[8] However, Jefferson succeed-

---

[1] See *supra*, p. 49.   [2] Advertisements in *Times*.
[3] *Athenaeum*, November 12, 1839, 782.   [4] *Ibid*.   [5] *Times*, May 4, 1833, 5.
[6] *Ibid*.

[7] Jefferson was a specialist in humorous American characterizations, including Asa Trenchard of *Our American Cousin*. His career had started at the tender age of four, when he climbed out of a large trunk and performed Jim Crow together with Rice, the pioneer in Negro minstrelsy. See *infra*, p. 78.

[8] The quarrel originated in a controversy about management of the Adelphi after the success of *Colleen Bawn*. (*Critic*, June 21, 1862, 613.)

ed in pacifying both the temperamental gentlemen into cooperation. Thus, the Adelphi version of 1865 bore the mark of both Boucicault and Jefferson, who wrote it in collaboration.¹

This dramatization played up the melodramatic aspects of the story in the Adelphi manner. The first act illustrated events before Rip's long sleep, the second the happenings in the village during his absence, the third his return. A thunderstorm in the mountains; a fight between Derrick, a villain who threw Rip down a precipice, and the hero; and Henry Hudson's spirit crew were used for special effect. The humour depended on the characteristics of Rip himself; stage Yankees were not introduced.²

The first performance took place on September 4, 1865. In that year, 101 performances were given; and when Jefferson left to play Rip in the provinces in March, 1866, the last Adelphi showing was billed as the 172nd.³

The critics unanimously praised Jefferson's acting. Rip gave him the opportunity to show the influence of age on a character, and a chance to develop numerous details like the drunkard's reluctance to swallow the first drink after some sober days. The reviews read like panegyrics:

... Mr. Jefferson's performance is one of the most remarkable which we have ever seen. It is a perfect delineation of Dutch character in accent, manner, and appearence... Mr. Jefferson is an actor-humourist. He has mastered all the inflections of a voice which is naturally sweet. He has a smile like sunshine. He has the power of drawing tears with a word, and sometimes with a look.⁴

... We have not often seen a finer, and never a less artificial or more easy piece of acting, than Mr. Jefferson's picture of the genial, quick, indolent, at once helpful and helpless loiterer, suddenly insulated from all the trifles in which he had lived, and made to realize at once that the busy world had not wanted *him*, but that he had no life except in *it*.⁵

The only criticisms had to do with the changes in Irving's original: Henry Morley called some of them »tasteless,» while delicacies had been »smothered in the garlic and onions of the melodramatist.»⁶ In general,

---

¹ Joseph Jefferson, *Autobiography* (London and New York, 1889), 308.
² *Lord Chamberlain MSS 7/1865*, i.e., Vol. 7 of 1865.
³ Playbills in *Enthoven Collection. Observer.* April 8, 1866.
⁴ *Reader*, VI, 494—495 (October 28, 1865).
⁵ *Spectator*, September 16, 1865, 1027—8.
⁶ Henry Morley, *Journal of a London Playgoer*, pp. 376—9. The same objection was stated by *The Examiner*, September 23, 1865, 603.

however, the *Rip Van Winkle* of 1865 was thought »a triumphant success.»[1]

As usual after a successful play, imitations and rehashes appeared. John Strachan and Henry Davis wrote a burlesque of it which was first presented in Newcastle in March, 1866. Here King Arthur and his knights deliver volleys of *bons mots* and *double entendres* around a bewildered Rip. The puns, most of them atrocious, are interspersed with topical allusions to the Emperor Maximilian of Mexico, the Monroe Doctrine, and similar questions of the day.[2]

The Theatre Royal, Norwich, staged a version written by W. W. Sidney and T. F. Phillips, which built heavily on the Boucicault-Jefferson script. Here Rip speaks a comic dialect, but no Yankees are to be found in the play. The additions to the Adelphi version consist mainly of puns uttered by Rip.[3] Theatre Royal, Oldham, also took advantage of the popularity of the theme, and staged its own variant on March 23, 1866.[4]

Even *Fun*, Hood's humorous magazine, printed a facetious suggestion for a new ending of *Rip Van Winkle* in its series »Continuations of Dramatic Histories.»[5]

The plays on the Rip-Van-Winkle theme of the thirties added the New-York Dutchman to the gallery of American stock characters on the English stage. Benjamin Brom Van Gunnery of *Monsieur Mallét* (1829) had anticipated this tradition, which was carried on by Peake in *The Emigrant's Daughter*.[6] This play was a revision of Dibdin's *The Banks of the Hudson*,[7] with the substitution of Diedrich Kidde, a brutal Dutch trooper, for the Yankee Jonathan Dobson of the original. Mynheer Van Stork was portrayed in *The Long Finn; or the Treasure-Seeker's Dream* of 1833.[8] Another American Dutchman, Van Huysen, was

---

[1] Further reviews: *Times*, September 6, 1865, 12; *Englishman*, September 9, 1865, 2; *Observer*, September 10, 1865, 6; *Illustrated London News*, September 30, 1865, 319; *Sketch*, May 30, 1900, 259. The words quoted are from *Athenaeum*, September 9, 1865, 350.

[2] *Lord Chamberlain MSS 4/1866*. [3] *Ibid*. [4] *Ibid*.

[5] Here the irate *vrouw* had learnt her lesson during Rip's absence, having been reduced to abject submission by Derrick. Ensues a scene of connubial bliss. The finish was even more melodramatic than that of the stage versions. (II n.s., 213 [February 10, 1866].)

[6] Performed in 1838, available in *British Museum Add. MS 42948*.

[7] See *supra*, p. 48. [8] See *infra*, p. 72.

included in *Life in America* by William Leman Rede.¹ A Dutch name reappears in the dramatis personae of one version of *Uncle Tom's Cabin* in 1852.² However, English interest in the Dutch-American type was never so intense as that in the Yankee, the Negro, or the frontiersman; his lethargy never gave him a chance to compete with shrewd Yankees or fiery westerners where vigorous action or humour was in demand. This can also be seen from the fact that the adapters of the thirties did not rely upon Rip's humour, but felt it necessary to insert comic Yankees into their plots. The success of the 1865 version built entirely on Jefferson's acting; here Rip became an individual and not a stock character.

CHAPTER V

1833—1839: THE ESTABLISHMENT OF A TRADITION

1. Nimrod Wildfire in England.

In addition to the previous plays, the audiences of the thirties had numerous opportunities to get acquainted with humorous Americans on the English stage. The basic stock characters had been introduced in the twenties, and the successes of some of the plays presenting them had created a demand for more. When the English had learnt to enjoy Jonathan's antics and his droll speech, a play title emphasizing his presence became an asset. In the thirties, humorous Americans became familiar figures of the English theatre.

James Kirke Paulding's *Lion of the West* has been called »the first drama to introduce a raw and uncouth frontiersman as its leading character.»³ It was a great success in the United States, where the

---

¹ First performed at Adelphi on November 7, 1836; available in *British Museum Add. MS 42939*.

² See *infra*, p. 115.

³ Nelson F. Adkins, »James K. Paulding's 'Lion of the West'», *American Literature*, III, 249 (November, 1931). It must be borne in mind that the American frontiersman had been introduced on the English stage *before* Nimrod Wildfire's appearance in *Lion of the West* in 1830; this had taken place in Moncrieff's *Monsieur Mallet* of 1829, which employed a character called Jeremiah Kentuck. See *supra*, p. 45.

popular Hackett played the main part.¹ After touring the West Hackett considered the time auspicious for another venture east of the Atlantic, and decided to transplant Nimrod Wildfire to the London stage.

In fact Wildfire's fame had spread across the ocean. As early as November, 1831, *The Athenaeum* wrote:

> A *Genuine Kaintuck.* — The Americans are as skilful in hitting off the ridiculous in their own countrymen as Mr. Mathews himself. In a little dramatic piece, now playing there with great success, the principal character is Nimrod Wildfire, who, to use his own language, is a *screamer.*

The magazine goes on to quote an episode from the play where Wildfire picked a fight with a raftsman:

> I am Nimrod Wildfire — half horse, half alligator, and a touch of the airthquake — that's got the prettiest sister, fastest horse, and ugliest dog in the district, and can outrun, outjump, throw down, drag out and whip any man in all Kaintuck ... An't I the yellow flower of the forest? and I'm all brimstone but the head, and that's aquafortis!²

The English version of Nimrod Wildfire's adventures was composed by William Bayle Bernard.³ It was called *The Kentuckian; or, A Trip to New York*, and classified as a farce.⁴

---

[1] The initial history of Paulding's play is of interest. In 1830 Hackett offered $ 300 as a prize for »an original comedy (in three acts) whereof an American should be the leading character.» A board of judges, Bryant and Halleck among its members, chose Paulding's MS as the worthiest. In the minds of contemporary Americans, Davy Crockett and Paulding's hero Nimrod Wildfire were soon identified. To avoid trouble the author wrote the Hon. David Crockett in Washington, and denied all such intentions in public. *Lion of the West* was first produced with »reasonable success» at Park Theatre, New York, on April 25, 1830. However, Hackett thought that the play was too preoccupied with Wildfire, and therefore a new version was written by John A. Stone (1801—34) with Paulding's permission. The new plot was more complicated and wove more characters into the action. Stone's version became a great success in New York, Boston, Philadelphia, and other large American cities, and record-breaking box-office intakes followed. (Adkins, *Op.cit.*)

[2] »Miscellanea,» November 5, 1831, 725—6.

[3] »It has been attributed, in the papers, to Mr. Bernard; but we have been informed, that that gentleman is responsible for nothing beyond cutting down an American comedy in three acts into the present farce.» (*Athenaeum*, March 16, 1833, 172.)

[4] There is a MS copy of this version among the Lord Chamberlain's license copies (*British Museum Add. MS 42920.* pp. 651—674). Since the original *Lion of the West* has not survived (Adkins, *Op.cit.*, 256), this MS may well be the most complete version we have of Paulding's play.

The characters illustrate the traditional contrast between Englishmen, Americans of the East, and the frontiersman. Nimrod Wildfire is the type of a frontier Kentuckian; Mr. and Mrs. Freeman represent the more polished Americans of the older communities. Freeman is a merchant with scanty interests in things non-material, while Mrs. Freeman's highest ambition is to be the mother-in-law of an English lord. Percival, an English businessman, represents honest John Bull, while Jenkins, another Briton, acts the villain by posing as Lord Grandby and availing himself of Mrs. Freeman's greatest weakness. Mrs. Luminary is a crusading Englishwoman, obviously modelled upon Mrs. Trollope, who wants to transform the United States into a civilized country by reforming American manners.

The action of the play is wholly subordinate to the characters. The plot consists of the age-old idea of exposure of the villain, and ends with a match between the honest Percival and young Miss Freeman among speeches emphasizing Anglo-American friendship and affinity. The play also expresses some other ideas and opinions. Mr. Freeman originally made a speech against hereditary titles, but this was deleted by Colman, the Licenser of Plays.[1] Freeman is careful to introduce Wildfire to the English audience by pointing out that he likes »native humour» and explaining that a frontier background is an ample excuse for lack of refinement. Wildfire is »a human cataract from Kentucky,» he says; »the Kentuckian is our National Gascon.» Mrs. Luminary's general horror of things American is exposed to ridicule. She was shocked beyond words when, at a dinner, in a company of twenty men nobody sat with his feet on the floor — what a »shocking familiarity with the furniture»! Wildfire does not make her adjustment easier. Even when wanting to explain to her »things in general on this here side of the big pond,» he »brings forward two chairs, sits on one, and just as Mrs. Luminary is about to sink into the other, he throws his legs on it.» His stories were not to her taste, either. Therefore it is understandable that the good Englishwoman was little attracted by Wildfire's next proposition: »I have ordered a good strong covered waggon for the Journey, there's a Parson close by who hitches teams quicker than any feller in the country — in five minutes we two will be hammered into one — and then . . .»[2]

In spite of the caricature, Wildfire's character was depicted with sympathy. Thus, when Jenkins challenges Wildfire to a duel, it is

---

[1] See *supra*, p. 20.   [2] *British Museum Add. MS 42920.* pp. 651—674.

Jenkins who has difficulties in retracting his challenge in front of Wildfire's impetuous bravery. In short, the play revolves around similar problems as Tyler's *The Contrast*.[1]

The Kentuckian was first performed at Covent Garden on March 9, 1833, and proved a minor success, although its run remained short due to external reasons. Hackett went on at Covent Garden until March 18 and gave six performances up to that date. On April 17 he moved to the Haymarket to continue. However, this theatre had to be closed »in consequence of the general prevailing Influenza,» and the next performance was not given until April 24. Hackett left for America at the end of May, having acted Wildfire in a total of 12 showings.[2] In any case Hackett's success was greater in 1833 than during his previous attempts to gain laurels by acting humorous American parts in London.

For an appreciation of the English reviews of *The Kentuckian* it is well to start with the comments passed by an Englishman who had seen the original version in New York. The following passage was written by E. T. Coke, a Briton of the military profession, who had visited the Park-Street Theatre in New York on a furlough trip:

> The first evening I was ashore, I attended the Arch [sic] Street Theatre (the most fashionable one, the Chesnut, being closed), for the purpose of seeing Mr. Hackett, who was in high repute with his countrymen, perform the part of »Nimrod Wildfire» in the »Raw Kentuckian; or, Lion of the West.» The play is intended to censure and correct the rough manners of the States west of the Alleghany mountains, and delighted the audience exceedingly; though to me the greater part of the dialogue consisted of unintelligible idioms. Mr. Hackett possesses great talent for broad comedy; and I was informed that th eeffect of his performance in the West was such as to excite a strong feeling against him; and so incensed the »half-horse, half-alligator boys,» »the yellow flowers of the forest,» as they call themselves, that they threatened »to row him up Salt river,» if he ventured a repetition of the objectionable performance. I was sorry, however, to see rather a bad feeling displayed towards the old country. In various parts of the performance frequent allusions were made to circumstances, which ought long to have been buried in oblivion; and which could only tend to diminish, or rather prevent, mutual good-will. These allusions, which ever told against the English, were much applauded by the audience.[3]

If the play was to be a success with Lieutenant Coke and his kind, revisions were called for. We may reason that some of Bernard's alterations and omissions in Paulding's and Stone's originals had to do with

---

[1] See *supra*, p. 10. [2] Playbills in *Enthoven Collection*.
[3] E. T. Coke, *A Subaltern's Furlough* (New York, 1833), p. 35.

such aspects that were either unintelligible or offensive to listeners like Coke.

Most of the critics of English newspapers and periodicals found the play strange. After a long description of the plot and Nimrod Wildfire's character, *The Observer* remarked:

> This little piece being excessively outlandish, we have not been able to describe it with the usual connected regularity. It is rather broad — and perhaps at first will not please — but those who are without prejudices, and who wish to see new characters, will not complain of it. The audience seemed very attentive, and the parts that were readily understood were immediately applauded. At the end of the piece Mr. Hackett was called for, and announced the piece for repetition amidst almost unanimous approbation.[1]

The Times devoted much space to a detailed series of comments. It thought the frontiersman »quite new to the English stage, and even almost unknown in England,» and praised both the novelty of the presentation and Hackett's acting, which were compared to Tyrone Power's stage Irishmen: »The Kentuckian is not a jot inferior to them in fun, and if we knew as much of him as we do of the children of the sister country, he would be quite as fully relished by the public.» The meagre plot and Mrs. Luminary's character were condemned.[2]

The same objections were stated by *The Morning Post*. The final verdict was favourable: the critic had been »exceedingly amused» by *The Kentuckian;* »the whole affair is an extravaganza, but is one of the most amusing we have witnessed for a long time, and was greeted throughout with shouts of laughter.»[3]

The Spectator also mentioned Mrs. Luminary among the defects of the play. It went on to commend Hackett's acting:

> Mr. HACKETT is a fine, manly fellow, with a frank look, a cordial smile disclosing a brilliant set of teeth, a sparkling eye, and immense heartiness of manner. He is none of your puny, sickly, cadaverous actors, whose pallor shows through the rouge and white lead; but a stout healthy yeoman, with a bronzed cheek, a voice as clear as a bell, and lungs that crow like chanticleer. His animal spirits lend to his performance that gusto which is essential to the truth of the character, as well as requisite to qualify its hardness.

---

[1] March 10, 1833, 3.

[2] March 11, 1833, 3. The English had, of course, never been irked by Mrs. Trollope.

[3] March 11, 1833, 5.

The same review contains a description of Wildfire's dress:

... a close buttoned frock, nankeen trowsers, with top-boots over them, and a cap of wild cat skin, the head grinning over one of his shoulders and the tail dangling over the other ...

The final verdict of this review was very favourable.[1]

The Examiner commented upon *The Kentuckian* in detail. It approved the satire of Mrs. Trollope and noted that Hackett used »far less breadth ... of dialect, than is bestowed upon the Yankee by our English actors.» This commentator considered Wildfire an old acquaintance: »a tarnation cute chap, such as Mathews has made us acquainted with long ago.»[2]

Other reviews called the play a »melange» and Wildfire a »gross exaggeration» and »a perfect brute in inexpressibles,» but mostly thought it a »decided success.»[3] *The Athenaeum* was sympathetic, but let it be understood that the audience had some difficulty in appreciating the strange humour: »The audience on Saturday took praiseworthy pains to understand the part, and as soon as they did, they relished it much and laughed heartily.»[4]

The Kentuckian was taken to Edinburgh, where the public had more trouble in understanding the fun.[5] It reappeared in London whenever Hackett was there looking for popular acclaim. Thus it was staged at the English Opera House in 1836. Now *The Athenaeum* was no longer enraptured by the play itself, but liked Hackett's acting as well as ever.[6]

The general consensus was much more favourable this time than during Hackett's previous visits to England. In 1833 the actor had a good play to work with, and although part of the dialogue remained unpalatable to an English audience, Hackett's efforts possessed sufficient appeal to warrant *The Kentuckian* a prominent place in the history of American humour on the English stage. As an external token of this appreciation, Hackett was chosen a member of the Garrick Club.[7]

---

[1] »Mr. Hackett's Kentuckian,» March 16, 1833, 234. [2] March 17, 1833, 166.
[3] Three unidentified clippings in the *Enthoven Collection*.
[4] March 16, 1833, 172.
[5] Lester Wallack, *Memories of Fifty Years* (New York, 1889), p. 194.
[6] August 6, 1836, 555. [7] *Sunday Times*, March 17, 1833, 3.

2. George Handel Hill as the Yankee Peddler.

George Handel Hill, better known as Yankee Hill, was one of the successful interpreters of the humorous Yankee.[1] Having received great acclaim west of the Atlantic Hill decided to try his luck in Europe. He came to England for the season 1836—7 and became celebrated for his Yankee parts, first in London, and then in the other theatrical centres of the United Kingdom. In 1838 he was in Europe again, acting both in England and in Paris.

The verdict of posterity is that although Hill excelled in Yankee parts, he was a man »of few gifts and of limited mentality.»[2] Yet he occupies a prominent place among the men of the stage who made American humour popular in England. Hill contributed his share to the movement started by Mathews and carried on by Hackett.

Hill's English debut took place in William Bayle Bernard's *The Yankee Pedlar; or, Old Times in Virginia* at Drury Lane on November 1, 1836.[3]

The play opens on a »High Road» in Virginia showing a tavern named The Jefferson's Head, and the house of Colonel Bantam. The Colonel is sleeping on two chairs, while the ubiquitous Negro slaves sing. He wakes up and improves his mood with another »jug of sling,» meanwhile commenting on his moderate habits:

> ... a »Julep» at seven, a jug of »toddy» at nine, an »Antifogmatic» when I went out a cock tail when I came in and a »Gum tickler» to settle it — nothing positively nothing, and yet my tongue is about as furry as a Beaver's tail...[4]

---

[1] See Oral Sumner Coad, »George Handel Hill,» *Dictionary of American Biography;* and *Scenes from the Life of an Actor, Compiled from the Journals, Letters, and Memoranda of the Late Yankee Hill* (New York, 1853). Hill was born in 1809. When he saw Alexander Simpson perform a Yankee part in 1825 his future specialty was determined. His versatility is reminiscent of the characters he portrayed: after his health had suffered from dissipation he failed in the middle forties, and became a practising dentist in New York City. Hill died in 1849. The parallel with Poe (1809—49) is striking.

[2] *Dictionary of American Biography.*

[3] The date (November 6, 1835) given in Hill's *Scenes from the Life of an Actor.* p. 128, is wrong. In the Lord Chamberlain MSS *The Yankee Pedlar* was licensed for the Olympic Theatre on December 29, 1836. (*British Museum Add. MS 42939.*)

[4] MS lacks pagination.

The gallant Colonel had no sympathy for Yankees and even less for peddlers. He had once been fooled by an itinerant Northern salesman at Williamsburgh; besides, he disliked the furious energy and unsociability of the breed: »Well now if there's any thing in the world I hate worse than fever and ague its a Yankee pedlar . . . An't those fellers always down here selling their wooden nutmegs pitcoal indigo and red flannel sausages . . .» Otherwise Bantam's principles embraced the traditional hospitality of the South: he considered it an insult if a visitor passed his house without having a drink with him.

By and by enters Hiram Dodge, the peddler, »A Wooden Clock under his arm and a basket in his hand»:

> Fancy ware, fancy ware — where's your pride gals where's your pride knives and scissors rale British manufacter cut thro' anything from Cotton to Cartrope Razors, razors only ile 'em well and put' em under your pillow & you'll wake up clean shav'd . . .

The furious Bantam drives Dodge away. The latter, however, soon succeeds in obtaining a letter of introduction (more or less by fraudulent stratagem), where he is given a good character and recommended to ride Bantam's horse to a sale. Now Dodge is allowed to enter Bantam's house, where he surprises Nancy, the latter's daughter, and a young man enjoying a surreptitious kiss. It cost Morlake five dollars to keep Dodge quiet:

> Five dollars to shet my clamshell — I conclude kissings rather dearer here than it is Down East Liz Baxter used to let me have them at a cent apiece but then I always dealt wholesale every Sunday arter meeting — I conclude I used to give her a pretty large order.

The climax consists of a horse race, where the Yankee thinks he is riding Bantam's horse and loses the race on purpose, while the mount actually belongs to Bantam's worst rival. The Colonel is in his best mood, and the play ends in general glee.

The Yankee Pedlar is the first play on the English stage to exploit the regional contrast between the North and the South. Bantam, the Virginia Colonel, was lazy, hospitable, and hard-drinking, while Dodge, the Yankee, was shrewd, money-minded, and active. Dodge also used many more Americanisms than Bantam; the actual pronunciation used by the actors must remain a matter of conjecture. The Yankee was a picaresque character: when selling razors proved economically unsound,

Hiram Dodge became a servant, confidant, carpenter, and jockey by turns.

The Yankee Pedlar ran at Drury Lane from November 1, 1836, to November 19, for a total of six performances. In January, 1837, Hill moved over to the Olympic, where the play ran through that month. The total in London during the 1836—7 season amounted to 27 performances.[1] The play was later taken to the United States, where it was first shown in St. Louis in 1841.[2]

When Hill first acted in England he was not sure of success. Some ten days before the first night he wrote:

> I suppose you will see by the papers what they think of me when they have seen me. I will send all to you, whether I hit or miss. It's more of a job than I thought for when I started; but I am in for it, and for the honor of Yankee land, I will put my best foot foremost the first time I have the opportunity of making my public bow to John Bull.[3]

A week after the first performance he had some experience of the reactions of an English audience to Yankee humour:

> They don't take all the Yankeeisms as readily as my audiences in the States do; therefore, without incurring too strong a charge of conceit, I take some of the applause as due to my talents as a comedian, apart from the peculiarity of character I represent.[4]

The fact that British audiences enjoyed the antics of Hiram Dodge is amply proved by the criticisms in the press.[5] According to *The Times*, Hill gave a »finished picture of what Mathews, Downing and Crockett tried to do.»[6] *The Globe* liked »the quaint dry humour of the actor, and the many odd phrases and similes interspersed throughout the dialogue.»[7] *The True Sun* expressed its admiration in more general terms: »Our heart always warms to an American in England; still more to an American on the English stage.»[8] *The Athenaeum* called Hill's debut »very

---

[1] Playbills in *Enthoven Collection*.
[2] Reed, p. 158. This version was by Morris Barnett.
[3] *Scenes from the Life of an Actor*, pp. 128—9.
[4] Ibid., 130, in a letter dated London, October 20, 1836.
[5] Many were published in a little volume *Opinions of the British Press on the Performances of George H. Hill*, »Collected by a Friend» (New York, 1837).
[6] November 2, 1836, quoted in *Ibid.*, p. 4.
[7] November 2, 1836, quoted in *Ibid.*, p. 6.
[8] November 2, 1836, quoted in *Ibid.*, p. 7.

successful»: »The audience relished the sly humour with which he told the barefaced lies set down for him, and the solemn mockery of seriousness with which he confirmed them; and he seemed established in favour with them before he had been two minutes on the stage.»[1] The following unidentified item is typical:

> An novel representation was given ... on Tuesday night by Mr. Hill, an American comic actor. Mr. Hill, it seems, has been extremely popular in America for the humorous fidelity with which he has portrayed the characteristics of Yankees, a race whose peculiarities excite no small degree of mirth among the nephews and nieces of Uncle Sam. The sketches of the late Mr. Mathews and the lucubrations of Major Downing and Colonel Crockitt [sic] have given us some notion of the oddities of the Down Easters. Mr. Hill's personation furnishes a finished picture, of the accuracy of which we have no reason to doubt, and of the whimsicality of which we readily bear witness to. The Yankees are said to be distinguished by a certain sleek, plausible cunning, great industry, some enterprise, a scanty and pliant honesty, a dialect which is not wholly unlike that of our own more eastern counties, and that humorous extravagance of speech which seems to pervade the lower classes of the United States. All these attributes are embodied in the Yankee pedlar, who is the hero of the slight one-act piece, which was brought out for the purpose of introducing Mr. Hill to a London audience ... The true merit of his acting is, that he gives a perfect picture of a very odd character, hitherto very slightly known on our stage, and proves that in that power of humour which is somewhat rare, and which is always highly attractive, he can fairly take his stand among the best low comedy actors we possess. He was received with great applause, his jokes produced abundant laughter, and the audience seemed so to relish the whim of the representation, that he can hardly fail to become a favourite ...[2]

In 1837, Hill performed the principal character in a farce written for him and staged at Queen's Theatre, *A Down East Bargain; or, Love in New York*.[3] He was also successful in a play called *Caspar Hauser; or, the Wild Boy of Bavaria*, in which he impersonated Dr. Lott Whittle, a Yankee »artist of all work.»[4] Having conquered the London public Hill left for Edinburgh, and continued his success there in February, 1837. In the Scots capital American stage humour and Yankee character were less well known than in London; Edinburgh critics therefore loved

---

[1] November 5, 1836, 787—8.

[2] Unidentified clipping in *Enthoven Collection*.

[3] First performed on January 26, 1837.

[4] Hill, *Scenes from the Life of an Actor*, Chapter XIII gives further details of the tour.

to dwell on the novelty and freshness of Hill's performances.¹ Even here the reviews were very complimentary, and the praise was clothed in terms like »dry,» »quaint,» »racy,» »broad» humour.

In 1838 Yankee Hill was in London again. He started in July by trying his talents on Master Stephen of Jonson's *Every Man in His Humour*, but was a miserable failure. An English critic excused his shortcomings by stating that they were not due to »want of talent,» but »want of fitness.»² Hill soon put his talents to better use. William Bayle Bernard had prepared a new play called *New Notions*, a farce in one act, which contained a part well suited to his taste.³

The plot was of the slenderest. It described a humorous Yankee in English surroundings. Major Wheeler was »a true image of his country — all trade & locomotion — has a tongue that would outrun a waterwheel and a pair of legs that wod kill a camel.» Wheeler possessed a strong dose of true Yankee inquisitiveness, and his ingenious ideas had no limit. He boasted about having sent a cargo of warming pans to the West Indies, where »the Niggers turn'd 'em into shovels & scoop'd up the sugar.» His military title came from the »Melishy,» *i.e.* the Penobscot Fencibles. Tall-tale jokes abound in his conversation: »About ten years ago — we'd a mortal dry summer in the States — hadn't had a drop of rain for as much as three months — ground gaped open jist like an Oyster bed — People got so dry — they couldn't cry.» When questioned about his passage across the ocean, he replied: »Oh — we come along mighty swift — we tired out a set of winds — & had to help ourselves into port with the fag eend of a hurricane.» When confronted with the English way of life, he reacted: »I'm darn tired of doing nothin! ruther think I shall wake up some morning and find a cobweb on my eyelids ... I guess now if you don't get up till noon — you can't call this a rising country.» Wheeler's Yankee ingenuity manifested itself in his urge to sell shares on his forthcoming patents. These included such inventions as feeding cattle with fine shavings, which the animals were supposed to enjoy as long as they wore green glasses; and a phrenological skullcap, partly steel-plated, which allowed the »good bumps» to develop

---

¹ *E.g.* notices of *Edinburgh Scotsman*, February 15, 1837, and *Caledonian Mercury*, February 16, 1837, quoted in *Opinions*, pp 27 ff..

² *Atlas*, XIII, 488—9 (August 4, 1838); *Examiner*, July 29, 1838, 469.

³ *New Notions* was an adaptation of a New-York success from Park Theatre, *Speculation*. (*Atlas*, XIII, 502 [August 11, 1838].)

freely, but kept the »bad bumps» down — the easy way to self-improvement![1]

New Notions was first performed at the Haymarket on July 21, 1838. It ran for every night until July 29, and then several times a week until August 17. The total number of performances was close to twenty.[2]

The reviewers still liked Yankee Hill. Many objections were stated to the slenderness of the plot, although it was understood that the continuity of the play was a secondary factor serving as a string for the jokes. Some commentators found fault with the acting: Hill suffered from a »want of power,» his voice was too weak, he was too quiet and too grave, his acting and speech too fast. The prevailing tone of the press notices was, however, laudatory, and the audience had reacted with »unanimous applause.» *The Atlas* noted that the English public was getting used to humorous stage Americans: »Now that this kind of caricature is beginning to be better understood in England than it used to be, such a piece of pure gasconade stands a better chance of being thoroughly relished by our audiences; and so it turned out.»[3]

Thus Hill carried on the tradition of comic Yankees in England. He was a skilful actor and a first-hand observer and analyzer of American humour; his acting, if anybody's, was the genuine product. Hackett's early failures in the late twenties and early thirties were partly due to the novelty of transatlantic fun; Hill's successes indicate that the Englishmen of 1838 were sufficiently trained to enjoy plays that built completely on native Yankee humour. The strangeness of Down-East character, speech, and behaviour no longer dumbfounded the British public, who had learnt to relax and enter into the spirit of the entertainment.[4]

3. Jonathans, Dutchmen, and Negroes.

Hackett's and later Hill's successes stimulated other playwrights and actors to try their hand at the portrayal of comic Americans.

---

[1] The play is available in *British Museum Add. MS 42948*.
[2] Advertisements in *Times*.
[3] XIII, 488—9 (August 4, 1838), a severe review; for other appreciations, see *Observer*, July 22, 1838, 2; *Times*, July 23, 1838, 5; *Morning Herald*, July 20, 1838, 5; *Examiner*, July 29, 1838, 469.
[4] It is not unfair at this point to ask: how many present-day Americans are able to enjoy regional English, *e.g.* Yorkshire, humour?

In 1833, the fancies of the English public were stirred by Bernard's dramatic version of Paulding's *Koningsmarke*. It was presented at the Adelphi under the heading *The Long Finn; or, the Treasure-Seeker's Dream*. The play was advertised as pure melodrama, but contained representatives of two humorous stock Americans: the Dutchman and the Negro. In addition to Mynheer Van Stork and Massa Brail the cast comprised other national types like Monsieur Fortbras and Senor Lobe Ferrara, all without distinct individuality. *The Long Finn* ran from June 18, 1833, to July 22, with a frequency of some three performances a week.[1] It was highly commended by *The Athenaeum*.[2]

William Leman Rede's burletta *A Flight to America; or, Twelve Hours in New York* was first performed at the Adelphi on November 7, 1836.[3] Frederick Henry Yates echoed Mathews by acting a French-American dancing-master.[4] More important was the minstrel element of the play: Thomas Dartmouth Rice appeared as Jim Crow, and the success of the play was due to the popular appeal of the limping, dancing, and singing Negro.[5] Among other humorous Americans were Van Huysen, a Dutchman with his familiar exclamation »Diebels!» and the language influenced by *Rip Van Winkle;* Mohawk, a Yankee repeating the eternal »I calculate»; and Pawks, »a reg'lar built Virginian» who does not like any Englishman »to undervalle us our Swamps — tarnation take me if I don't lick you elegant!» The only significant difference between the various types of white Americans consists of their language and their local references. Bad roads, vehicles stuck in the mud and similar items borrowed from stereotype travel-books go to complete the picture. The plot is confusing. Jim Crow is the only new character type; the other characterizations follow previous traditions.

In 1838 William Thomas Moncrieff, the author of *Monsieur Mallét*,

---

[1] Playbills in *Enthoven Collection*.   [2] June 22, 1833, 404.

[3] Available in *British Museum Add. MS 42939* under the title *Life in America; the Flight — the Pursuit — the Voyage*.

[4] While manager of the Adelphi (1825—42) Yates showed his versatility by taking any humorous parts that happened to be vacant and were difficult to fill by the remaining cast. (Joseph Knight, »Frederick Henry Yates,» *Dictionary of National Biography*.)

[5] Reviews tended to stress Rice's part. (Unidentified clippings, *Enthoven Collection*.) For a more detailed discussion of Negro minstrelsy in England, see *infra*, pp. 76—94.

presented another play on humorous American character.¹ The title page of his manuscript shows his idea of the theme:

Tarnation Strange;
or
More Jonathans
An Anglo-American Drama
Of National Humour, Characteristics & Peculiarities
In
Two Acts
1838

In the late thirties, Jonathan's peculiarities were attractive enough to be advertised as the central theme of a play.

The plot of *Tarnation Strange* was simple, and its main virtue consisted of the fact that it served as a string holding together the pearls of melodrama and humour. There were two English ladies, Mrs. Swallow and her pretty daughter-in-law, and two gentlemen, Jonathan Jonah Goliah Bang, a bumbling and boisterous American, and the English Cornet Wimbledon. After the necessary complications the beauty gets her Cornet, and Mrs. Swallow gets Bang.

Jonathan Jonah Goliah Bang came from West Tennessee County, Kentucky. Moncrieff's analysis of his character was not concerned with regional distinctions: Bang was half Yankee, half frontiersman, showing both the common sense of the former and the impetuosity of the latter.² A double set of »Jonathans,» as American jokes were then called, was collected in the play and used to maximum advantage.

Tarnation Strange was advertised as a farce. The first performance took place at the New Strand Theatre on August 3, 1838. It proved a success, and after the initial run was completed it was revived on Friday, October 12, 1838, »by particular request.» The October 12 performance was billed as the fortieth.³

Both the melodramatic and American features were used by the writer of the playbill blurbs. In the first scene alone, the audience was promised

---

¹ Available in *British Museum Add. MS 42948*. Printed in *Dicks' Standard Plays* (687).
² It should be remembered that even Sam Slick was a composite of Yankee and frontiersman.
³ Playbills in *Enthoven Collection*.

Animal magnetism, Sublimated spirit of steam, its wonderful effects — Jonathan's account of himself and his countrymen — Improvements in machinery — Wonderful shingle machine — Self acting mechanical shipwright — Surprising Instances of animal instinct — Sagacious dogs, astonishment for the *natives* ...

A long paragraph on American humour followed:

So great has been the March of Intellect of later days, that the Louisville Journal, United States, credibly informs its readers, that a Bear was in the nightly habit of frequenting the Pit of the Theatre during Miss Ellen Tree's Performances in that Town, and that he one evening took a Crocodile friend of his with him, who was so fascinated by her exquisite acting of the Wife, that he actually shed tears, real Crocodile tears! and the Vermont Mercury asserts that during one of the representations of Mr. Power in Paddy O'Rafferty, in that state, a young Colt who happened to be stabled at the back of the Theatre, accidentally thrusting his head through some dilapidated boards, had his risible faculties so much excited by what he saw, that he indulged in several involuntary horse laughs, to the great edification of the swinish multitude, who happened to be in front. It is not intended to be inferred, that these instances of sympathy in what Coleridge has oddly enough called the mute creation, towards our national representations on the other side of the Atlantic, should be followed by a corresponding observance in the present attempt to display some genuine specimens of American humour on this; it is only trusted that on this occasion our biped public will not be more fastidious than the quadruped auditors of Louisville and Vermont, but will allow their smiles to be elicited by those humorous peculiarities and eccentricities which have already afforded Cousin Jonathan so much amusement, and which can have no other end than to extend our stores of harmless mirth, and enlarge the good fellowship already so happily existing between the Mother and Sister Countries.[1]

The reviewers were satisfied with the play. The vogue of American humour in the England of the thirties was reflected by *The Sunday Times:*

We are soon likely to be deluged with Jonathanisms; all the freaks, foibles, and exaggerated sentences of our Trans-atlantic neighbours are transferred with the view, not of »holding the mirror up to nature,» but of holding the Yankee up to laughter ... There are some smart good things said through it. All the *outre* speeches, strange stories, and adventures that ever have been written or said, seem to have been collected together, and given to *Mr. Jonathan Bang.* The audience enjoyed them, and at the fall of the curtain were warm in their plaudits at the announcement of its repetition till further notice. Miss Daly as the *Paymaster's Widow*, and Hammond as the *Kentuckian*, were excellent.[2]

The Morning Herald called the piece »commonplace in plot and incidents,» but admitted that many of the »Jonathans» were new. It noticed

---

[1] *Ibid.* Several misprints and spelling errors have been corrected.
[2] August 5, 1838, 2.

that Bang was neither a pure Yankee nor an out-and-out frontiersman: ». . . in designing his hero a Kentuckian, instead of a Yankee, he has wholly mistaken the phraseology, the dialect of the two being as distinct as that of a Yorkshireman and Cockney.»[1]

The Morning Post liked the »Jonathisms,» but added a remark on Hammond's, the English actor's, deficiencies as a portrayer of American character: »He certainly acted the part exceedingly well, but still he was not quite the American. He might get a wrinkle from Mr. Hill.»[2]

Richard Brinsley Peake's *The Emigrant's Daughter* affords an example of how a playwright could concoct a new play on the basis of old ones.[3] It is a close copy of Dibdin's *The Banks of the Hudson*,[4] but some innovations can be found: de Leslie, a French-American cut to the Monsieur Mallet tradition; and Diedrich Kidde, an Irvingesque Dutch brute, were added to the original. The humour was provided by Hector Titmouse, a timorous Englishman who never got rid of the fundamental trait of his character when fighting the Americans as an English soldier during the Revolution. The play was melodramatic rather than humorous.[5]

Another of Peake's efforts, *Job Fox, the Yankee Valet*, was performed at the English Opera House in August, 1838.[6] The plot gave Fox a chance to demonstrate his native ingenuity: he had been hired by Mr. Testy to keep out visitors from the house, while Mrs. Testy loved guests. Fox satisfied both parties and collected ample tips from the visitors in the process. As a sample of his way of expressing himself one of his first remarks to his master:

Well Suare — I've done my feed — your cider's purty good — but your pork an't fat enough to grease a cat's whiskers. — Well I guess now, I am a spry crittur for the day — what work are you going to set me to, to feed the hogs or turn up a

---

[1] August 6, 1838, 5.

[2] August 6, 1838, 5. The same review was printed by *Observer*, August 5, 1838, 2.

[3] *British Museum Add. MS 42948.* Licensed on August 3, 1838.

[4] See *supra*, p. 48.

[5] This was also the opinion of *Sunday Times*, August 12, 1838, 2.

[6] *British Museum Add. MS 42937*, pp. 605—633. Listed by *Nicoll* under «Unknown Authors.»

pumpkin patch — or have you got any old cheers and tables you want me to jine or perhaps you've got an old sheaf of wheat you'd like me to trash.[1]

To sum up, the thirties were the decade when humorous presentations of American character became firmly entrenched on the English stage. The Yankee, frontiersman, Negro, or immigrant were no longer new and revolutionary characters. The patterns had been set and the traditions established; in the following decades playwrights and actors elaborated the models without instigating new precedents. If we compare the vogue of transatlantic humour on the stage with the popularity of humorous American books in England we cannot fail to note that the drama was ahead of the printed word as a medium. The English stage of the eighteen-twenties and thirties initiated the popularity of American humour in England and paved the way for the subsequent appreciation of more literary works in this genre.

CHAPTER VI

NEGRO MINSTRELSY IN ENGLAND, 1836—1870

1. The Birth of Minstrelsy.

A study of humorous American characters in English stage entertainment should not be limited to legitimate drama alone. To place British appreciation of American humour into its proper framework the investigator must remember that he is dealing with popular trends and currents; higher aesthetic considerations do not suffice. When dealing with the channels through which transatlantic fun came to nineteenth-century England we must needs include one, whose apparent vulgarity and lowness has discouraged comprehensive investigation. This channel is Negro minstrelsy.

The ancestry of Negro minstrelsy is traditionally traced from the annals of the stage Negro. Various authorities list plays with coloured characters considering their facts pertinent to the discussion of pure minstrelsy, although the latter should perhaps more properly be called

---

[1] *British Museum Add. MS 42937*, p. 607.

an independent development than a direct consequence of an old dramatic tradition.¹ However, some items having more direct bearing upon the birth of minstrelsy have been listed in the literature.

Thus George Augustus Sala, whose extensive knowledge of things American was based on the years this *bon vivant* spent west of the Atlantic as a correspondent, had heard a story concerning the first appearance of minstrelsy on the stage:

> On the day that Washington died, in 1799, there was being performed at a lowly playhouse, in Boston, the drama of »Oroonoko»; and between the acts, one of the performers, all unconscious of the loss the Republic had sustained, *sang in character a comic negro song*. This was the first instance on record of nigger minstrelsy as public entertainment; and from this humble beginning sprang the Woods, the Pells, and the Christies, who have made the anthology and the lyricism of Ethiopia famous from Indus to the pole.²

The song was called »The Gay Negro Boy,» and the name of the actor who sang it was Gottlieb Graupner, if we are to believe Charles White, an old coloured minstrel manager and comedian, who based his statement on Russell's *Boston Gazette* of December 30, 1799.³

This isolated occurrence led to no extensive vogue of Negro songs. Other equally isolated instances have been quoted. Either Andrew Jackson Allen, Edwin Forrest's personal slave, cook, and *fac totum*, who was deaf, loquacious, and interested in acting, or some more mythical character called »Pig-Pie Herbert» or »Hop Robinson» sang a Negro song in Albany, N. Y., in 1815. When Edwin Forrest himself performed a coloured part in Sol Smith's farce *The Tailor in Distress* at Globe Theatre, Cincinnati, in 1823, he added some singing and dancing to the role. An Irishman called Bernard Flaherty is supposed to have sung and danced Negro material at Vauxhall Gardens, The Bowery, in 1838.⁴

East of the Atlantic, a few events should also be included. »Juba» was sung at Drury Lane in 1816; however, the text had little to do with Negro themes. More important was Charles Mathews' contribution in

---

[1] For the outline history of the stage Negro, see *supra*, pp. 14—15.
[2] *My Diary in America* (London, 1865), II, 30.
[3] Hutton, *Curiosities of the American Stage*, p. 99.
[4] For histories of minstrelsy, see Hutton, *Op.cit.*; Carl F. Wittke, *Tambo and Bones* (Chapel Hill, N.C., 1930); Harry Reynolds, *Minstrel Memories* (London, 1928); and Dailey Paskman and Sigmund Spaeth, *»Gentlemen, Be Seated!» A Parade of the Old-Time Minstrels* (Garden City, N.Y., 1928).

1824. His »Possum up a Gum Tree» was a great hit and can for all purposes be considered a minstrel song.¹

Thomas Dartmouth Rice was the man who crystallized Negro minstrelsy proper.² Various accounts are given about the origins of Rice's conception of the new stage character. In any case, after Rice had performed his Jim Crow on the stage and it had become an obvious hit, William Cumming Peters of Pittsburgh published the song, which became a tremendous success.³

2. Thomas Dartmouth Rice in England.

In 1836, Thomas Dartmouth Rice appeared at the Surrey Theatre in London. He stayed in England for several years; on June 18, 1837, he married Charlotte B. Gladstone, a London girl.⁴ Rice's London performances established Negro minstrelsy in England; if any one man shaped the popular entertainment of nineteenth-century England, it was he.

His first appearance in England took place on July 9, 1836, at the Surrey, and the name of the piece was *Bone Squash Diabolo*. It consisted of one of his own original burlesques that had been so successful in America. The entire show revolved around Rice's singing and dancing of »Jump Jim Crow.» Jim Crow now became the rage: men wore

---

[1] It is not improbable that the recurrence of the possum theme in later minstrel songs was due to Mathews' influence: an instance where American humour is indebted to an English comedian. An obvious modification of »Possum» is »Zip Coon»:

> »Ole Zip Coon he is a larned scholar,
> Sings 'posum up the gum tree an' coony in a holler.
> 'Posum up a gum tree, Coony on a stump,
> Den over dubble trubble, Zip Coon will jump.»

(Wittke, *Op.cit.*, pp. 179—180.)

[2] Carl Wittke, »Thomas Dartmouth Rice,» *Dictionary of American Biography*.

[3] Incidentally, Rice introduced the celebrated Joseph Jefferson (of Rip-Van-Winkle fame) to the stage at the age of four. Jefferson was carried onstage in a bag by Rice, and he jumped out, face blacked, while the latter sang:

> »Ladies and gentlemen, I'd have yer for to know,
> I'se got a little darkey here, to jump Jim Crow.»

(Matthews and Hutton, *Actors and Actresses of Great Britain and the United States*, V, 155.)

[4] *Dictionary of American Biography*.

Jim-Crow hats and smoked Jim-Crow cigars. *Punch* soon labelled a turn-about politician »Jim Crow.» After a series of equally successful shows entitled *Mephistopheles*, *The Virginian Mummy*, and *The Black God of Love*, Rice's fortune in England was well established. It is not difficult in 1951, when we are well used to the inescapable popularity of hit tunes, to apply our imagination to the London of the autumn of 1836:

> The nigger mania broke out with a virulence that has never since wholly subsided. The infection was brought from America, inoculated into the blood of Englishmen by an operator of the name of Rice, who blackened his face and dressed himself like a negro — I suppose from the cotton, the sugar, or rice plantations — and sang a very silly, if not utterly stupid song, which he called »Jim Crow,» and of which the burden, repeated at the end of every stanza, accompanied by a grotesque dance, was —
>
> > Turn about and wheel about,
> > And do just so;
> > Turn about and wheel about,
> > And jump Jim Crow.
>
> Nothing like it was ever before seen or known in England. To use a common phrase, »it took like wildfire.» The famous dancing mania of the Middle Ages cannot have been a worse epidemic than this was; and the small beggar-boys of the streets — some of whom, it is to be hoped, are by this time well-to-do citizens at the Antipodes — drove a flourishing trade by imitating the fashionable comedian of the Adelphi, and »jumping Jim Crow» in the public thoroughfares by day and by night. It became an indescribable nuisance. Many must have been the sermons, the poems, the plays, the leading articles, the forensic arguments, and the mathematical calculations that it spoiled by its horrible iteration under the windows of studious men! But, worst phase of all in its unhappy history, its popularity was so great that it became the first of a series, which has lasted — with an occasional oasis of something better — until the present day, to disgust and plague the real lovers of music, and put them out of humour with the divine art that can be perverted to such monstrous purposes. The thing must have been in vigorous existence from 1836 to 1841, when two or three competitors of a similar kind, but somewhat better in quality, began to struggle for and obtain a hearing.[1]

After three successful months at the Surrey, Rice moved to the Adelphi and opened in Rede's *A Flight to America*.[2] This burletta was a glorified elaboration of Jim Crow with added American characters,

---

[1] »Musical Epidemics in London» in Charles Mackay, *Through the Long Day* (London, 1887), I, 132—4.

[2] See *supra*, p. 72.

both black and white; a »Grand Procession of Niggers» on July 4th was one of the high spots, where Jim Crow appeared as an uncrowned Negro king on the back of a white horse. Of this performance a reviewer wrote:

> *A Flight to America* is a »new, musical, characteristic, and ollapodrical extravaganza,» got up for the purpose of introducing an American actor, Mr. Rice, in the famous part of *Jim Crow*. We will not say that we like Mr. Rice's performance, but there cannot be a doubt of its extraordinary reality. The shuffling gait, the strange whistle, and the more strange laugh, could never have been invented by Mr. Rice . . .[1]

Rice's powers were used for the Adelphi Christmas pantomime, which was called *Cowardy, Cowardy, Custard; or Harlequin Jim Crow and the Magic Mustard Pot*.

After Rice had visited England in 1838, the Adelphi recovered his services in 1843 for Stirling's *Yankee Notes*, where he made a success in the part of Julius Caesar Washington Hiccory Dick.[2] Two more farces, *Jim Crow in His New Place*, and *The Foreign Prince*, complete the list of Rice's appearances in England.[3] He also performed in Dublin, where the profit was $ 1800 for one performance, and at Cork, where the intake was larger still: $ 1900 for one night.[4]

Rice's great fortune with the English public soon resulted in the spreading of the new genre. As early as 1843, two more of the American minstrels, Joe Sweeney and Ned Harper, came to London to profit from the Englishman's love of burnt-cork entertainment. Both gentlemen were famous in their own way. The legend has it that Sweeney was the man who invented the banjo by cutting a cheese-box in half, covering it with a skin and stringing it with five strings; until then a four-string instrument had been used. Harper was famous for his burlesques of Negro character.[5]

The hack writers who lived by topical booklets did not leave the Jim-Crow craze unutilized.[6] One of these curious pieces of fiction set out to dramatize the story of Jim Crow in the form of a first-person

---

[1] Unidentified clipping, *Enthoven Collection*.
[2] Printed in *Duncombe's British Theatre* (46).
[3] Reynolds, *Op.cit.*, 76—8.   [4] Wittke, *Op.cit.*, 29.   [5] Reynolds, *Op.cit.*, 78.
[6] *The Origin of Jim Crow* (London, 1837), price 6d. Reviewed in *Athenaeum*, June 17, 1837, 440. John Briggs, *The History of Jim Crow* (London, 1839).

narrative, allegedly by the hero himself, about slave life. Jim learnt to read and write, which was punishable by law; consequently, his Virginia owners sold him to the West. The story is full of echoes of travel books; Americans rush to the dinner-table and gulp down their victuals with amazing speed, they duel brutally and utter Yankeeisms. Finally Jim got the idea of staging a Negro show and became a celebrity. The following description of Jim Crow's clothes is probably based on the appearance of Rice on the stage:

> It consisted of an iron roan-coloured Monmouth cap, with a hole on one side that showed some of my hair through it; — a light grey serge frock-coat, out at the elbows, and without buttons, except on the flaps of the pockets; the cape, cuffs, and mouths of the pockets being soiled with grease and soot; — a brick-coloured cloth waistcoat, with only one button, about midbreast, so as to show a coarse narrow-eyed chequered shirt, and equally coarse broad-eyed chequered handkerchief, loosely tied round the collar as a cravat; — a pair of deep blue shorts, without button or any other fastening at the knees, the fronts of the thighs greasy, as if they had been used for towels, and a hole rubbed through the middle of the greasy part of the right thigh with a bit of the shirt sticking out; — a pair of yellow stockings, secured under the shorts so that they might not fall, but hang in folds about my legs; — a pair of thick leather shoes the colour of the waistcoat, with a hole in the left one, so situated as to allow of my great toe being protruded entirely through, showing the stocking on it, except at the end of the toe and nail, which were bare; the soles of both heels much twisted inwards; and for a tie, what is known in the Southern States as plantain-string, being the fibre of the leaf-stalk of the plantain-plant.[1]

When reviewing this *History of Jim Crow*, *The Athenaeum* significantly reflected upon the great vogue of minstrelsy in the England of 1839:

> This book is one of the signs of the times. A few years since, the most romantic authoress connected with a Minerva press would never have dreamt of choosing a black man for the hero of a tale. She would never have thought of him, but as Lady Somebody's footman or a cymbal-player in the Guards. Now, however, the case is altered. Twenty millions have been paid on Sambo's account, and, on a parallel principle with Desdemona's affection for the moor, loving him for the dangers he had passed, we like him for the money he has cost ... He is no longer a nigger, but a gentleman of colour, a favourite low comedian, the hero of a novel, and a jet ornament to society ... From internal evidence, this book is by an American, and an abolitionist. The style is quite Transatlantic, magniloquent, and mercantile ...[2]

---

[1] Briggs, *Op.cit.*, 176—7.

[2] »The History of Jim Crow,» February 1, 1840, 94—5. The Slavery Abolition Act of 1833 had granted twenty million pounds sterling as a compensation to slave-owners in the West Indies.

Contemporary prints also illustrate Jim Crow's appearance and popularity.[1]

Thomas Dartmouth Rice's shows and plays from 1836 to 1843 started the fashion of Negro minstrelsy in England. The new type of popular entertainment began auspiciously and put its imprint on daily life with surprising speed.

3. American Character and Humour in Minstrelsy.

Although Rice's discovery of the public attractions of minstrelsy sprang from a theatrical tradition, he had unwittingly started an entirely new form of entertainment with his Jim Crow. However, it took some time before the new genre developed into the channels that we tend to think of today when talking about Negro minstrelsy. The theatre was where Rice presented his Negroes, and in the thirties or forties there was no question of what suited the stage and what did not. Theatrical managers were eager to stage anything, even pure minstrel shows, as long as they proved popular with the public and filled the coffers with jingling shillings and half-crowns. At first minstrelsy sought expression through the existing theatres, and the arrangements were no different from the ordinary theatrical routine. Negro minstrels were simply specialized comedians who could easily be fitted into the traditional system of short-term engagements.

At the beginning, minstrel influence invaded ordinary English comedy and farce. Burnt-cork numbers could be inserted into any suitable play. Thus in *The Knight and the Sprite; or, The Cold Water Cure* by two such typically English playwrights as Gilbert à Beckett and Mark Lemon, one of the actors, Mr. Hall, was dressed up as a watersprite with webbed hands and feet. Even this outfit did not prevent him from singing funny minstrel songs to the accompaniment of a banjo.

Minstrelsy developed much during its half-century of vigorous existence. In the thirties and forties the success of burnt-cork entertainment depended largely on novelty: the catchy tunes and the queer dialect of the performers, their odd dancing and their unheard-of instruments of accompaniment, all still had a freshness of their own. The

---

[1] »The Gallery of Comicalities,» *Bell's Life in London* (London, 1836), available at the British Museum Print Room.

humour, both verbal and humour of situation, was very important, too. All these elements could be fully used by one individual or by small groups of minstrels.

These simple attractions gradually wore off, and a more complicated machinery was adopted by the performers. Groups became larger, and minstrelsy developed into an independent institution which no longer fit into the routine of theatres. By the middle forties troupes were large enough and their shows sufficiently elaborate to warrant the renting of separate halls or theatres. Thus an American troupe called The Ethiopian Serenaders opened a series of performances at Hanover Square Rooms, London, in January, 1846. It soon afterwards moved to the fashionable St. James's Theatre, which became one of the usual haunts of the minstrels. In 1859 St. James's Hall in Piccadilly[1] became permanently associated with minstrelsy, and remained the London headquarters of this type of entertainment until it was pulled down in 1904.[2] If burnt-cork performers had started out as specialized comedians of the legitimate stage, they now found themselves representatives of another, independent type of entertainment, which for several decades usurped some of the functions previously held by the theatre. Perhaps the minstrels absorbed the least attractive sections of the general public and left the legitimate theatre freer to lift its standards from their all-time low.

The changes in the entertainments themselves can be attributed to various elaborations of Rice's original performances. At first the emphasis was on the songs, dances, and character of the Negro performer. A special character type emerged:

[They were] lazy, shiftless fellows, careless of the morrow. The stage Negro loved watermelons and ate them in a peculiar way. He turned out to be an expert wielder of the razor ... He always was distinguished by an unusually large mouth and a peculiar kind of broad grin; he dressed in gaudy colors and in a flashy style; he usually consumed more gin than he could properly hold; and he loved chickens ...[3]

Gradually the shows developed towards something »bigger and better.» Instead of the single actor, minstrels now appeared in troupes, and their programmes occupied entire evenings. By the early eighties troupes could consist of one hundred members, of them over sixty actual stage performers.[4] The brilliancy and elaborateness of the later shows were

---

[1] At the site of the present Piccadilly Hotel. [2] Reynolds, *Op.cit.*
[3] Wittke, *Op.cit.*, p. 8. [4] *Ibid.*, p. 219.

important elements, but the humour remained equally basic until the extinction of the genre. The fundamental attractions remained the same.

In Negro minstrelsy in England, should the characters and the humour be called American? The answer is yes. The immediate origins of minstrelsy were American, not English. The main character of minstrel shows was the American coloured man. The jokes belonged to a peculiar vein outside the traditions of English humour. The language of the minstrels was always the language of the American stage Negro, even in the cases where the performers were Englishmen.[1] Finally, English commentators had a feeling, at least during the early decades of the minstrel vogue, that they were dealing with something outlandish and strange. Contemporary spectators did not hesitate to include burnt-cork performances under the heading of American humour.

Rice's performances at the Surrey and the Adelphi exemplify early minstrel humour. Samples of the performances of the later, more elaborate period can be studied in Samuel French's series *The Darkey Drama*.[2] In the first part of this collection the dates and places of first performances are given; most of the pieces were originally staged in the United States in the sixties.

These sketches are short, time of playing about ten minutes. Most of them use two or three actors; sometimes the number of characters is larger, and often the co-operation of other troupe members is indicated (music, effects). Those humorous elements that can be examined from the texts consist of humour of situation and action, straight jokes, character humour, and humour of language.

The situation humour and the humour of action are very closely akin to those of low comedy in general. There is little difference between the practical jokes of minstrelsy and of the music-hall.[3]

---

[1] Reynolds, *Op.cit.*, p. 58. [2] Full title: *The Darkey Drama, a Collection of Approved Farces, Interludes, Scenes, Etc.* (London and New York, n.d.)

[3] Tricks with chairs, *e.g.*, were common, as in the following scene between Orfeus and Plato, two coloured minstrels:

»*Plato:* Why don't you come in?
Orfeus: I didn't hear nobody knock.
Plato: Knock? who — what?
Orfeus: You just tol' somebody to come in!
Plato: Get out. (*Orfeus rises*) Sit down! (*moves Orfeus's chair.*)

»Orfeus falls in sitting, and, in falling, kicks away Plato's chair. — Plato has half risen, laughing, when, in sitting down, he falls. — Picture of the two sitting

The character humour of the typical minstrel sketch shows the peculiarities of the comic stage Negro in their most caricatured form. The burnt-cork Negro was lazy and good-humoured. He possessed great musical talent and a facility for witty repartee in his own vein. His dress was gaudy, but tattered and torn; stage directions give us detailed information about his appearance and costume.[1] He was often aggressive, and much of the dialogues consists of half-friendly quarrel. His concerns had to do with the most concrete aspects of everyday life, while his outlook was hedonistic in a childish and blue-eyed way. In short, minstrelsy developed an unrealistic character type. Rice's original may have had actual, living models; his followers stereotyped blackface character into a set pattern, exaggerating and standardizing it beyond all verisimilitude into the realms of pure clowning.

The jokes of the minstrel shows were of the simplest kind. No knowledge of the subtleties of topical questions or of the problems of man's adjustment to society was necessary for their proper appreciation. The actual background of the American Negro was not used in minstrel sketches; Sambo and Joe were not toiling in cotton-fields, but performing their antics in settings familiar to nineteenth-century city-dwellers — that is, when the settings were given any prominence at all, which rarely happened. In Rice's original shows there was a decided effort to put the coloured comedian into plausible surroundings, and to weave his songs, dances, and jokes into the plot of a play. Later the plot lost its importance. Sometimes the basis of the jokes moved away from pure caricature towards social comedy: the incongruity of blackfaced men acting up to social standards beyond their comprehension was used for humorous effect. The characters, however, remained obvious

---

on the floor eside one another, looking at one another.» («Deaf — in a Horn,» *Darkey Drama*, I, 13.) Such crude practical jokes are not distinctive of minstrelsy, but used by most types of low comedy.

[1] Samples:

»*Dismal:* Patched blue coat, with brass buttons, no waistcoat — plaited bosom to his striped shirt, red necktie — black trousers patched on both knees — a boot and a shoe — black chimney-pot hat — large carpet-bag with large purse in it, travelling-rug — pocket-book in coat breast-pocket. White hair and beard long.

»*Joe:* Battered white hat, without brim — shirt of calico, red check on pink ground, with broad collar turned up on one side — tight striped trousers coming to just above the ankle — blue stockings — heavy shoes.» (»16000 Years Ago!», *Darkey Drama*, I, 66.)

caricatures. And where references to things American can be found, they have no essential significance for the sketches, and can be substituted by local English references without disrupting the effect.

The characteristics of the language of the minstrel Negro can be grouped under four headings. First, certain sounds of standard English were thought to cause difficulty to the coloured man; thus, *d*'s were regularly used for *th*'s. Secondly, the Negro was fond of long, solemn-sounding words of Latin and Greek extraction, which he used without due regard for meaning in a way reminiscent of Mrs. Malaprop. These words were often real tongue-twisters and were mispronounced. Thirdly, certain typical »Negro-words» were used. Finally, the grammar was substandard; *e.g.* the forms of »to be» were used in a most unorthodox manner.[1] Puns were an important part of the bill of fare.

After 1836, the humorous American Negro on the English stage was essentially a development of the coloured man of the minstrel show. The stage could not always exaggerate its caricatures so much as the minstrels could. However, the popularity of blackface entertainment shaped the English man-in-the-street's ideas of the American coloured man, and presumably many lower-class Britons might have believed that minstrel and stage caricatures were based on actual traits of Negro slaves. In any case the burnt-cork Negro became the inspiration of the humorous coloured man of the legitimate stage; *Punch* adopted him to represent his race in jokes and cartoons and used him extensively during the Civil War; the »Sambo-myth» attained a most widespread popularity.

We may say, then, that the humour of the minstrel shows should be considered American rather than English, and that burnt-cork entertainment was one of the many channels through which American humour spread into nineteenth-century Britain. On the other hand, Britons rapidly became so expert in handling the new genre that it would be of little practical consequence to differentiate between American and English origins of individual minstrel shows. The two worlds

---

[1] A short sample from »De Trouble Begins at Nine,» *Darkey Drama*, I, 48, will illustrate these characteristics:

»Let's sot down. Relaxavacation arter a long day's work at de sub*lime* study of whitewashing, an' de sweeping arguments ob carpet-shaking, am a great inwention. If I on'y get a few hours' quiet, I'll practize dat new song dat I mean to astonish de fokes wid. Dis coat o'mine is gittin' shaky in de j'ints — it's like a *wheat*-eran among de *tares!* . . .»

of minstrel entertainment on either side of the Atlantic were so closely allied that the present-day investigator does wisely in considering them one. Minstrel troupes travelled back and forth across the ocean, and the same jokes and songs and characterizations were laughed at by both Americans and Englishmen. Although of American origin and based on American character, Negro minstrelsy was adopted wholesale by the cousins in the Old Country.

4. *Minstrelsy in England after Rice.*

The full history of Negro minstrelsy in England has not yet been written. The following makes no pretense of being a complete account, but will provide a few representative examples of facts and data pertinent to a full appreciation of the importance of minstrelsy in nineteenth-century entertainment in Britain.[1]

The history of Rice's undertakings in England has been outlined. His great success and the popular vogue of the new genre soon incited others to follow his example. How soon trueborn Britons learnt the trade can be seen from the fact that as early as 1839, a group of English minstrels left for the United States to make their fortune presenting shows to the American public. These gentlemen were the Buckleys, James and his sons Bishop, Swaine, and Fred. They assumed the professional name of »Congo Melodists» and became a sensation west of the ocean both by their skill and their novel ideas. They are said to be the first to harmonize minstrel melodies and to introduce operatic music into minstrelsy. After their great American successes the Buckleys visited England twice, in 1846 and 1860. In the latter year they performed both at Liverpool and St. James's Hall, Piccadilly.

In 1843, soon after Joe Sweeney's and Ned Harper's arrival in England, a four-man group called The Virginia Minstrels (violin, banjo, bone castanets, tambourine) toured Britain and met with some success in Liverpool, Manchester, and London. However, they did not encounter the interest they had reckoned with, and after an economic failure they were forced to disband and return to America. The fate of The Ethiopian Serenaders at St. James's Theatre was better: giving two performances daily, one in the morning and one in the evening, they

---

[1] Where not stated otherwise, the present account is built on Wittke, *Op.cit.*, and particularly Reynolds, *Op.cit.*

could carry on for six weeks in 1846. Sir Robert Peel and Gladstone were in the audience. Minstrel entertainment was indeed becoming fashionable: The Ethiopian Serenaders were invited to perform at parties in noblemen's houses, and the climax of their stay in Britain was a show for Queen Victoria herself at Arundel Castle.

George Augustus Sala's name has been mentioned in connection with his account of the origins of burnt-cork showmanship. In 1847 Sala, an author of considerable contemporary renown, wrote the song »De Long Tail Blue» for a troupe called The Lantum Serenaders while the latter were expected to perform at Princess Theatre, London. Sala was an addict: he bought a large photographic album, »bound in embossed morocco,» and pasted it full with pictures of various minstrel performers; he was supposed to value this treasure highly.

On September 14, 1852, when *Uncle Tom's Cabin* was starting its London run, »an Ethiopian Extravaganza» was staged at the Strand. The author was G. H. George. For plot he chose a simple triangle and studded it with the usual minstrel songs and blackface characters. It was christened *A Colour'd Commotion*. Notable among the dramatis personae were Dandy Jim (»A Fast Black»), Sam Snap (»A Gloomy Darkie»), and Miss Sukey Snubber (»Not fair, but Fickle»).[1]

Several American minstrel troupes toured Britain in the fifties. Raymor & Pierce's Christy Minstrels stayed in England from 1857 to 1860; Campbell's Minstrels arrived in September, 1859, at the very point when minstrelsy acquired a permanent home at St. James's Hall.

Eph Horn, called »the Yorick of Negro Minstrelsy,» came to England in 1865. Among his great roles were »The Four Crows,» »The Locomotive Nigger,» and »Woman's Rights.» The last was a great success; Horn dressed up in feminine garb and delivered a comic oration on his subject. Many other famous minstrel comedians could be seen and admired in England in the sixties, among them Wash Norton, Francis Leon, Jerry Bryant, and Joe Brown. Sam Hague, an Englishman who had moved to the United States in the fifties and established Hague's Georgia Minstrels, returned in the sixties to his native land with his American troupe and performed in London in 1866.

In the United States vaudeville was in many respects a continuation of the traditions established by minstrel shows and museums.[2] Consid-

---

[1] *Lord Chamberlain MSS 6/1852.* Listed by Nicoll under »Unknown Authors.»
[2] It should be remembered that a typical »museum» in the newer sections of mid-nineteenth-century America based its attraction on two types of entertain-

ering burnt-cork entertainment one aspect of these transatlantic *circenses*, it is not surprising that the Christy Minstrels added a new attraction to their London show of 1866. This was Japanese Tommy, a dwarf three feet tall, hideous and grotesque. He failed to impress English critics; *The Observer* concluded that »the pleasant melodies, the broad humour, the strong sense of fun of the regular corps of minstrels» had proved more attractive than the dwarf.[1]

On October 16, 1868, The Royal Original Christy's Minstrels had the honour of a command performance at Balmoral.[2]

The minstrel vogue lasted well beyond 1870. Several outstanding performers of this later period have been mentioned by the commentators. Among the most celebrated were John R. Kemble, an »interlocutor,» who was an Englishman but had assumed an American accent and manners; Charles Sutton, an American comedian who appeared in correct evening dress with a corset instead of a waistcoat and who had obviously learnt much from Artemus Ward;[3] Seamon and Somers; Willis P. Sweatnam, and many others.

Even these few facts suffice to show that Negro minstrelsy was a most popular type of entertainment in England between 1836 and 1870. From modest beginnings inside the framework of stage comedy or farce minstrelsy developed into an independent institution with its own traditions, managers, actors, and playhouses. The shows were elaborated by both English and American performers, but the basis remained the same: humorous, very exaggerated caricature of the American Negro. Because of their popular appeal the minstrel shows assume some importance as a medium of introduction of American humour and presentations of transatlantic character in England. Everybody, from Queen Victoria to the chimney-sweep, laughed at minstrel jokes and the antics of blackface performers.

---

ment. There was a freak show displaying curiosities like Bertha Mills's feet, 19 inches long, or Jo-Jo, the dog-faced boy; and a variety show, often with minstrelsy as the burden of the performance. (Douglas Gilbert, *American Vaudeville* [New York and London, 1940], pp. 4—6.)

[1] December 9, 1866, 3.

[2] Mentioned on the cover of the sheet-music of »Plantation Melodies,» published by C. Sheard (London, 1868).

[3] Artemus Ward (Charles Farrar Browne) visited England in 1866—7 and died there in the latter year. Both Ward and Sutton inserted completely irrelevant statements into their discourses with extreme solemnity, and achieved a very humorous effect by this »*dementia praecox* method.»

5. Contemporary Comments.

Considering the great vogue of minstrelsy in England we may take it for granted that the *vulgus* enjoyed the genre. And whatever the more fastidious commentators said about the low aesthetic value of minstrel entertainment, it has to be admitted that minstrelsy formed one link in a long chain of popular pastimes spanning from a remote past via Elizabethan bear-baiting to the music-hall and television show.

When Rice introduced minstrelsy in England the reviewers wrote about his acting, singing, and dancing without realizing that they were describing the germ of a new type of popular amusement. It was in the nature of these farces that their plots were weak and lacked unity. Nevertheless the commentators usually praised the plays in which Rice appeared, and let it be understood that his individual attainments were their greatest merit. To quote one sample:

... [*Yankee Notes*] came at last to relieve their patience and reward their perseverance. The piece has, of course, been written for Mr. Rice, and for a medium for the exhibition of his very peculiar powers. Mr. Rice is, as the majority of people know, the original »Jim Crow,» he [has] »turned about and wheeled about» to his own advantage, and to the injury of nobody, and has deservedly become popular, almost beyond any contemporaneous buffoons, for his exact representation of a negro of the United States, and his native humour and correct representation of life as it actually is in a pretty considerable class of his native country. The farce itself is cleverly written, and abounds with pointed jokes, sharp repartees, and happy allusions to politics and plans ... Mr. Rice, however, was the Magnus Apollo of the evening; he was not exactly the classical deity of antiquity, but he was the most perfect representation of the emancipated negro of the United States that can be imagined. He was received last evening with great applause, and encored with most vociferous approbation.[1]

It was typical of the early reviews that critics commented upon the realism and verisimilitude of the minstrel Negro. Later even English reviewers learnt to call burnt-cork character an exaggerated caricature.

Charles Mackay was tortured by the constant repetition of »Jim Crow,» the hit tune.[2] Many others failed to see any values in the shows. Howard Paul, the American who lived in London and dabbled with humorous writing, was among those who condemned minstrelsy because

---

[1] *Times*, December 27, 1842, 5. For further comments on *Yankee Notes*, see *infra*, pp. 94—95.

[2] See *supra*, p. 79.

of its childishness and lack of moral and didactic principles. In particular he lamented the increased popularity of »vulgar» transatlantic melodies at the expense of »more refined» ones:

> The truth seems to be, that American songs grow popular on this side of the ocean, not because they possess poetic excellence or harmonious melody. The more refined the production, the more slender its chances of becoming known, while some jingling tomfoolery dashed with a spice of quaintness is in the mouth of the whole nation. Abundant illustrations of the truth of this statement are afforded in the universality of the »Dan Tuckers» and »Uncle Neds» of past times, the versification of which would disgrace the puerile muse of the dullest of schoolboys.[1]

However, even Paul had to abandon his principles and bow to popular taste when compiling a book of American songs for the English market.[2]

Yet there were many who liked minstrelsy. It was George Augustus Sala's favourite entertainment.[3] Thackeray emphasized the katharsis which could be derived from minstrel shows:

> I heard a humorous balladist not long ago, a minstrel with wool on his head and an ultra-Ethiopian complexion, who performed a negro ballad that I confess moistened these spectacles in a most unexpected manner. I have gazed at thousands of tragedy queens dying on the stage, and expiring in appropriate blank verse, and I never wanted to wipe them. They have looked up, be it said, at many scores of clergymen without being dimmed, and behold! a vagabond with a corked face and a banjo sings a little song, strikes a wild note, which sets the heart thrilling with happy pity.[4]

In his memoirs John Hollingshead forthrightly announces his great love of burnt-cork entertainment and mentions the »Squash-Holler,» a »collar-flap breakdown,» as his particular favourite.[5] Many items in newspapers and periodicals echo similar sentiments.[6]

---

[1] Howard Paul (ed.), *The Book of American Songs* (London, 1857), p. iv.

[2] »Aunt Dina Roe,» »Uncle Sam,» »Ginger's Wedding,» »Tinkling of the Banjo,» »Rosa May,» »Good Old Hut at Home,» and similar items were included and advertised as »Ethiopian songs» or »Ethiopian melodies.» A modern reader will prefer many of these simple items to the artificial sentimentality of several of the »refined» songs.

[3] See *supra*, p. 88.

[4] Quoted in Wittke, *Op.cit.*, p. 53; and in Brander Matthews, »The Rise and Fall of Negro Minstrelsy,» *Scribner's*, LVII, 759 (1915).

[5] *My Lifetime* (London, 1895), I, 140—1.

[6] *E.g.*, a passage in the *Era* of 1862 shows the importance of humour in later minstrelsy: ». . . Their budget is filled with new original jokes, which are delivered

When minstrelsy was divorced from the legitimate theatre and lost its initial fashionable appeal, current publications stopped paying attention to it. Only occasionally, when a large or otherwise celebrated troupe staged a better-than-ordinary show, did the press deign to print anything like real reviews or criticisms. As usual, *Punch* is here a better mirror of its time. As early as 1841, in its very first number, a short list of phrases translated to various languages called »Nouveau Manuel du Voyageur» includes »Jump Jim Crow.»[1] Judging from the amount of space granted to discussions of minstrelsy in the spring of 1847, the popularity of the genre had another peak period at that time. Perhaps the editors had decided at one of the sessions around the famous mahogany table at their Fleet-Street office to try to ridicule minstrelsy out of existence, or to show that it was but an idle type of entertainment. Whatever the matter, volume XII of *Punch* contains more material on minstrelsy than any other. Thus *Punch* complained:

> There are no less than four-and-twenty sons of Ethiopia at this present moment requesting Old Dan Tucker to get out of the way, and lamenting the fate of Lucy Neal, every night, in London, to say nothing of the numerous parties of the children of the sun, or sons of their fathers, who are perambulating the provinces, in the shape of Ethiopian Serenaders. We should be glad if Mr. HUME would move for a return of all the Ethiopians at present in this country, whether Lantum, Ohio, or otherwise; as, in the present paucity of provisions, every unnecessary addition to the population is a serious evil.[2]

> We have on previous occasions called attention to the Ethiopian mania, but have not yet succeeded in checking it. Ethiopians are to be found in every quarter of the town and every corner of the Kingdom; for a pennyworth of bones and a banjo, a ha'porth of soot, and an ounce of suet, will set up a party of four, without outlay... It must be admitted that the public has not dealt out its patronage with a niggard hand to these niggered melodists. We shall not be surprised if the rage for Ethiopian blackness extends to the occupants of the boxes as well as to the performers on the stage, and we shall expect to see Ethiopian head-dresses, and Ethiopian masks for the upper part of the face, becoming popular as the COSTUME DU SOIR.[3]

In the same spring, *Punch* predicted that minstrels »will disappear in due course, with the spread of enlightenment,»[4] and stated: »Every one

---

in such a manner as to keep the audience convulsed with laughter from the commencement to the end of the entertainment.» (»The Christy Minstrels,» XXIV, 10 [September 7, 1862].).

[1] I, 28 (1841). [2] »Glut of Ethiopians,» XII, 122 (1847).
[3] »Ethiopian Fashions,» *Ibid.*, 138. [4] »What is Ethiopia?» *Ibid.*, 167.

is tired of the Ethiopians, and we get so angry as nearly to turn black in the face whenever we hear them mentioned.»[1] Optimistically, *Punch* could say: »Now that the rage for black vocalists is just over, we may look for a healthier complexion in the aspect of public amusement . . .»[2] This optimism was unfounded on fact; in 1870 the humorous periodical still deplored minstrelsy as a nuisance: »From Camberwell to Highgate, from Kensington to Hackney, there is scarcely to be found a so-called quiet street but all day long it echoes with the rattling of the bones and the twanging of the banjo.»[3]

These comments show that sentiments both pro and con were aired by the inhabitants of nineteenth-century England. The popularity of minstrelsy in England between 1836 and 1870 was great; nevertheless the genre died out completely, and only occasional survivals *e.g.* in BBC programmes remind the Briton of 1951 of the previous glories of blackface entertainment. Reynolds gives an appraisal of the extent of the minstrel vogue in England in the form of an anecdote, which may serve as a fitting conclusion to the present discussion:

> It almost seemed at one time that England was divided into two classes — those that wanted to become minstrels and those that did not, and the first were apparently in the majority, including all classes of people, anybody in fact whose mother or neighbours had rashly told him he could sing. Many were absolutely hopeless and some quite a nuisance. The worst cases from sheer irritation were at times made to contribute to the minstrels' enjoyment themselves. If a very bad case came along he was told, »You'll have to turn somersaults and to do trapeze work if you come here. Don't worry, we'll teach you.» So the minstrels would strap a belt around his waist, hook the belt to a rope that ran through a pulley overhead and haul him up nearly to the ceiling, then after pelting him with cushions they would leave him suspended while they went out to get a drink. On their return the aspirant was usually ready to return to his former occupation.[4]

---

[1] »New Musical Prodigy,» *Ibid.*, 206.

[2] »The Last of the Ethiopians,» *Ibid.*, 249.

[3] »Our Nigger Highwaymen,» *Ibid.*, LVIII, 241 (June, 1870). Other items: »Britannia and the Blacks,» *Ibid.*, XII, 176 (1847); »The Billstickers' Exhibition,» *Ibid.*, 226; »An Ethiopian Serenade,» *Fun*, IV n.s., 67 (October, 1866); »A Derby Nigger, »*Ibid.*, VII n.s., 121 (May, 1868); »Amateur Theatricals,» *Punch's Almanack*, LIV (1868).

[4] Reynolds, *Op.cit.*, pp. 114—5.

CHAPTER VII

THE FORTIES

Humorous American characters continued to haunt the English stage of the forties. In that decade the interest of the Britons in things American was exemplified by Dickens's *American Notes*.[1] East of the ocean they were received as a faithful and true report by a famous author; west of the Atlantic they caused indignation and anger. Even dramatic treatments of American character were assured of popular acclaim. The stock types had been established, the grooves were set; it remained for dramatists to elaborate existing patterns.

Edward Stirling's farce *Yankee Notes for English Circulation* was first performed at the Adelphi on Christmas Eve, 1842. Stirling was noted for his series of dramatizations of Dickens's novels, and the title *Yankee Notes* shows that he and the Adelphi had the popular novelist in mind, although the play has nothing to do with Dickens's travelbook.[2] It was of course advantageous to link one's play to a book then prominent on bookstore shelves and drawing-room tables.

The plot of *Yankee Notes* consisted of the usual love-affairs, elopement plans, and mistaken identities of nineteenth-century farce.[3] The confusion is brought to an end by a *dénouement* in the garden of a Saratoga Springs hotel, where all the important male characters try to make love to a coloured girl by turns. The minstrel characters of Julius Caesar Washington Hiccory Dick, acted by Rice,[4] and of Miss Zip Coon were the major attractions. Other Americans were included: Bilberry Wad, a New-York merchant; Silas Solomon Sprawl, Jr., the son of a Kentucky businessman; and Major Dowbiggen, a frontiersman, were the main ones. A few English characters were added.

In spite of Wad's New-York background, Stirling made him use frontier language. Thus he speaks about »bells like ring-tailed monkies; knockers like rattle-snakes.» But the Yankee traits dominated his character: he was money-minded and would fain have married his daughter »as per agreement and invoice with Sprawl & Co., Mud River,

---

[1] First edition 1842.

[2] The title may have been an afterthought: as late as on December 19, the Adelphi playbills referred to the forthcoming play without mentioning any title. (*Enthoven Collection*.)

[3] Printed in *Duncombe's British Theatre* (46). [4] See *supra*, p. 90.

Kentucky,» because young Sprawl was a »saleable article.» Even Pippin, one of the Englishmen, mastered the art of frontier speech when impersonating Major Dowbiggen (whom he had never seen): »I'm the boy, just imported from old Kentucky — half horse, half alligator — a sprinkle of an airthquake, and a bit of a steamer — a regular screamer, I guess.»

The reviews show that the minstrel element formed the basis of its popularity. The Adelphi was »crowded to excess every evening during the week,» and it was predicted that *Yankee Notes* »must inevitably fill the Adelphi coffers.»[1]

The several dramatizations of *Martin Chuzzlewit* in 1844 fail to employ transatlantic characters.[2]

The Strand Theatre followed its presentation of *Chuzzlewit* with a package of two one-act farces written by the American playwright Cornelius Ambrosius Logan.[3] The first of these was *Yankee Land; or, the Foundling of the Apple-Orchard*.[4] A paternity case served as basis for the slender plot. Both English and American characters were included. Lot Sap Sago, a Yankee, was contrasted with Otto Mannikin, a fop who used the transatlantic euphemism »gentleman cow» for the shocking word »bull.» Lot Sap Sago is one of the most finished and consistent humorous Americans to be presented on the English stage. His independence and resourceful self-reliance are characteristic; there is

---

[1] *Era*, January 1, 1843, 2; see also *Observer*, January 1, 1843, 4; *Sunday Times*, January 1, 1843, 3; *Times*, December 27, 1842, 5; *Examiner*, December 31, 1842, 838.

[2] Martin Chuzzlewit's and Mark Tapley's American journey was only alluded to in these plays; the dramatic unity would have been endangered by the introduction of another setting, which actually had little to do with the central plot. The Strand Theatre version indicated that a string of American melodies were to be played at the end of Act I to indicate the departure of the heroes. Dramatizations were written by Stirling, Thomas Higgie and Thomas Hailes Lacy, Charles Webb, and an unknown author. The Higgie-Lacy version is available in *Lacy's*, Supp. I; the others in *British Museum Add. MS 42976*.

[3] Logan was born in 1806 of Irish parents. After a motley career as a newspaperman and a sailor he began to act in the middle twenties, and moved from Philadelphia to New York in 1826. He advanced to theatre manager in Pittsburgh, and later to the manager of a travelling theatrical company in the Middle West. In his plays he was one of the early American dramatists to use Yankee character for comic purposes. In addition to the two farces under discussion, Logan's daughter attributed *The People's Lawyer*, performed in England in 1856, to him, saying that J. S. Jones merely revised Logan's original. (Edwin Francis Edgett, »Cornelius Ambrosius Logan,» *Dictionary of American Biography*.)

[4] *British Museum Add. MS 42978*.

a touch of the frontier in the lusty exaggeration of his stories. Two representative quotes will illustrate the point:

> I ain't no beggar — never seed one — never want to — never begged but once. and that was when I took Ike Jasper for a Moose and shoved a bullet thro' his shoulders, then I begged his pardon . . .[1]

> Tell you them Oxen of mine won't travel single. Cause why, they an't got but one tail between them. I'll tell you how it happened. One day I was dragging a stick o' red pine timber down to the Steam boat landing in Castine, & just afore I got to the Wharf, one of them are Oxen hawed right into a hole — I laid the switch on him like a trip hammer — but the more I licked him the more he wouldn't budge, he laid right down in the mud — so what should I do, but run right down to the Steam Boat that was just a going over to Fox Island — seized hold of a Coil of Rope & making one end fast to the Boat I run up to the mud hole & bent t'other end onto that are Ox tail. The Engineer didn't know what was stopping the Boat, so he piled on more steam & the tail began to crack — for more than 5 minutes it was pull Bullock — pull Boat — but the beef gave way first, for the critter's tail broke short off & now that quadruped had to hire t'other one to switch the flies off.[2]

Yankee Land ran from October 7 to October 26, 1844.[3] It was but a trailer farce and did not receive so much attention as the main play of the evening.[4]

The other of Logan's pieces staged at the Strand Theatre was the one-act farce *The Vermont Wool-Dealer*.[5] It ran from September 28 to October 12, 1844.[6] The plot consists of the story of an elopement, and there are the usual mistaken identities; in the end Deuteronomy Dutiful, the Vermonter, is fooled, promises to pay for the champagne consumed, and returns to Vermont. Dutiful's speech is bombastic and his actions fiery in the frontier fashion:

> I'll whip te hull boodle of you at once! Make me mad, and I'll lick a thunderstorm! . . . I'll fight you with rifles loaded to the muzzles with three cornered slugs, and rammed into each other — Git me my Ebenezer — riz — and you'd think somebody was blowing rocks — I have the almightiest notion to pick up this awful nigger and knock out somebody's brains with his shin . . .

In addition to frontier speeches of this type, Deuteronomy displays the Yankee virtues of practicality, money-mindedness, and shrewdness, but comes to grief in the play in spite of these qualities.

---

[1] Scene 1.   [2] Scene 4.   [3] Advertisements in *Times*.
[4] The same fate followed its performances in New York in 1834 (*Reed*).
[5] Available in *British Museum Add. MS 42978*.
[6] Advertisements in *Times*. The date 27. 2. 1845 in *Nicoll* is wrong.

The other characters include Con Gormley, an American Irishman who displays no transatlantic characteristics; Slap, a hotelkeeper who is just as reluctant to serve his guests as the travel-books said him to be; and Betty and Bob, two Negroes. The two latter are not made vehicles of coloured humour to any considerable extent.

The Yankee parts in these two farces were acted by Danforth Marble, an American actor who specialized in this type of entertainment. Little is known about him.[1] Judging from the reviews criticizing his London performances of 1844 he was a skilful follower of Hackett and Hill; his acting was commended as the best part of the performance. Marble's analysis of Lot Sap Sago and Deuteronomy Dutiful seems to have stressed the Yankee traits rather than the frontier ones; the comments of the critics on the quietness and slyness of the acting indicate that that was the case. The press notices also show how little trouble the English audience of 1844 had with American humour and the New-England dialect when these were handled by an expert showman. A typical piece of criticism is that of *The Morning Post:*

> This is a genuine Yankee article, manufactured in the States, and presented for approbation by a regular down-easter. Mr. Marble is an actor whose peculiar excellence in the impersonation of American character is not to be repudiated. His quietude is perfectly refreshing. The twinkle of his eye and sly smile that accompanies the enunciation of each good thing is exceedingly amusing. The staple of the piece is of questionable quality... Mr. Marble's dialect is unmistakably legitimate, and his quaint nasal tones and droll action form a perfect portrait of the members of that section of the »Union» of which Mr. Marble is the honourable representative. Some of the remarks with which the character is interspersed have the right *Sam Slick* stamp, and would pass current from Passmaquody [sic] in the South to Chippewa in the North, describing the unrest he suffered on board the steamer by the tremendous snoring of a *contingent* passenger. He says, »I shoved his tarnal head through a butter-firkin — greased his nose, and then the varmint snored easier.» He kisses the lady, and swears she »blushed to such an almighty extent that he burnt his shirt-collar.» Vows that his grandfather's orchard is so thickly planted that he was obliged to split the trees to let the sun rise — had a horse that got so old that he wouldn't die, so was obliged to place him against a tree and borrow another horse to help him draw his [last] breath. The effect of these Americanisms was much enhanced by the mode of delivery, and elicited shouts of laughter. The house was well filled.[2]

The critic of *The Sunday Times* called *The Vermont Wool-Dealer* a bad play, »almost as uninteresting as any we ever saw,» but thought that

---

[1] See Carson, *The Theatre on the Frontier*, pp. 286—7, 300 ff.
[2] *Morning Post*, October 5, 1844, 5.

Marble's »quaint drolleries, uttered with that peculiar nasal twang that distinguishes the real Yankee» saved the performance. Marble was also favourably compared to Hill; the former was said to have »greater breadth and force,» a »bolder and firmer» technique and »a more decided and striking effect.»[1] Another reviewer considered it necessary to explain that Marble was not a minstrel, »but of the Sam Slick genus.»[2] *The Sun* found »truth of life» in Marble's portrayal of the Yankee, and also »the common feelings and passions of man.»[3] The critic of *The Era* availed himself of the opportunity to pass comment upon American humour:

> Both [farces] were written for the special purpose of introducing Mr. Marble (not the Marble of Fenimore Cooper's last novel!) to an English audience, and developing the »outré» notions, clothed in the marvellous diction of the new world. It is an all but untrodden path upon the stage, though the Washington Irvings and the Coopers of America, bearing peculiarly in mind the Sam Slicks, as well as our own Trollopes, Marryatts, and Bozzes, have, in their writings, rendered us, to an extent, familiar with the habits and customs of the embryo population, in which semi-barbarism develops the strangest compound of shrewdness and folly, of fancied superiority and innate distrust, of vanity and arrogance, and of envy and jealousy ... Let but some talented dramatist wing them for the stage, and Marble will be amongst the very first to bring them down with a volley — of applause! What we like about this gentleman's acting is his standing aloof from every school and style, and trusting to his own indigenous resources. His humour is broad, but distinctive; and his by-play imbued with the art that constitutes its nature ... The nasal twang, and the monotonous drawl of Brother Jonathan, with his vulgar attempts at ease, and his quiet mode of occupying a chair with his boots, making a species of a rocking-horse of it when not adapted to the original intention of the cabinet-maker, were exquisitely hit off; whilst Munchhausen himself would have been jealous of the rival skill and masterly effect with which the »long-bow» was handled.[4]

Several shorter reviews echo the same opinions and give further details of Marble's success at the Strand. He was dubbed »an excellent performer,» »the best representative of the Jonathanisms of his countrymen,» and the possessor of »comic talent that we shall be glad to see developed in a better drama.»[5]

---

[1] October 6, 1844, 2. [2] Unidentified clipping in *Enthoven Collection*.
[3] October 8, 1844, 3. [4] October 13, 1844, 5.
[5] *Evening Sun*, October 15, 1844, 1; *Era*, October 20, 1844, 5; *Spectator*, October 5, 1844, 947; *Ibid.*, November 2, 1844, 1042; *Sunday Times*, October 20, 1844, 2.

From the Strand Marble transferred to the Haymarket, where *Yankee Land* ran from October 29 to November 2, 1844.[1] Now Marble's ambition got the better of his judgment. He appeared in another hastily concocted farce called *Sam Patch the Jumper*, which was first performed at the Haymarket on November 4, 1844.[2] It was a whopping failure. The piece consisted of a mixture of Yankee humour and melodrama including one kidnapping story and a fight at the verge of Niagara Falls. There was no trace of dramatic unity, and the jokes were old and worn-out. The failure of *Sam Patch* abruptly terminated Marble's acting in London. However, his previous success proved a sufficient excuse to make a critic praise his acting, although the disdain for the play was expressed in straightforward terms.[3] But the kind words written by *The Times* when it moved in for the kill were of no avail. After his failure Dan Marble's name disappeared from the annals of the English theatre; this had been the lot of his predecessor Yankee Hill.

James Barber's *Jonathan; or, the Man of Two Masters* contains no American characters.[4] *The Wigwam*, performed at the Lyceum Theatre in January, 1847, takes the audience to an Indian encampment near Montreal, but uses no comic Americans; the fun is mostly dependent on the Cockney characters.[5]

In January, 1848, the Royal Standard Theatre of Shoreditch played *The Mysteries of an American City; or, I Vonders How That'll Vork*. The plot is a mixture of Gothic melodrama and Dickensian sentimentality in American settings. It contains no extensive treatment of humorous American character.[6]

Towards Christmas, 1848, the usual crop of pantomimes contained two with American elements. The Royal Amphitheatre performed

---

[1] Advertisements in *Times*.
[2] Available in *British Museum Add. MS 42979*. Sam Patch was a Rhode Island folk hero; the legends about his jumping feats had been used as a basis of humorous treatment by Seba Smith. See Rourke, *American Humor*, p. 74; and Spiller et al. (eds.), *Literary History of the United States*, II, 732.
[3] *Times*, November 5, 1844, 6.
[4] Performed at the Royal Amphitheatre in June, 1845. (*Nicoll*.) Available in *Dicks' Standard Plays* (983).
[5] *British Museum Add. MS 43006*; *Athenaeum*, January 30, 1847, 130.
[6] *British Museum Add. MS 43009*. Nicoll lists it as property of the Britannia Theatre, while the MS bears the name of the Standard.

Yankee Doodle upon His Little Pony, and, a few weeks later, Nelson Lee's *Harlequin and Yankee Doodle*.[1]

In the last year of the decade, Adelphi audiences had the dubious pleasure of enjoying another Cockney comedy with a transatlantic setting. This time it was J. Stirling Coyne's *Cocknies in California*.[2] The first performance took place on February 26, 1849. In addition to the fun of the Cockney Chiffinses the play uses the humour of Peter and Julina, a coloured couple:

> *Peter:* Julina!
> *Julina:* What am dat, Peta?
> *Peter:* It strike me berry hard — dis 'ere colour gen'lman dam fool, to stay for nigga help any longer wit massa Bunker. What for I dig for him when ebbery body in Callumfornia dig for himself?
> *Julina:* Berry true, Peta — berry true!

The adventures of these forty-niners in their hectic search of gold contain no further elements relevant to the present study. A few references to coons and gum-trees sufficed for local colour.

Marble's English tour was the most important event in the history of humorous American characters on the English stage in the forties. Otherwise this decade was a time of intensive Anglo-American contacts in the dramatic field. Forrest visited England, Macready America, and the disgraceful riots of 1849 proved that the theatre could kindle Anglo-American enmity into open flame. Lesser actors undertook Atlantic crossings. American plays were taken to England, English plays to America; even if a few enthusiasts like Dickens and Talfourd directed attention to the copyright question, plays were practically free for anybody to use. In the forties the London audiences no longer considered humorous American characters unheard-of curiosities; after the pioneer work of Mathews, Hackett, and Hill, the English had a good yard-stick by which to measure the achievements of Marble and other presenters of comic Americans.

---

[1] *Nicoll.*
[2] Printed in *Webster's National Drama*, XV.

CHAPTER VIII

THE FIFTIES

1. Caricature in Social Comedy: Fashion.

The beginnings of native American humour owed a great debt to folklore. The most important comic stock characters who represented the United States were descendants of non-literary types shaped by popular fancy and imagination. By 1830 they had crystallized into their permanent stage forms, and reigned for decades as the only representatives of humorous American character. On the English stage they were usually presented as exaggerated caricatures without much reference to any social framework or to the problems of man's adjustment to his environment. The Yankee and the frontiersman were extreme individualists, whose chief concern was their own profit and welfare; when they philosophized, their remarks were of the cracker-box type, shrewd and egocentric.

In the development of American humour the general tendency has been away from folk patterns towards social patterns. This gradual change of emphasis can be seen *e.g.* in the works of Mark Twain, where the tall-tale Calaveras County had to yield to the socially more significant Hadleyburg. In our day much of the best-known humour of American writers is focussed on social problems like man's adjustment to the viciousness of the mechanized everyday. This increased emphasis of the social aspect of humour may be interpreted as one manifestation of the gradual stabilization of American society. In the West of yore, a man's main business was himself and his family; the pioneer could not be expected to think in wider terms. With the passing of the frontier era the complex questions of man's integration with society and his relations to his fellow-men had to be solved, and solved anew since the experiences of other nations could not be applied without modifications to the problems of the rapidly growing United States. Early American humour was largely based on frontier life; later transatlantic entertainment dealt with man's existence in settled and stable communities. The dating of a change so fundamental cannot be exact; it is both convenient and justifiable to consider the Civil-War period an important dividing-line.[1]

---

[1] In *Literary History of the United States*, II, 729, Thompson and Canby date this change »some time between 1860 and 1875.»

The increasing emphasis on social problems can be seen in American stage humour as well. Because of the absence of clear strata in American society, early new-world writers of social comedy, *e.g.* Oliver S. Leland, had preferred English settings. About 1860, the supreme reign of caricature was over, and plays more akin to social comedy began to appear.[1] Where the laugh had previously been on the Yankee, the frontiersman, or the Negro, it could now be shifted on social evils like intellectual dependence on worthless foreign models, oversophistication of manners, class distinctions, and similar topics. The transition was gradual, and caricatured characters could often be found in plays dealing with social problems.[2] In the present study the history of such caricatures will be traced on the English stage: more comprehensive discussions of pure social comedy fall outside the scope of this work.

On the English stage the trend towards the treatment of problems of American society can be stated in terms of a change from farce to comedy. In the thirties and forties the vehicles of American humour *par préférence* had been the comic interlude and one-act trailer farce, which merely provided the audience with its wonted guffaw between more important pieces. In the fifties humorous American characters appeared in several long plays occupying central places in the programmes.

After Tyler's *The Contrast*, one of the early examples of American social comedy is Anna Cora Mowatt Ritchie's *Fashion; or, Life in New York*.[3] In a short preface the authoress stated her purpose:

> The Comedy of *Fashion* was intended as a good-natured satire upon some of the follies incident to a new country, where foreign dross sometimes passes for gold, while native gold is cast aside as dross; where the vanities rather than the virtues of other lands are too often imitated, and where the stamp of *fashion* gives currency even to the coinage of vice.[4]

Among the characters is Adam Trueman, a farmer from Catteraugus and an honest and virtuous American in the best Colonel-Manly tradi-

---

[1] See John Geoffrey Hartman, *The Development of American Social Comedy*. In *American Drama to the Present Day*, p. 1, Quinn calls the sixties and seventies »transition decades.»

[2] »The comedy types appeared frequently in delightful confusion in the same play.» (Quinn, *American Drama to the Civil War*, pp. 324—5.)

[3] First performed in March, 1845, at Park Theatre in New York City. Such a discerning critic as Poe »hailed the play as a sign of vitality in American drama.» (Quinn [ed.], *Literature of the American People*, p. 391.)

[4] This preface was included in a version printed by W. Newberry in London in 1850, available in *British Museum Add. MS 43024.*

tion. He is contrasted with Mrs. Tiffany, the epitome of the transatlantic *nouveaux riches*, who prefers to call her arm-chair »fow-tool.» A humorous Negro servant, Zeke, is contrasted with an equally humorous French maid called Millinette. The necessary impostor poses as Count Jolimaitre, while two more characters, Twinkle the poet and Fogg the bored young aristocrat, further prove the degeneration of Mrs. Tiffany's social circle. Trueman's honest simplicity is brought out from the very beginning. He enters the Tiffany residence with customary vigour, having known Mr. Tiffany years ago when the latter still was a poor man, and protests when told that Mrs. Tiffany would not receive him: »Where's this woman that's not *at home* in her own house? May I be shot! if I wonder at it! I shouldn't think she'd ever feel *at home* in such a show-box as this!» When confronted with Mrs. Tiffany's notions of what is important, Trueman airs his feelings:

Trueman: Fashion! And pray what is *fashion*, madam? An agreement between certain persons to live without using their souls! to substitute etiquette for virtue — decorum for purity — manners for morals! to affect a shame for the works of their Creator! and expend all their rapture upon the works of their tailors and dressmakers!
Mrs. Tiffany: You have the most *ow-tray* ideas, Mr. Trueman — quite rustic, and deplorably *American!*[1]

The first performance of *Fashion* in England took place at the Olympic Theatre, London, on January 9, 1850. Mrs. Mowatt, herself an accomplished actress, did not take part in the performance.[2] She was, however, present at the London opening of her play and was called before the curtain, which was tangible evidence of her success. *Fashion* ran at least to February 9, 1850; a minimum of twenty performances.[3]

In the opinion of some reviewers the play proved a »decided success» and »triumph.» The fact that it was a social comedy emphasizing the necessity of simple virtue and ridiculing blind obedience to the dicta of outlandish modes did not escape the critics; this time there were greater principles involved than mere presentation of typified, inherently ridiculous characters. Thus the reviewer of *The Morning Herald* phrased his comments in terms of social adjustment and completely failed to

---

[1] *Ibid.*, Act IV, Scene 1 (p. 39).
[2] However, she acted in George Henry Lewes's *The Noble Heart*, which was staged at the Olympic after *Fashion* had finished its initial run.
[3] Playbills in *Enthoven Collection*.

discuss Trueman as a comic Yankee. He emphasized the fact that many of the elements of *Fashion* were well known on the English stage; the play was preoccupied with a problem which may have assumed similar shapes on both sides of the Atlantic. These remarks show that in the reviewer's mind the humour was not based on the antics of a Yankee in a social vacuum, but on more fundamental problems of man's relations to his fellow men.[1]

The same commentator went on to say that the characters of *Fashion* were superior to the plot. Life in New York, he thought, must be queer indeed if the characters were not exaggerated caricatures. In any case he congratulated Mrs. Mowatt on »literary dexterity» and a neat dialogue, which compensated for its lack of delicacy with humour. The good acting also received its share of the praise.[2]

The Athenaeum gave an affirmative answer to the question whether *Fashion* gave a true picture of life in America.[3] The critic of *The Sun* realized that *Fashion* was different from the other plays presenting humorous American character on the English stage:

> ... but America had not given us, until last night, any play that would stand the test of representation before a London audience. Rough and ranting melodramas have formed the staple of what America had hitherto sent us, but last night this reproach was wiped out, and there was represented at this theatre, with the most deserved success, an original American five-act comedy, the scene of which is laid in New York, and which delineates American manners after the same fashion as our own Garrick, Colman, and Sheridan were accustomed to delineate English manners, and which, as regards plot, construction, character or dialogue, is worthy to take its place by the side of the best of English comedies.

This critic preferred Prudence, Mrs. Tiffany's Puritan and maidenish Yankee sister, to all the other characters.[4]

The Observer noted that English parallels of *Fashion* should be sought in early nineteenth-century comedy. It found some fault with the play, the characters of which »possess very little novelty.» Yet the »portraitures are considered accurate by persons perfectly competent to judge of them, seeing that the play has been acted with success in every chief city of the American union.» The critic was willing to grant the play an excuse for its shortcomings:

---

[1] January 11, 1850, 4.   [2] *Ibid.*   [3] January 12, 1850, 51.
[4] January 10, 1850, 3.

To appreciate this work properly, however, all its circumstances must be taken into consideration. It was originally produced at the Park Theatre, in 1845, when the authoress was extremely young; and it was worked out in a country where the traditions of dramatic writing are almost wholly unknown.[1]

The Spectator centered its remarks around the native American element of *Fashion*. It was not charmed by the framework of the social comedy, and thought the attractions of the play were due to the illustrations of American character and setting.[2]

All these reviews were favourable rather than condemning. But the critic of *The Era* started off by severe statements like »although it occasionally provoked our laughter, it never once excited our admiration.» He pointed out that there was no »epigrammatical satire» nor any »sparkling novelty,» both necessary in good comedy. The final paragraph displays the tendency of some Englishmen to call all original American letters crude and vulgar, and all those that were based on European models mere imitation:

> The piece, as a whole, was cleverly acted. If it failed to meet the expectations of any one present, the fault was decidedly not on the side of the performers. Its great defect was a want of truth, and the absence of original and striking ideas. The Americans graft their literature to ours, and contend that even such productions as Sheridan's *School for Scandal*, and Tobin's *Honeymoon*, and comedies of still later date, are as much American as English, else we might regard *Fashion* as a remarkable production. It would be no compliment to the fair author to say it is extraordinarily excellent for an American piece, although we may probably state as much with fairness. Still, judging as we do, there is much to amuse in it, and with some curtailment, it is likely to remain for some time on the bills of the Olympic.[3]

The Examiner had no kind words for *Fashion*. Having quoted one of the above reviews *in extenso* the critic went on:

> ... we are bound to add that we do not in the least agree with it. The piece seemed to us to have no merit whatever, negative or positive. For the most part it was nonsense, nor was it nonsense void of offense ... for what has here drawn praise and glory to Mrs. Mowatt, Mrs. Trollope would have been denounced to the tar-barrel ... Humour, character, plot, morality, and good sense, were all upon the level below toleration.[4]

---

[1] January 13, 1850, 7. [2] January 12, 1850, 34.
[3] XII, 12 (January 13, 1850). [4] January 12, 1850, 22.

The Morning Post was savage in its comments, too.[1]

Mrs. Mowatt's *Fashion* was the first American social comedy to be presented on the English stage. The emphasis was on a social problem, but the caracters remained essentially caricatures.[2]

2. *Josh Silsbee as the Yankee Ploughboy.*

In the autumn of 1851, English society became acquainted with one of the early manifestations of militant feminism. At this time Mrs. Bloomer's ideas of emancipation and of feminine garb arrived in England, and a whole crop of plays made fun of the suggested innovations.[3] In an age when the display of a well-shaped feminine ankle proved a source of male inspiration the Bloomer plays had certain attractions; to quote an Adelphi playbill: »The Farce was perfectly and uproariously successful — the display of PRETTY BLOOMERS being irresistible.»[4] The only one of these plays to include a caricatured American character was C. A. Somerset's *The Bloomer Costume! or Brother Jonathan in England!*, licensed on October 6, 1851, for the Grecian Saloon, where the first performance took place on October 13.[5]

In this play, Mr. Humphrey Grogram, president of a parish board in an English town, was visited by his American brother Jonathan. A third brother, also an American, had willed a sizeable legacy to Humphrey and his family on one condition: the female Grograms must immediately adopt the Bloomer costume. After some consternation, they did.

Most of the play revolves around the bloomer theme rather than around Brother Jonathan; in the first scene the transatlantic visitor is given some prominence. He is introduced by a letter he wrote from

---

[1] Quinn, *American Drama to the Civil War*, pp. 317—8.

[2] Mrs. Mowatt's novels *The Fortune Hunter* and *Evelyn* were also known in England. They were said to »give us a higher idea of Mrs. Mowatt's talents as an authoress than her plays did.» (»Our Library Table,» *Athenaeum*, November 23, 1850, 1215.)

[3] From September to November, 1851, the following were licensed: *Bloomerism or Follies of the Day*, Adelphi, 26. 9.; *The Bloomer Costume*, Queen's, 30. 9.; *The Bloomer Costume! or Brother Jonathan in England*, Grecian Saloon, 6. 10.; *The Bloomer Wives, or the Birds of Bloomsbury Bower*, 10. 10.; *The Two Bloomers*, Surrey, 10. 10.; *The Bloomers*, Olympic, 3. 11. (*Lord Chamberlain MSS.*)

[4] *Enthoven Collection.*

[5] Available in *British Museum Add. MS 43037.*

America announcing his imminent arrival, and when he comes, his conversation is typical of the comic stock American:

Jonathan: (without) Hallo! Hallo! open the door in a flash of blue Lightning or I'll thunder it about your ears — *(knocking again)* well, and who are you? one of the helps I guess? — The *Tiger*, eh? if you bite me damme but I'll blow your brains out! — Where's brother Humphry? upstairs — enough — I'll condescend to ascend and see him — *(enters)* I guess your name is Mr. Humphry Grogram, oh yes?
Grogram: That is my name.
Jonathan: Then I'm your brother, and tarnation glad to see you *(embrace)*.
Grogram: Mercy! he's nearly squeezed all the breath out of me.
Jonathan: We're so much used to the Backwoods dye see — and the *Bears* — that we hug rather tightish I guess. Oh yes! So you're brother Humphry — eh? and that slick old woman is your wife I calculate?
Grogram: That — brother is Mrs. Godiva Grogram.
Godiva: Slick old woman! what an uncouth fellow he is tho' after all —
Jonathan: Godiva Grogram! *Godiva!* I'm not much of a Scholar, but I've read of you Ma'am — how d'ye do? an't you the Lady that rode once on horseback thro' the streets of Coventry — in a state of — I don't like to say how — in a tarnation state of comical Niggledegee — you know what I mean, I guess. Oh Sister in Law Godiva, I'm ashamed of you — but you're an immortal deal older and know better now, I calculate — Oh yes —
Godiva: Sir — if you came from America to insult me —
Grogram: Pshaw nonsense! no such thing: Brother Jonathan merely confounds your name with another that he has read of in History — nothing more —
Jonathan: And those three tarnation spruce & slick, shy and sly young female Buffaloes are your Daughters, I guess... My dears — I am tarnation glad to see you — give us a Buss, in the true Kentucky fashion — a smack that you might hear from Boston to New York... And now brother Humphry if you won't be jealous — darn my jacket, if I don't have a Buss from your wife, the old She-Buffalo as well...[1]

And Jonathan the frontiersman proceeded to kiss his female relatives with loud and thorough relish.

A more notable event was the Adelphi production of the historically important *The Forest Rose and the Yankee Ploughboy*, a comedy in two acts by Samuel Woodworth, the American playwright, editor, and literary man.[2] The first performance in London took place on September 23, 1851.[3]

---

[1] *Ibid.*, pp. 17—19.

[2] Jonathan Ploughboy of *The Forest Rose* has been called the first of the descendants of Tyler's Jonathan of *The Contrast* to become popular in the United States. See Quinn, *American Drama to the Civil War*, p. 294.

[3] Playbill in *Enthoven Collection*.

The setting of *The Forest Rose* was a New-England farm. The main plot dealt with the love-affairs of two idealized rustic girls; the villain was Bellamy, a city slicker from New York. Jonathan Ploughboy was the comedian of the piece. He was the butt of practical jokes: when agreeing to kiss his Sally blindfolded, he was made to kiss Rose, a coloured girl smelling of onions. His characteristics are better revealed in the dialogue. When meeting strangers he avoided giving straight answers to questions and tried to find out as much as possible about them with true Yankee inquisitiveness. He was a shopkeeper selling »almost anything.» When Bellamy, the villain, tried to bribe Jonathan to aid his machinations, the Yankee interest in material things did not facilitate virtuous action:

> I don't calculate I feel exactly right about keeping this purse — and yet I should feel worse to give it back — twenty three dollars is a speculation, that ain't to be sneezed at — but will it be right to keep the money when I don't intend to do the job. Now if I was at home down at Taunton I would put that question to our debating society and I would support the affirmative side of the question...[1]

Shrewd, inquisitive, talkative, and business-minded, Jonathan boosted his ego at all occasions. However, his actions were righteous, and since Bellamy's villainy bore the brunt of the ridicule, Jonathan's character escaped comparatively unscathed.

Jonathan's part was played by another of the American actors who came to Britain to specialize in stage humour, Josh Silsbee. Little is known about him.[2] He arrived in London at an auspicious moment: Madame Celeste, the manageress of the Adelphi, was just about to leave for the United States, and attractions had to be found for the period of her absence. Silsbee fully realized Madame Celeste's most ambitious and optimistic hopes. *The Forest Rose* was an immediate success. By January 1, 1852, it had reached its 84th performance, and the last successive evening, January 10, 1852, was billed as the 93rd. In an 1854 edition of the play the preface stated that Silsbee had performed it in London for more than one hundred consecutive nights. Silsbee was advertised as »the only living Successful Delineator of

---

[1] *British Museum Add. MS 43037*, Act II, Scene 3, p. 16.

[2] Rourke, *American Humor*, pp. 21—22, mentions Silsbee as one of the actors who carried on the traditions of Yankee Hill by portraying Yankee character. There is no mention of Silsbee in *Dictionary of American Biography*.

Yankee Peculiarities,» and the playbills promised »Enormous Success of and Roars of Laughter at the celebrated Yankee Comedian, Mr. Josh Silsbee.» The Adelphi promptly suspended the free list for the duration of his visit.[1]

In addition to *The Forest Rose,* Silsbee went on to act Hiram Dodge in Yankee Hill's old success *The Yankee Pedlar* for 27 nights beginning on January 12, 1852. On February 18th he left for the provinces, having played at the Adelphi for 120 nights.[2] The Edinburgh and Manchester audiences liked him just as well as the Londoners. The Manconians saw Hill inaugurate a new farce, *Love and Larnin'*, in spite of a severe cold.[3]

Upon his return to the English capital Silsbee acted Nathan, a Yankee, in a piece called *A Wife for a Day.* This play was first staged at the Standard and then at the Adelphi, at the latter theatre from November 8 to 15, 1852, for at least seven performances. On November 16 *The Yankee Pedlar* was revived for one night.[4] Then *Uncle Tom's Cabin* arrived on the London stage, and due to its enormous and sudden popularity everything else was crowded out. After November, 1852, there is no record of Silsbee in England.

Numerous reviews extolled Silsbee's virtues. A representative example is that of *The Times:*

> Mr. J. Silsbee, an American delineator of »Yankee eccentricities,» who made his first appearance last night, is probably the best actor of his class ever seen by a London public. Mr. Hill, whose line of character he adopts, was smart and lively, but small in his style, whereas Mr. Silsbee's humour is large, unctuous, and broad. He is grave without being dry, and the solemnity of his countenance, as abundant Yankeeisms roll from his tongue, is one of his most amusing peculiarities. Nature has done much to qualify him as a low comedian. His face is large, and capable in itself of exciting the risible muscles, and his thick-set figure is susceptible of the most ridiculous make up. His dialect is the broadest that has yet been heard, and his articulation is so rapid that, though he has a sonorous voice, great attention is required to catch the whole of his words. His effect on the audience was immense. A roar greeted his entrance, and a roar accompanied him throughout his performance. This is of itself an evidence of rare merit, for Yankee peculiarities have almost been done to death, and with an inferior actor would be all but intolerable. In Mr. Silsbee's manner there is, however, such evident originality that he imparts freshness to a school of drollery which was fast becoming ineffective . . .[5]

---

[1] Playbills in *Enthoven Collection;* »Chit Chat,» *American Magazine,* I, 112 November, 1851); Quinn, *American Drama to the Civil War,* p. 294.

[2] Playbills.

[3] »Provincial Theatricals,» »Music and the Drama at Manchester,» *Era,* XIV, December 12, 1852, 11.

[4] Playbills in *Enthoven Collection.*   [5] September 24, 1851, 6.

The Morning Post preferred the acting to the script, and made a remark about American social standards:

> The author, as we have said, has selected his hero from the lowest grade of society in a country where even the highest is not remarkable for polish; consequently, without considerable coarseness and vulgarity, his picture could scarcely be deemed faithful.[1]

The comments of *The Sun* were enthusiastic; here Silsbee was said to have given »an *original* picture» of the Yankee and to possess the very qualifications needed for the part.[2] *The Spectator* pointed out that the success was due to the acting and not the play. In this critic's opinion American stock characters were already worn out:

> In the first place, what can be regarded as more unattractive than the announcement of drama constructed for the purpose of showing »Yankee eccentricities»? Some ten or twelve years ago, we were literally dosed with Yankeeisms; no kind of wit was so abundant as that hybrid between the Irish bull and the Munchhausen tale, which is distinguished by the name of Jonathan ... the »fun» of the first year became the »bore» of the second ...[3]

The Sunday Times had a high opinion of Silsbee's Yankee imitations, but not of »his artistic excellence as a comedian.» The play was thought devoid of any merit.[4] *The Era* called the production »wretched,» but hailed Jonathan with an eager welcome:

> ... Brother Jonathan has now furnished us with precisely what we wanted — what we cannot »raise» at home — a veritable Yankee low comedian — the faithful portrayer of that unadulterated material which is so interesting to the Britisher — the type of a class, about which, generally speaking, we read so much and know so little. Here he is, having made what the playbills, and truly for once, announce as an immense hit.[5]

Other reviews repeated similar statements.[6]

The popularity of the Yankee ploughboy in London in 1851 shows that the English public still liked stage caricatures of American character.

---

[1] September 24, 1851, 5. [2] September 24, 1851, 3.
[3] September 27, 1851, 924—5. [4] September 28, 1851, 5.
[5] XIV, 11 (September 28, 1851).
[6] *Atlas*, September 27, 1851, 619; *Ibid.*, November 13, 1852, 728; *Examiner*, September 27, 1851, 614; *Observer*, September 28, 1851, 2; *The American Magazine*, I, 53 (October, 1851); *Ibid.*, 112 (November, 1851); *Era*, November 14, 1852, 11; unidentified clipping in *Enthoven Collection*.

The same currents that had made Mathews, Hackett, Hill, and Marble appreciated in Britain in the previous decades, led to Silsbee's successes in the early fifties.

3. Uncle Tom's Cabin.

The traditional and established types of treatment of American themes continued on the English stage in the fifties. In 1850 The Surrey Theatre staged a dramatic version of Cooper's *The Red Rover*,[1] and the Royal Pavilion performed *Magawisca; or, the Indian Chief's Revenge*, in June, 1851.[2] These plays contained no humorous American characters. More important were the versions of *Uncle Tom's Cabin*, where comic relief was inserted in the form of caricatures of Yankees, frontiersmen, Negroes, or immigrants.

It is not surprising that Mrs. Beecher Stowe's novel was repeatedly dramatized. It was a tremendous popular hit.[3] The book possessed

---

[1] Written by Edward Fitzball. John Leslie, an American artist, had painted a moving panorama showing the entire passage from Newport, Mass., to the final destination of the ship. (*Athenaeum*, March 2, 1850, 243.)

[2] *British Museum Add. MS 43035*. The licenser's approval was also secured for *Alzine ou les américains* (*Ibid. 42884*).

[3] *Uncle Tom's Cabin* was first published in weekly parts in *National Era*, Washington, D.C., between June 5, 1851, and April 1, 1852. In America alone, 100 000 copies were sold in eight weeks, 200 000 within one year, and 313 000 by April 1, 1856. In England the success was great, too. The first edition with a London imprint came out in May, 1852. By September »the London publishers furnished to one house 10 000 copies per day for about four weeks, and had to employ 1 000 persons in preparing copies to supply the general demand.» By October 1, over twenty editions could be found in the London bookstores, and one publisher was reported to have sold more than 18 000 copies. One month later, Smith's railway bookstores sold 300 copies daily. Charles E. Stowe estimated the total number of copies circulated in Great Britain and the colonies to amount to more than one and a half million. (Charles E. Stowe, *Life of Harriet Beecher Stowe* [Boston and New York, 1889], pp. 189—190; Gohdes, *American Literature in Nineteenth-Century England*, pp. 29 ff.; S. Austin Allibone, *Critical Dictionary of English Literature* [Philadelphia, 1870] II, 2278—9; »Slavery in the United States,» *Edinburgh Review* [April, 1855]; »Gossip of the Literary Circles,» *Critic*, XI, 519 [October 1, 1852]; *Ibid.*, 576 [November 1, 1852].)

Basking in the popularity of the original came a number of imitations or refutations, which received their share of the popular acclaim. In the autumn of 1852 alone, reviews of the following have been found in English periodicals: *Uncle Tom in England, or a Proof that Black's White; Life at the South, or, Uncle*

great topical interest and contained elements that could be made into both melodrama and farce, the two leading dramatic forms of the mid-nineteenth century. It was not difficult for a playwright or a hack writer to transform the vigorous action of Mrs. Beecher Stowe's volume into equally forceful action in front of the footlights. The characters of her work show affinities with previous traditions like the noble savage, the stage Yankee, and other representatives of transatlantic man. There was some humour, too, in the original, and the nature of the plot and its people facilitated the introduction of further humorous characters. *Uncle Tom's Cabin* was popular; the story was well-nigh ideal for dramatizations; foolish indeed was the English theatre director or producer who did not avail himself of his obvious chance.

Uncle Tom's Cabin was first dramatized in America in August, 1852, without permission of the authoress. In fact Mrs. Beecher Stowe never possessed the dramatic copyright to her story, and thus never received remuneration for the stage performances.[1] It did not take long until London audiences had a chance to see Tom, Eliza, and Legree in their own theatreland.[2]

Tom's Cabin as It Is; Mrs. May H. Eastman, *Aunt Phillis's Cabin, or Southern Life as It Is;* C. H. Wiley, *Life in the South;* Samuel Glover and Charles Jeffreys, *The Uncle Tom Ballads.*

[1] Annie Fields, *Life and Letters of Harriet Beecher Stowe* (London, 1897), p. 178.

[2] A list of first performances of *Uncle Tom's Cabin* in England; the versions marked with * have been read by the present writer in the *Lord Chamberlain MSS* of 1852—3:

1852. September 13: *Uncle Tom's Cabin; or, the Negro Slave.* Standard Theatre.*
              20: Eliza Vincent, *Uncle Tom's Cabin; or, the Fugitive Slave.* Victoria Theatre. *
              20: *Uncle Tom's Cabin; or, the Negro Slave.* Queen's Theatre.
              20: Edward Fitzball: *Uncle Tom's Cabin; or, the Horrors of Slavery.* Olympic Theatre.*
      October 4: *Uncle Tom's Cabin; or, Life among the Lowly.* Marylebone.
               9: C. D. Pitt, *Uncle Tom's Cabin.* London Pavilion.*
              25: Edward Fitzball, *Uncle Tom's Cabin.* Grecian Saloon.
      November 1: John Courtney, *Uncle Tom's Cabin.* Surrey.*
               8: *Uncle Tom's Cabin.* Living Marionettes.
              22: H. Young, *Uncle Tom's Cabin.* Hippodrama, Astley's Amphitheatre.*
              29: Tom Taylor: *Slave Life; or, Uncle Tom's Cabin.* Adelphi. Written in collaboration with Mark Lemon.*

The humorous elements of Harriet Beecher Stowe's novel revolve around a few characters who provide comic relief to the otherwise tragic — or sentimental — story. The most definite white comedian is Ophelia, the Yankee old maid with her caricatured traits, who found it difficult to apply her Puritan standards of behaviour to the life of the Southern Negro. The humorous Negroes are Aunt Chloe, the irrepressible Topsy, the very volatile Sam and Andy, and Sambo and Quimbo with their songs and dances.[1]

The playwrights or adapters did not follow the original plot closely. Their main problem was to give *Uncle Tom's Cabin* the unity which is necessary for a stage plot. Where a novelist may carry on several parallel plots simultaneously and allow them to diverge and converge at will, the playwright has to exercise great care to make every scene of every act contribute to the main plot. The novelist may take his time and let his volume expand, whereas the playwright is restricted to severe limits. This was particularly the case in nineteenth-century melodrama, where the dramatist had to concentrate on action if he wanted to avoid the pandemonium of an irritated gallery.

Consequently, what the adapters of *Uncle Tom's Cabin* did was to choose one of the several parallel plots of the original novel for main plot, and to select a number of suitable incidents from the work and proceed to fit them into this central theme. Since the number of characters on the stage had to be limited, they often amalgamated several of the original characters into one. A very clear example of this process is afforded by Tom Taylor's Adelphi version; the author felt it his duty to explain what he had done to the public, who could be expected to be familiar with Mrs. Beecher Stowe's book.[2] Thus one cannot expect the humour of the stage presentations of *Uncle Tom's Cabin* always to be based on the humour of the novel.

	December	27: Edward Fitzball, *Uncle Tom's Cabin*. Drury Lane.*
1853.	January	3: *Uncle Tom's Cabin*. City of London Theatre.*
	February	1: Charles Hermann, *Uncle Tom's Cabin*. Theatre Royal, Manchester.
1882.	September	13: *Uncle Tom's Cabin*. Standard Theatre.
1892.	October	31: Charles Hermann, *Uncle Tom's Cabin*. Princess Theatre.

(*Nicoll*.)

[1] The edition consulted was that of Routledge, London, 1852.

[2] Playbills in *Enthoven Collection*. For more information on Tom Taylor, see Winton Tolles, *Tom Taylor and Victorian Drama* and *infra*, p. 125 ff.

8 — *Soc. Scient. Fenn., Comm. Hum. Litt. XVIII. 1.*

In other respects Tom Taylor's version provides a representative sample of the caricatures of American character that could be included in English dramatizations of *Uncle Tom's Cabin*.[1] In the very first scene, Taylor presents a humorous dialogue between Topsy and Mrs. Shelby, who has also taken over Ophelia's original part. This dialogue follows the novel closely. A comic treatment of Negro life is included: among a crowd of slaves the humorous Sam is seen to burn his fingers on Cleopatra's corn cake. Follows a Negro dance, and the choice of banjo, bones, and fiddle for the accompaniment reveals the influence of Negro minstrelsy.

In the second scene of Act II, we see Aunt Chloe and Uncle Tom with their children in an animated scene. The little pickaninnies, full of animal spirits, are warned by Tom: »Ye'll all stick togeder wid de molasses and neber get clar again,» when they participate in the simple pleasures of slave life. The language is the traditional dialect of the stage Negro.

At the Ohio River ferry-house we meet Sol, a lazy Yankee, who is an obvious stock caricature; his laziness is his only novel feature. In spite of his expostulation: »If any stranger comes he'll have to sit on his thumbs,» a Mrs. Spicer gets him to work in a comic scene.

In the same act Taylor describes events at a tavern named The Jefferson's Head. George, the noble refugee half-cast, pretends to be a Lousiana dandy. Skunk, a frontiersman, starts an inquisitive conversation in the overcrowded tavern, where a snoring Judge Tarbox from Wisconsin makes life even more difficult. This humorous episode reveals Taylor's familiarity with travellers' accounts of America; in numerous travel-books descriptions of inns and hotels in the United States were standard items.

In the third act George arrives at Legree's house impersonating a Southern cotton speculator. In the ensuing dialogue Taylor reveals his inability to distinguish between Yankee and Southern character; both gentlemen speak like Yankee peddlers:

Legree: Travelling on pleasure, Sir?
George: Wa'al, I guess pleasure is a thing folks differs about — one man's pleasure you know is another man's pison.
Legree: Stoppin' here tonight Straanger?
George: Wa'al — guess I didn't think o'goin' on ...[2]

---

[1] This account is based on the MS in *Lord Chamberlain MSS 8/1852*.
[2] Act III, Scene 2.

True Yankee inquisitiveness and taciturnity are presented in this dialogue, where George tries to dupe Legree into believing that he has invented a new cotton gin, unheard-of in its efficiency, and into exchanging the specifications of this machine against Eliza and Cassy, Legree's lawful slaves.

The other scenes are pure melodrama. The high point of suspense consists of the escape over the ice of the Ohio.

In the Standard Theatre version both Negro and Yankee humour can be found. The Yankee bears the Irvingesque name of Van Tromp; the coloured comedians are Sam, Andy, and Aunt Chloe. The hostess of the ferry station is dubbed Prudence Charity.[1] An unidentified manuscript introduces a full-fledged Yankee peddler, Jonathan Slingsby. He enters towards the end of the first act with a pack on his back and snow on his feet praising his goods, »all slick bran new, I guess,» and reappears towards the end of the play sleeping under a tree.[2] The Surrey Theatre adaptation drew upon the humorous aspects of Sam and Andy.[3]

C. D. Pitt's version, written for the Royal Pavilion, built on the humorous contrast between Billy Bombast, a Cockney from Whitechapel, and Snowball, the blackest of black maidens, who wanted to marry Billy. When the latter was suspected of being a runaway slave and protested by proclaiming himself one of Her Majesty's loyal subjects, Snowball exclaimed: »Me never helps no englis savage.» Legree's diction was in the tradition of the humorous stage American. When Little Eva fell overboard in the river-boat scene, he exclaimed: »Thunder and pigsarce! ... She'll be tarnation careful another time I reckon ... Sarve her right!»[4]

At the Olympic Theatre Haley was conceived as a caricatured American with a copious supply of »I calculate» and similar stock phrases. The ferryman's name was Jonathan. Most of the humour of this version was due to Topsy's utterances and behaviour.[5]

These instances suffice to show that there was a tendency among the English dramatizers of *Uncle Tom's Cabin* to attempt caricatured portrayal of American character. There efforts were strongly coloured by such stereotype conceptions of the Yankee and the American Negro

---

[1] *Lord Chamberlain MSS 6/1852.*
[2] *Ibid. 8/1852*, licensed December 20, 1852, theatre and author not mentioned.
[3] *Ibid. 6/1852.* [4] *Ibid. 7/1852.* [5] *Ibid. 6/1852.*

as had previously been presented on the English stage either in legitimate plays or in minstrel shows.

The reviews in newspapers and periodicals reveal that humour was an element the critics reckoned with in their evaluations of the dramatizations of *Uncle Tom's Cabin*.

When discussing the Adelphi version, the critic of *The Times* praised Miss Collins's Aunt Chloe because of her humorous Negro dialect.[1] Mrs. Keeley's humorous Topsy was praised by *The Atlas* and *The Sunday Times*.[2] *The Examiner* commented upon the humorous traits in Legree's character and their effect on the audience:

> An addition to the picture which made it even more revolting was the thorough American slang of it. If there is anything more shocking than the violence of such a ruffian as Legree, it is his attempts at humour or comedy.[3]

The reviews of the Surrey version state that Legree, acted by Mr. T. Mead, was the only one of the characters to speak with an American accent. Miss Lebatt's Topsy was praised as »humorous and characteristic ... and ... effective.»[4] Mr. Hoskins's Haley at the Olympic proved attractive to the reviewers. Hoskins had visited the United States and knew how to make Haley a traditional Yankee with all the »dry humour,» nasal twang, phraseology, odd gait, and costume that were expected from such a person.[5]

Fitzball's Drury-Lane version was much abused. Legree and Topsy, acted by Mr. Selby and Miss Newcombe, received the best favours of the commentators. An actor named George Wild acted the part of the Yankee peddler with »broad strong humour.» *The Observer* noted the difference between Uncle Tom and the comic minstrel Negro:

> The Uncle Tom of Drury is not the silly and absurd »nigger» we have seen him represented elsewhere, but one of those natural creations which powerfully enlist our feelings.[6]

The Times observed that the version had failed to keep on the right side of the borderline between pathos and bathos:

---

[1] November 30, 1852, 8.

[2] *Atlas*, XXX, 776 (December 4, 1852); *Sunday Times*, December 5, 1852, 3.

[3] December 4, 1852, 773.

[4] *Sunday Times*, November 7, 1852, 6; *Era*, XIV, November 7, 1852, 10.

[5] *Sunday Times*, September 26, 1852, 3; *Observer*, September 26, 1852, 7; *Era*, XIV, September 26, 1852, 10.

[6] January 2, 1853, 6.

... the most lachrymose provoked nothing but the hilarity of the audience, which ultimately burst into a positive roar just as Mr. H. Betty, who made his first appearance in the part of George Harris, called down »retribution» on the devoted head of Legree ...[1]

Perhaps some of the difficulty was due to the fact that most regular theatre-goers had seen previous *Uncle Tom's Cabins* and that the Christmas audience was bent on pantomime and light amusement.[2]

A review of the Victoria production is of interest both because it reveals what a theatre specializing in melodrama could make out of Mrs. Beecher Stowe's novel and because it illustrates the goings-on at such a playhouse in the early fifties:

> George Harris was tremendous, in a pair of crimson and white trousers, and fought a terrific combat with Haley and his men in a manner that can be seen nowhere to perfection except in the haunts of the old domestic and nautical drama. Visions of jack tars shivering their timbers floated before one's eyes as the click-click of the one, two, three, and over, and double cuts all across the stage struck on one's ear. George was quite the hero of the piece, for besides this combat, in which, whenever his cutlass was used up, he fixed pistols like minute guns, he had no less than two more, in all of which he distinguished himself to the great delight of the spectators. Haley during part of the drama invested himself in a high fur cap, and what with that and his whip, during this phase looked more like a Russian or Bokharian than the American slave driver. The escape over the ice elicited the loudest applause, and Uncle Tom's pious moralities, which from the Babel of sound [from the audience] were almost the only parts heard, and Legree's death, that gentleman being shot by Cassy in the last scene, were also highly prized.[3]

To sum up, the English adapters of *Uncle Tom's Cabin* to the stage were familiar with stereotype caricatures of American character. The relief characters of Mrs. Beecher Stowe's original were often played up into stage comedians according to established tradition; Yankee and Negro elements were drawn upon for these analyses. Some dramatizers felt it advantageous to insert further humour into their plays in the form of comic Americans or Cockneys. Even when the basic theme was tragic and its stage treatment thoroughly melodramatic, caricatures of American character were of importance in the adaptations of *Uncle Tom's Cabin* to the English stage.

---

[1] December 28, 1852, 2.

[2] For other reviews, see *Critic*, XII, 26—7 (January 1, 1853); and *Atlas*, XXXI, 8 (January 1, 1853).

[3] *Times*, December 28, 1852, 8.

4. A New Attraction: the Yankee Gal.

In November, 1852, the Lord Chamberlain's Office approved a one-act dramatic sketch entitled *Paul; or, the Fortunate Slave*.[1] This play was full of Negro humour of the most robust type in the minstrel tradition;[2] the unknown playwright also inserted a Brother Jonathan into his concoction.

The American playwright Howard Paul wrote copiously for the English stage in the fifties and sixties. His farces and comedies did not, however, build on stock types of humorous Americans.[3]

Edward Ranger's *The American in England* was licensed for the Theatre Royal, Manchester, on May 13, 1855.[4] In this comedy an American, Benjamin Franklin West, comes to England looking for his long-lost parents. He meets an English girl, goes to Bath and mixes with society, woos and wins, and ultimately finds that a sympathetic member of the English aristocracy, Duke de St. Victor, ist his own brother. The English characters range from Lord Singleton to Mrs. Filter, the Bath lodging-house keeper, who overcharged and drank West's brandy when he turned his back. An aunt with anti-American sentiments completes the dramatis personae, who were to enable the author to compare English and American institutions. The attitude was generally sympathetic towards the United States: things English take most of the ridicule. West and his coloured slave, Cicero, are treated as comic stock Americans; however, the play emphasizes social aspects instead of concentrating on these two as caricatures in a social vacuum.

The American in England was largely a one-man effort: West was acted by Ranger himself. The first performance took place on April 16, 1855, and the play was repeated two days later.[5] The critic of *The Manchester Guardian* stated that it could not be produced in London because the actor-managers of the metropolis were »too fond of playing

---

[1] *Lord Chamberlain MSS 7/1852*.

[2] Thus four coloured characters sing quartets. There were no minstrel dances; Caesar's trousers were so tight that all his movements were hazardous.

[3] Paul was interested in American humour; he published an anthology of transatlantic fun, a book of American songs, and wrote short stories and Yankee tales in *The American Magazine*, of which he was editor.

[4] Listed by Nicoll under »Unknown Authors.» Available in printed form (Long Sutton, John Swain, Printer, High Street, n.d.) in *Lord Chamberlain MSS 3/1855*.

[5] Advertisements in *Manchester Guardian*, April 14—18, 1855.

the first characters themselves,» which was contrary to Ranger's wishes. He observed that America was kindly treated in it, »... and we think Mr. Ranger has the United States in his mind in the production of his drama. It will take there better than in this country.» After an exhortation to Ranger to prune the text the critic's remarks show that he was comparing Ranger's West to a definite ideal of American characterization:

> In the acting, Mr. Ranger had all the peculiarities of the Yankee except his restlessness and perpetual motion. His delivery was also a little too slow and sententious, instead of being quick and decided. On the whole he was well supported, and the piece will doubtless go better after one or two more representations.[1]

In 1856 a later celebrated American actor couple visited England and profited from the vogue of transatlantic stage humour. This couple was the Florences, William Jermyn and his wife Malvina, *née* Pray.[2] They appeared at Drury Lane on April 28 in a farce named *The Yankee Housekeeper*, expressly written by Florence to allow his wife to display her talents.[3]

The story contained plenty of action and numerous stock characters. Mr. Florence played Barney, an Irish servant, while Mrs. Florence impersonated Peg Ann Mehitable Higginfluter, a Yankee girl from Maine with her two hat-boxes, a bird-cage with a cat and several kittens in it, an umbrella, and a collection of further personal effects. Peg was engaged by a Quaker goodwife as a maid-of-all-work, and got much involved in the farcical intrigues and love-affairs that constituted the staple of the product. The plot has nothing to do with American society; American humour was introduced both into the title and the content of the play by making a Yankee girl its main character. Both her language and her flippant New-England sauciness and vigour formed the centre of the fun. Her two songs »Polly, Won't You Try Me, Oh?» and »Bobbing Around!» were »encored nightly three times,» if one is to believe the playbills.[4]

---

[1] *Manchester Guardian*, April 18, 1855, 5.

[2] They reaped laurels in B. E. Woolf's *Mighty Dollar* of 1875 in New York, where Mr. Florence created the famous Bardwell Slote and Mrs. Florence acted the part of Mrs. General Gilflory. (Matthews and Hutton, *Actors and Achesses of Great Britain and the United States*, V, 115—130.)

[3] Listed by Nicoll under »Unknown Authors.» Available in *Lord Chamberlain MSS 2/1856*.

[4] *Enthoven Collection*.

The Florences acted in *The Yankee Housekeeper* at Drury Lane from April 28 to June 7, 1856.[1] On May 26 they staged Dion Boucicault's *The Young Actress*, where Mrs. Florence could show her versatility: the part required changing from Maria, a young actress, to Paul Bertin, a French boy; then to Corney Gray, and Irish lad; further to Effie Heatherbloom, a Scots lass, and finally to Jemsha Joyful Lobb, a Yankee Gal. This »protean farce» ran for six performances. A run of equal length was the fate of *Mischievous Annie; or, a Lesson for Husbands*, a similar »protean farce» written for the Florences, where the leading female part required a change to Hezekiah Slocum, a Yankee boy, and to Frou Sligiterskypipesfunderknickelpoppelsox »With her Great DUTCH ORGAN SONG.» Mr. Florence modestly stuck to his stage Irishmen.[2]

In the same summer (1856), another American actor couple, Mr. and Mrs. Barney Williams, appeared at the Adelphi; Mr. Williams specialized in Irish parts, his wife in the portrayal of Yankee girls.[3] They acted in several plays. *Our Gal* achieved a total of 51 performances between July 26 and November 1, 1856. In another slight farce, *Customs of the Country*, Mrs. Williams played Melissa, a Yankee girl. *Irish Assurance and Yankee Modesty* ran for twenty-five nights from August 12 to September 19. A further item in their repertory was *Lucifer Matches; or, the Yankee* —!, which ran for 18 performances beginning on September 25. The Williamses were supposed to tour the provinces as well, but were repeatedly re-engaged by the Adelphi because of their box-office success.[4]

In *Irish Assurance and Yankee Modesty* a certain Mr. Buffer hired Pat, the Irishman, to do odd jobs around the house and to make love to his maiden sister. Enter Nancy Stoker, the Yankee girl:

How de due, mum. I'm Nancy Stoker, from Seconk Plain, not a mite or grain more... Yes, I'm the slickest critter you ever did see. In travelling here, I must say, it is wonderful to observe the operations of nater on a big scale, and them 'ere young chaps all fall in love with me and giggle so when I speaks to 'em; I

---

[1] Advertisements in *Times*. [2] Playbills in *Enthoven Collection*.

[3] Mrs. Williams was the sister of Mrs. Florence, which partly explains how the Williamses were able to follow the example of the Florences so soon. The Williamses acted in London from 1855 to 1859. See *The Oxford Companion to the Theatre* (London, 1951), edited by Phyllis Hartnoll. The author was not able to consult this recent work of reference until the present study was in final proofs.

[4] Playbills in *Enthoven Collection*.

expect it's my ellegant figure. I don't know what else it can be ... I guess I'm spunky, right up and down, like a yard of pump water. No two ways about Nancy. I am a screamer ...¹

As we might expect, Nancy soon frightens the entire Buffer family when her »dander is up.» Pat, the Irishman, is the only person capable of handling her, and much of the fun consists of dialogues between the two, both talking to each other in their respective dialects and phrases. Pat of course makes love both to Miss Buffer and Nancy.

The reviewers liked the Drury Lane performances of the Florences. *The Atlas* was content to state that »the lady's representation of Yankee peculiarities was a decided success.»² *The Spectator* stressed the fact that the actors were to be thanked for the success, not the farce itself, when commenting upon *The Yankee Housekeeper*. It opined that the »portraiture of the Yankee 'gal' is coloured to a degree that leads us to suspect that the fair citizens of Maine are a little caricatured...»³ The unusual traits of Miss Higginfluter and their contrast with those of ordinary Victorian women gave a starting-point to *The Observer:*

... The dialect is of the strongest, the prosaic shrewdness accompanying an almost boisterous vivacity betokens a development of the 'cute organs that the dull citizens of the Old World would scarcely associate with their notions of the feminine nature; the gestures are of the strangest and, at the same time, of the most significant kind, but all so perfectly free and spontaneous as to leave no doubt that a real type of Anglo-Saxon family has been truly apprehended by a quick and observant intellect; in brief, the Yankee »gal» of humble life, as delineated by this actress, is a being to whom half-measures are wholly unknown. If she is abashed, she buries her face in her apron — if she is kindly disposed to an admirer she pokes him in the ribs — if she feels her dignity compromised, her first tendency is to slap the face of the offender — if the desire of gaining the »hard dollar» steals upon her mind, she scorns everything like a hint, and with the utmost businesslike air, asks, »What will you gi'e me?» All this is heartily done, with intrinsic frankness and good nature; while the movements acquire a sort of grace from their wildness. Mrs. Florence sparkles with vivacity; though much of her attraction undoubtedly depends on the novelty of the character she represents, she is, in fact, an intelligent and efficient actress ... The farce is a very primitive affair, but it allows the Yankee »gal» full opportunities to display her peculiarities.⁴

The reviewer of *The Era* remarked that Mr. Florence's Irishmen had nothing to do with the United States, but were »a quiet version» of the

---

[1] Printed in *French's American Drama* (XVII, New York, n.d.). A copy is included in *Lord Chamberlain MSS 3/1856*. The quote is from p. 7.

[2] May 3, 1856, 279. [3] May 3, 1856, 469. [4] May 4, 1856, 7.

traditional sons of Erin. Mrs. Florence was praised more. Her costume was said to consist of a huge bonnet, an elaborate parasol, and a »shawl of unheard-of pattern» and other »fixings.» Her »briskness of style» joined to a »vivacity of speech» made her like »an eccentric sunbeam.» Having mentioned Hackett, Hill, Marble, and Silsbee, this writer went on:

> ... not only is Mrs. Florence the first American comic actress that has ever visited this country, but she presents us for the first time with a faithful transcript of that remarkable character, the regular down-Eastern Yankee help, who slaps faces, shakes tablecloths, pokes ribs, drives bargains, tells smart stories, and sings odd songs, all with equal coolness, quaintness, and rapidity.

In spite of all this praise, the critic wound up by calling *Yankee Housekeeper* »a severe drawback upon their talents being fairly exhibited.»[1]

The criticisms of the Williamses at the Adelphi were not equally favourable. *Irish Assurance and Yankee Modesty* was criticized as follows:

> The piece is one of those indescribable works that now seem peculiar to the other side of the ocean, but are evidently based on the English farces of that happy period when a defiance of possibility, a voluntary ignoring of all social regulations, a huddling together of situations, and a perpetual change of scene were deemed important elements of the broader kind of dramatic humour.[2]

This commentator was no longer satisfied with mere caricature of transatlantic character; in his opinion a good play had to possess other virtues as well. An unidentified review thought it a pity that the Williamses should act in such a bad play.[3] *The Observer* praised the acting, but condemned the script because of a lack of interest, plot, and continuity.[4] Even »the flattering approval of a crowded auditory» did not induce the other critics to like the play any better.[5] Nevertheless the runs show that the general public did not share the sentiments of the more fastidious critics.

In February, 1858, the Williamses revisited the Adelphi in *Yankee Courtship; or, Away Down East*.[6] The setting of this farce was Con-

---

[1] XVIII, May 4, 1856, 10.   [2] *Times*, August 13, 1856, 7.

[3] Clipping in *Enthoven Collection*.   [4] August 17, 1856, 3.

[5] *Sunday Times*, August 17, 1856, 3; *Era*, XVIII, August 17, 1856, 11; *Examiner*, August 16, 1856, 518.

[6] Available in *Lord Chamberlain MSS 1/1858*; licensed on February 12. According to *Nicoll* the first performance took place on February 15.

necticut. There were two Jemimas, aunt and niece; the aunt owned a goodly sum of dollars in railroad property and was constantly wooed by the Hon. Augustus Gas, a Member of Congress, who is made to go through the motions of a Connecticut courtship involving the necessary offers of apples and gingerbread. Gas proves an impostor, and after he has been thoroughly scared by remarks about tar and feathers his wife appears on the scene. The entire affair ends with a reel.

The farce has abundant action, and the humour is humour of situation rather than of character. Thus Twitcher, Gas's accomplice, seeks refuge in a mechanical churn, which is put to use to the great delight of the spectators while the unfortunate wretch still is inside. The language of the manuscript is full of colloquialisms, but does not sustain a consistent Yankee dialect at length; this may have been supplied by the actors. Caesar, a Negro servant, speaks the language of the coloured comedian.

This time the reviews were kinder. Even if *Yankee Courtship* was »scarcely distinguishable from any one of the dozen pieces already brought out for the display of New England humour,» Mrs. Williams's acting was said to »infuse life into anything — even a worn-out subject.»[1] *The Atlas* called the play »most admirably got up,»[2] while *The Observer* went on to state that »perhaps no drama yet produced at the Adelphi more completely exhibits the thorough command the lady possesses over American character and manners.»[3]

During their 1858 visit the Williamses also acted a piece named *Latest from New York*. Here Mr. Williams played his usual Irishman, this time under the name of Phil Mullegan, while his wife impersonated two Yankee women, Mrs. Serephina Serena Sprout and Mrs. Abbadiah Painter, and added a touch to her characterizations by a song called »Yankee Fixins.»[4]

C. M. Wolcott's *Nothing to Nurse* and Boucicaults *The Poor of Liverpool*, both acted in England, afford good examples of Anglo-American theatrical contacts in the fifties.[5]

---

[1] *Spectator*, February 20, 1858, 202.
[2] February 20, 1858, 122.   [3] February 21, 1858, 7.
[4] Playbills in *Enthoven Collection*.
[5] Wolcott was an English actor resident in New York City. The transatlantic setting of the farce has little to do with plot, action, or characters. A certain Mr. Muddle pretends to be married to get the sympathy — and money — of a rich uncle. When the latter pays a visit to him and demands to see Muddle's

To sum up. Humorous caricatures of American character continued on the English stage in the fifties. Transatlantic social comedy had first been introduced into Britain in 1850, but caricature remained the basis of portrayal of comic Americans. The Yankee girl for the first time became the main character of a series of plays. In the fifties the drama began to lose relative importance as a medium of American humour in England; the emphasis was shifting from the stage to the book. This was due to the rise of the cheap book, which brought American humour to masses of Britons at a very low cost.[1] This development was to continue in the following decade.

CHAPTER IX

THE SIXTIES

1. Our American Cousin.

The sixties were the decade in which American humour became firmly entrenched in the consciousness of the British public. The development of the cheap-book business made it possible to bring transatlantic fun to large audiences at low cost. Artemus Ward came to Britain to

---

nonexistent wife and child, the housekeeper rushes out and borrows a baby. When the curious old gentleman starts removing the swaddling-clothes, the baby proves to be a Negro child. The rest of the play displays Muddle's hectic endeavours to straighten out the situation. T. H. Lacy added a preface to his printed edition of *Nothing to Nurse* where he aired his views on international copyright on the basis of the eye-for-eye and tooth-for-tooth principle.

Boucicault's play was first performed in New York in December, 1857, as *The Poor of New York*. When Boucicault came to England he found that Stirling Coyne had already produced a version of it called *Fraud and Its Victims*. Boucicault now renamed his product *The Poor of Liverpool*, and later *The Streets of London*. By the simple substitution of Liverpool or London for New York the play was given local colour. That such a process was possible shows that drama was sufficiently identical on both sides of the Atlantic to permit settings to be changed by a mere change of words.

[1] On the history of the cheap book in England, see short list of sources in Gohdes, *American Literature in Nineteenth-Century England*, p. 19; and Michael Sadleir, *Yellow-Backs* (London, 1938).

deliver his humorous lectures and delighted the public with them. James Russell Lowell, Oliver Wendell Holmes, and Charles Godfrey Leland were widely known, and names like that of Jack Downing could be seen in the cheap-book lists. The interest in life beyond the ocean received an additional impetus from the Civil War. The English had displayed a keen curiosity about things American ever since the early decades of the nineteenth century; now the United States was a topical subject even more than before. British interests were involved in the outcome of the Civil War; the aristocracy at first tended to sympathize with the Confederacy, the lower classes to support the North. Correspondents were sent to America to report on the events, and G. A. Sala, the most discerning of them, availed himself of the opportunity and acquainted himself with American life and letters, including humour. In the sixties all these facts are more evident in the history of written American humour in England than on the stage. Yet this is the background to be considered in the discussion of humorous American characters on the English stage in the sixties.

One of the most typical writers of Victorian comedy was the versatile Tom Taylor.[1] The Exhibition of 1851, that striking show of mid-Victorian enterprise and economic optimism, attracted large numbers of transatlantic visitors. Taylor could not help observing them and their strange manners. Perhaps he was reminded of the successes of colleagues who had ventured to apply their talents on comic Americans; in any case he set off to compose a comedy contrasting British and American manners. The title was *Our American Cousin*.

At first there was little to indicate that the play was to become one of the great comic hits of the nineteenth-century stage in both England and America. The play opens at Trenchard Manor, somewhere in England. A letter arrives from young Trenchard, who was visiting the United States, about a discovery he had made: there was an American branch of the family, and Asa Trenchard, heir to much property in Britain, was on his way to the Old Country. Asa was duly recommended to the Trenchards, and the female members of the family began the inevitable conjecturing about his person:

---

[1] Born in 1817 he emerged on a varied career: lawyer, editor of *Punch* and Professor of English Language and Literature at the University of London, he had found time to write numerous plays ever since his early boyhood. See Tolles, *Tom Taylor and Victorian Drama;* and Charles Kent, »Tom Taylor,» *Dictionary of National Biography.*

Auguste: I can imagine the wild young hunter — an Apollo of the Prairie.
Florence: With strong nasal twang, and a taste for smoking Cigars and drinking Coblers ... He's seven feet high ... and has long hair and a red skin, and shoots with a bow and arrows and scalps people who offend him.

When Asa arrives he proves odd according to English standards. His introduction was given in the bragging frontier manner:

I'm Asa Trenchard raised in Saginaw, suckled in the Bloody Creek, about the tallest gunner and the slickest dancer, and the loudest critter in all pints, by snakes in all Michigan...

Asa washed under the kitchen pump, devoured a whole ham on his way down to lunch, and always »felt dry»; he threw the entire Trenchard family into consternation when offering them part of his daily refreshment schedule: »julip, gin-sling, cobler, cock-tail, and chain-lightning,» or of his more innocent victuals, mess o'mush, corncob, slapjack, oysters, and clam chowder. His bathroom monologue was well worth overhearing:

Waal now, they didn't ought to keep their pig saltin' tubs in their chambers. That's kinder nasty that is. (*turning over towels on towel horse*) And what an all fired dirty people these Britishers must be to need such a deal of towels to clean themselves...

As luck would have it, Asa soon found the Trenchards practising their archery, which gave him the deep-seated conviction that the English were just as savage as the Indians. The Trenchards thought Asa equally savage, and it did not add to their admiration that he always sat with his legs nonchalantly thrown over the side of a chair, unless he placed them on a table or a window-sill.

The other important comedian of the piece was Lord Dundreary, whose ultra-snobbish behaviour was planned to contrast with the straightforward crudeness of Asa.

The plot of *Our American Cousin* consisted of the usual mixture of farce and melodrama. Sir Edward Trenchard was in financial trouble thanks to an unscrupulous agent, Coyle. Asa arrived to collect his English property, but found Mary Meredith, a penniless girl of noble descent, serving as a dairymaid at Trenchard Manor. Mary was to inherit the property if no will was presented, and the noble Asa does not hesitate to destroy the document in order to help the damsel in distress. Furthermore, Asa drank Coyle under the table, stole his keys, broke his desk with an axe, discovered documents proving the rascally agent a felon, and blackmailed him into paying all Sir Edward's debts and giving up his claims on Miss Trenchard. In the end Mary accepts Asa's proposal of marriage.[1]

It can be seen from this outline plot how little Lord Dundreary originally had to do with the play. He was a mere relief character of very minor stature, thrown in to provide a contrast with Asa. In the original version, Dundreary had about a score of repliques. However, fate would have it otherwise. Joseph Jefferson, a well-established comedian at this time, played Asa, but Dundreary's part was given to Edward Askew Sothern, another of the actors equally well known on both sides of the Atlantic.[2] The latter was not happy about his new role; he felt slighted in the choice and given a part too insignificant for his talents. However, he noticed his chance and began improvising freely and adding to the part. He invented new gags nightly, made Dundreary walk in a queer way, stutter, sneeze at unexpected moments in unexpected ways, and, in short, transformed the entire part into the main attraction of the play. To everybody's surprise, the New York audience loved it. The »Dundreary hop» became famous, and his »twisted aphorisms» (»Birds of a feather gather no moss») were uttered with an irresistible lisp and stutter. Even the dress was characteristic: in an »ankle-length coat, peg-top plaid trousers, a flowing cravat, long weeping whiskers, and a monocle»[3] he became one of the remarkable stage characters of the century. No wonder Sothern spent most of the following ten years in this guise.[4]

Our American Cousin was a great success in the United States.[5] The first performance in England took place at the Haymarket in Lon-

---

[1] The version consulted was that of *Lord Chamberlain MSS 9/1861*.

[2] On Sothern, see *Dictionary of American Biography*, and T. E. Pemberton, *A Memoir of E. A. Sothern* (London, 1890).

[3] Tolles, *Op.cit.*, p. 178.

[4] Moncure D. Conway, *Autobiography* (London, 1904), I, 229; Joseph Jefferson, *Autobiography* (New York, 1889), pp. 197—8; Lester Wallack, *Memories of Fifty Years* (New York, 1889), p. 165.

[5] Taylor had sent his manuscript to New York hoping to have it produced there, and Bancroft Davis, a predecessor of today's more organized dramatic agents, took the opus to Lester Wallack. The latter did not wish to produce it, but forwarded it to Laura Keene, who did not display any particular enthusiasm, either. However, her business manager, John Lutz, noticed its merits, and a *force majeure* precipitated the first performance: the painters and carpenters were not up to schedule in the preparations for *A Midsummer Night's Dream*, and in this emergency *Our American Cousin* was taken to fill the gap. It was first per-

don on November 11, 1861.¹ What better example of the close relations between the theatres of the two great English-speaking nations can be found: a caricature of an English lord, originally conceived by an English playwright, but developed by an American actor, finally performed in London by the latter after a tremendous success in the United States!

A London success was by no means assured. The people involved, including Sothern, were rather pessimistic.¹ The first night was a fiasco, and Buckstone, the Haymarket manager, hastened to put up a notice that *She Stoops to Conquer* was to be performed in a few days' time. But Charles Mathews the Younger, a shrewd judge of public taste since his own and Madame Vestris' initial troubles, came to see Buckstone and urged him to »push this piece.» »But it is an offense to all the swells,» said the latter. »Don't you believe it,» replied Mathews; »you push it and it will please *them* more than anybody else.» This convinced Buckstone, *Our American Cousin* ran for a record-breaking and unheard-of four hundred consecutive performances, and Sothern told his friends that the Haymarket made a profit of thirty thousand pounds on the play.³ Dundreary coats and Dundreary whiskers became the fashion of the day just as Jim-Crow cigars had conquered London in the thirties, and Sothern's dressing-room was full of clothes provided by publicity-minded firms for advertising purposes.⁴

Due to the great popularity of the play there are ample review materials on English opinions. *The Observer* called it weak, badly constructed, and worthless, but praised Sothern's acting. Buckstone was cast as Asa Trenchard, and his acting possessed »amusing comicality» although he was »by nature too genuinely English to shine much in the garb of Yankeedom.»⁵ The reader will remember that this was not Buckstone's debut in humorous American parts; as a young man he had acted Jeremiah Kentuck in *Monsieur Mallet* of 1829.⁶

The critic of *The Era* similarly characterized the play itself as »a hasty work manufactured to suit the American market,» and a »dramatic

---

formed at Laura Keene's Theatre, New York City, on October 18, 1858. (See Wallack, *Op.cit.*, pp. 159 ff., and Jefferson, *Op.cit.*, pp. 193—4.)

Our American Cousin acquired more sinister associations: when Lincoln came to see it for the second time he was assassinated at Ford's Theatre in 1865. (Rourke, *American Humor*, p. 147; John Gross, *Lincoln's Own Stories* [New York and London, 1912], p. 133.)

[1] *Nicoll.* [2] Pemberton, *Op.cit.*, pp. 27—8. [3] Wallack, *Op.cit.*, p. 165.
[4] Pemberton, *Op.cit.*, pp. 30—1.
[5] November 17, 1861, 7. [6] See *supra*, p. 46.

curiosity.» Having praised Sothern and compared his art to that of Gillray and Cruikshank he went on to comment on Asa, who »could not fail to secure the laughter and the sympathetic good wishes of his audience whenever he appeared, and he vigorously addressed himself to the task of bringing out all the points of gallantry in the character.»[1]

The Sunday Times disliked *Our American Cousin* as exaggerated, wanton, and reckless caricature. Of Asa, it said: »Mr. Buckstone's Yankee twang is but occasional. Nevertheless, he is throughout irresistibly droll.» This critic was also ignorant of the authorship of the play, and called Dundreary the American idea of an English nobleman.[2] *The Athenaeum* liked the play and noticed the contrast between Dundreary and Asa.[3] Henry Morley recognized the latter as one of the factors of the success.[4] *The Times* ended its criticism as follows:

> This Yankee hero, as sustained by the ever popular Mr. Buckstone, is almost as amusing a spectacle to the audience as the ridiculous aristocrat, but surely all that they do might easily have been brought within the limits of two short acts, and we need not have had a »three-act comedy,» in which a number of meritorious actors are made to perform most unthankful parts.[5]

English commentators generally thought *Our American Cousin* an American play.

Although Sothern's performance was the cynosure of attraction in its humorous novelty, the English reviewers spent part of their space on Asa Trenchard and Buckstone's acting of the part. Asa often functioned as a trigger upon whose actions Dundreary reacted, or as a peg on which the latter could hang his jokes. Yet he was also funny in his own right as a humorous American character, and formed one of the attractions of the play.[6]

Our American Cousin was one of the successes to be revived on the English stage at frequent intervals.[7] It was largely modified during the months and years of its popularity.[8] Cartoons on Dundreary themes

---

[1] November 17, 1861, 10. [2] November 17, 1861, 3.

[3] November 16, 1861, 659. [4] *Journal of a London Playgoer*, pp. 280—1.

[5] November 12, 1861, 10.

[6] In the United States Dundreary may have eclipsed Asa to a greater extent. Cf. Rourke, *American Humor*, p. 147.

[7] Thus, in January, 1862, the Haymarket took it up once more, and *The Athenaeum* commented upon it as favourably as ever. (February 1, 1862, 159.) It was still popular in 1870. (*Ibid.*, February 19, 1870, 270.)

[8] Extensive additions and changes had to be licensed. In *Lord Chamberlain MSS 1/1864*, there is an item labelled *Additional Scenes to Our American Cousin*

9 — *Soc. Scient. Fenn., Comm. Hum. Litt. XVIII. 1.*

appeared.¹ Sothern himself grew tired of his creation, but the audience wanted him to go on as Dundreary and give up all thought of other parts.² Where imitators ventured to portray the English aristocrat they were often denounced as mere echoes of Sothern's original.³

Our American Cousin was the first of several plays to profit from the vogue of Lord Dundreary. John Oxenford's *Sam's Arrival* was the second; beyond occasional American expressions there are no attempts at portrayal of transatlantic character in the play.⁴ Henry J. Byron wrote another specimen of the same cycle of plays and named it *Lord Dundreary Married and Done For*. Here Asa Trenchard appears very much in his original character. He had now married an Englishwoman and lived in Britain for a while; a haircut was his only concession to the English way of life.⁵ A third item, *My American Aunt; or, Dundreary in Difficulties*, can be found in the Lord Chamberlain's manuscripts.⁶

Dundreary's fame lasted through most of the sixties and spread from London to the provinces, where audiences also got their chance to laugh at the lord and at Asa.⁷ For the Haymarket *Our American*

---

containing a series of such alterations and additions. More emphasis was given to both Asa and Dundreary, but particularly the latter. A completely new farcical scene was inserted, where Asa went to bed in Dundreary's room, practised pistol shooting from between the sheets, smoked cigars, and misbehaved in other ways to the lord's horror.

¹ *E.g., Fun*, II, 125 (June 14, 1862); III, 168 (January 10, 1863); VII, 123 (December 10, 1864). The latter used Dundreary to make fun of the new Civil-Service entrance examination; inane, stupid answers were given to equally silly questions.

² He tried to act *David Garrick* and *Bunkum Muller*. See *Athenaeum*, November 5, 1864, 607; *Ibid.*, December 3, 1864, 754; *Reader*, III, 274 (February 27, 1864).

³ *Observer*, September 14, 1862, 7.

⁴ Staged at the Strand Theatre in September, 1862; available in *Lord Chamberlain MSS 6/1862*. For reviews, see *Observer*, September 14, 1864, 7; *Sunday Times*, September 14, 7; *Reader*, V, 636 (June 3, 1865); *Athenaeum*, September 13, 1862, 347.

⁵ Prince of Wales Theatre, Liverpool, December 14, 1863; then taken to the Haymarket on June 13, 1864. Available in *Lord Chamberlain MSS 4/1864*. For reviews, see Morley, *Op.cit.*, p. 341; *Reader*, III, 790 (June 18, 1864); *Observer*, June 19, 1864, 7; *Athenaeum*, June 18, 1864, 843.

⁶ *Lord Chamberlain MSS 5/1864*.

⁷ Dundreary's popularity in the provinces manifested itself in instances like the following: when Sothern played the part of Claude Melnotte in *Lady of Lyons* at Glasgow in the autumn of 1866, he finished the performance by giving the

Cousin was a veritable gold mine.¹ It should be remembered that a caricature of American character was the second most important element of this great stage success of the nineteenth century.

2. Traditions Continued.

The Lyceum Theatre initiated the history of caricatured American characters on the English stage in the sixties by importing an American melodrama named *Pioneers; or, the Maid of the War Path* to London.² The setting was the frontier in 1755, when the English and the French were fighting one another on American soil. One of a group of renegade villains bears the Irvingesque name of Moses Van Smart. The pioneers were conceived as noble heroes, not as robust and humorous men. Thus one of them, Philip Lancey, is a far cry from Nimrod Wildfire:

> The sun is speeding towards the West, leaving in its track a golden hue that sends the weary labourer smiling to this repose — Repose did I say! Alas! I fear that blessing is denied my suffering countrymen until their sinewy arms have driven back these bloodthirsty despoilers who seeks [*sic*] to wrest from us the land our fathers won — and spread desolation in their track . . .³

In addition to the jet-black villains and noble and romantic gentlemen there is one prominent character closer to humorous traditions. This is Jocko, a deformed Negro, a most efficient woodsman and Indian fighter, whose character shows a blend of the comic Negro, the frontiersman, and the noble savage. A specimen of his dialogue will illustrate the point:

> *Philip:* What have you been doing?
> *Jocko:* Roastin Injins — I went back for my ole coat — but when I got dar I seed de house a burnin and a couple ob niggers comin out ob it an one of em

---

audience a speech of thanks in the Dundreary manner, and was duly interrupted by peals of laughter and cheers after every few sentences. (*Sun*, November 14, 1866, 1.)

¹ Buckstone was proud of the success and liked to dwell upon it in after-curtain speeches and at benefits. (*Era*, July 23, 1865, 11; *Observer*, August 5, 1866, 7.) The *Athenaeum* went so far as to compare Dundreary to Falstaff. (December 7, 1867, 771—2.)
² *Lord Chamberlain MSS 8/1860*, licensed October 20, 1860.
³ Act I, Scene 2.

had dat ole coat — I was nound dat it shouldn't go off de premises and dar was no oder way dan to make de Injuns stay dar too. But now youd better push ahead wid me, for dem deblish Injuns are pooty near us.¹

The ubiquitous Jocko performs miracles: he is instrumental in all the last-minute escapes, he shoots French rascals, burns houses, throws people out of windows, drowns them in wells, and behaves in manners fitting a melodramatic hero in general. The feats are performed with appropriate humour and an easy *nonchalance*. No wonder a reviewer felt sorry for Mr. H. Watkins, the actor, who had to do the work performing all these physical feats.²

Another melodrama in an American setting was staged by the Britannia Theatre, London, in September, 1861. Its title was *Red John the Daring; or, Settlers' Perils*, and it consisted of two acts of blood and thunder at »Mr. Powell's Station» among escaped Negro convicts and other sources of horror. One of the coloured men, Sambo, speaks the language of the humorous Negro; otherwise there is no caricature of American character in the play.³

One of the death-blows to the noble-savage theme was John Brougham's burlesque *Pocahontas; or, the Gentle Savage*. It had been performed in New York in 1855, and was taken up by Princess Theatre, London, on October 19, 1861. The success was followed by a revival at St. James's Theatre on November 27, 1869, when it was called *La Belle Sauvage*.⁴ The humour is burlesque, based on puns, *bons mots*, *double entendres*, topical allusions, and flagrant incongruities. The Tuscarora Indians are made to possess an Italian academy for their young ladies, and the setting of one of the scenes is described as an »Indian Trafalgar Square.» The fun was well received by the English public.⁵

In September, 1862, Drury Lane staged a one-act, one-scene farce called *The Yankee Legacy*.⁶ The author has not been identified. Mehitable Ann from New Hampshire had inherited a farm inhabited

---

[1] Act I, Scene 3.

[2] *Athenaeum*, October 27, 1860, 558.

[3] *Lord Chamberlain MSS 8/1861*, licensed September 18.

[4] *Nicoll*. Available in *Lord Chamberlain MSS 8/1861*, and in *French's Acting Edition*.

[5] For reviews, see *Athenaeum*, October 26, 1861, 549; *Ibid.*, December 4, 1869, 746; Lester Wallack, *Op.cit.*, pp. 147—150.

[6] Available in *Lord Chamberlain MSS 5/1862* (no pagination).

by Joe and his fiancée, and according to the will Joe had to marry Mehitable Ann. He was saved by the timely appearance of Briggs, a Cockney. The humour consisted of much Yankee and some Cockney fun. When Mehitable Ann first entered the farm, nobody was at home, and she monologized:

This must be the location I guess — nobody at home — don't see no poppilation round, — gone to a meetin' praps — well, here's a kind o' smell of breakfast — ain't thar — yes (*lifts cover*) thar's pork & tea & fixins — somebody's been & took measure of my feelings (*sits LC*) Ah — pooty good pig considerin — not up to Cincinati sugar cured — wall — that ud fetch 16 cents by the barrel — jest about.

Mehitable Ann's stories are among the best ever heard from an American character on the English stage. Bunker Hill was the name of her previous boy-friend, and Mehitable Ann was by no means shy in giving Briggs the details:

Bunker Hill & me was courtin one night after the old folks had gone to bed when I heerd Pa stirring over head he opened the door & sung out — who's there. Well, we was both awfully skeered. Well, I couldn't put Bunker Hill into the closet cos Ma'am had the key & we couldn't get the pesky window open — it had got iced down hard, well, there was our big churn in the kitchen & I told Bunker Hill he must get into that & he got in & I put on the kiver — well the old man come down & wanted to know what on airth I wanted up at that time o'night so I just told him I got up to do the churning he was kind of suspicious & sez he Mehitable Anne there's some sort of contraption going on but since you're so all fired smart — just you put the cream into the churn & go to work! I hung back & said I guessed it was so early I'd better go to bed again & he said I shouldn't and told me to go and fetch the cream, well I fetched the cream in a big tin pail about two gallons & a half & father he lifted up the kiver of the churn & I souced it all over Bunker Hill — up he jumped — I had to laugh right out (*laughs*) and out he crawled like a fly — I ran away while the old man kicked him through the window.

Another story of the best Yankee brand tells us how Josiah Dodger went broke on a black mare:

You see, Josiah was in the funeral line, & amongst his horses was a crittur called Rose who in her day could her mile under 3 minutes. Wall he started Rose in a one horse hearse pacing as grave as was becoming that mournful occasion. They was on the Plank Road when the procession was overtook by a feller in a light wagin & a fast trotter — Josiah then pulled up sharp. Rose got her tail out straight as a handle — ready in case bein called on — »Ain't that old Rose» says the stranger — guess it's nothing else. — Ah'. It's a pity to see she's broke down — poor old crittur, she's worn out that's a fact —, & he took a start & gave

Joe his dust dodging round & across. I won't go it sez Joe. The mare pulled at him — no sez Joe — but he felt a rash coming out over him — She ain't more 'an two legs & a half to stand on cries stranger. Aint she by thunder roared Joe & he let her go Hi Rose — neck & neck up the hill — down the streack — two forty five two forty — Rose passed him — two thirty with a dead weight behind & as Joe looked back there was the mourners looking out of their carriage — waiving their weepers. It was a grand sight — but it broke Josiah cause Boston is a serious place & folks thare don't think it orthodox to encourage fast funerals.[1]

No wonder Mehitable Ann was proud of her large supply of Yankee stories; she bragged she had »more than there's in the Arabian nights.»

The Yankee Legacy was overshadowed by many greater attractions like *Colleen Bawn*, Boucicault's great hit; a troupe of saltatory Beni-Zong-Zong arabs; and the vigorously melodramatic *Relief of Lucknow*. Yet it ran for 18 performances between September 1 and 20. 1862.[2] Mehitable Ann's part was acted by Mrs. Hough, an American actress, whose performance was praised in spite of the necessary »hoydenish manner,» »unmusical voice,» and »abrupt ill-breeding» as an admirable performance. Again the script was blamed, the acting praised by the reviewers.[3]

The Civil War did not provide the English stage with materials for very large numbers of plays. Nevertheless some dramatic pieces were based on the topical appeal of the American conflict. *The Sons of Columbia: A Story of the American War*, first staged at the Britannia on March 10, 1862, dealt with the American Revolution; the characters included Hukey Slick, a Yankee settler, and Hans Vanderduken, a Dutch farmer. Both used the language characteristic of their types.[4] *A Leap for Liberty*, performed on April 17, 1862, at Queen's Theatre, was a melodramatic triangle drama in a Southern setting. An impertinent slave girl, closely reminiscent of Topsy of *Uncle Tom's Cabin*, and a Negro swell gave a humorous touch to the beginning of the play; Morton Desmond, the white villain, spoke American English.[5]

A Southerner Just Arrived, a one-act farce staged at the Olympic Theatre, London, in October, 1862, made fun of the idealistic abolitionists east of the Atlantic.[6] It contained one caricatured American, Jabez

---

[1] This story was borrowed from F. A. Durivage's *The Fastest Funeral on Record*. The latter had been included in Haliburton's anthology *Traits of American Humour*, Vol. III (London, 1852).

[2] Playbills in *Enthoven Collection*.

[3] *Sunday Times*, September 7, 1862, 3. For other reviews, see *Sun*, September 2, 1862, 2; *Era*, September 7, 1862, 10; *Athenaeum*, September 6, 1862, 315.

[4] *Lord Chamberlain MSS 2/1862*.   [5] *Ibid. 3/1862*.   [6] *Ibid. 7/1862*.

Julep, »Columbian confectioner, compounder o' brandy smashes gin sling & cocktail.» Julep pursued a young man whom he had surprised in the act of making love to Mrs. Julep. The young lover escaped into a chimney, emerged black with soot, and was taken for a fugitive slave by the abolitionist Ebenezer Franchise, who essayed to protect him from his Southern pursuer. Julep's speech is illustrated in his dialogue with Franchise:

Julep: Guess the critter caant be far off I've follered him up and daown and all raound and I'll fix him ez slick ez grease sure as my names Jabez Julep.
Franchise: Well Sir What's your business.
Julep: (looking round) Waal stranger ta'ant business ta'ant pleasure — but sorter kinder haaf and haaf like guess you'll hev to cipher pooty considerable some afore you fix it h's haow! ... Wa'al citizen my names Julep but you wont get much out of that — you see I've come into these diggins after a loafer.

Julep shows the Southern or frontier tendency to brag as well: »When I'm streaked I wake snakes and cut up ugly,» he says, and indicates his determination to find the culprit by promising to »stick like a skeltin on a buffalo» until »the consarned coon» is found.[1]

In March, 1864, Drury Lane took up an old farce originally called *The Spitfire* with added American elements under the title of *The Alabama*.[2] This slight farce contained no caricatures of American character.[3]

The Confederate's Daughter; or, The Tyrant of New Orleans was a melodrama in two acts staged by the Britannia Theatre, London, in July, 1865.[4] The heroine is Frances, a Southern belle; the Confederates are depicted as noble, patriotic defenders of honour and glory, while the Federal troops are brutal barbarians. The only humorous character is an Irishman; Pompey, Frances's faithful slave, and Seth and Captain Hirer, Federal soldiers, speak the traditional language of the Negro and the Yankee.

H. R. Beverly's *The Last Slave* was refused a licence in August, 1865, because owing to its melodramatic treatment of Lincoln's as-

---

[1] *A Southerner Just Arrived* was reported an adaptation of a French play. (*Athenaeum*, November 8, 1862, 600.)
[2] *Lord Chamberlain MSS 2/1864.*
[3] This farce was a trailer to Byron's *Manfred*, and its only virtue was said to consist of sending the audience home »insured against nightmare of Manfred.» (*Reader*, III, 340 [March 12, 1864].)
[4] *Lord Chamberlain MSS 6/1865*, licensed on July 26, 1865.

sassination. the change in American affairs a licence was granted in July, 1867, for the New Adelphi Theatre, Liverpool.[1] The play was extremely melodramatic; the only relief consists of Negro songs sung by a chorus, and of the sayings of Lissy, a female Negro of considerable temperament.

The People's Lawyer, a farce by C. A. Logan, the American playwright, which was rewritten by J. S. Jones, was licensed by the Lord Chamberlain for the Strand Theatre on May 19, 1856, but not acted until July, 1865, when the Adelphi took it up.[2] The plot is melodramatic, but uses a Yankee character, Solon Shingle, for humorous relief.[3] Shingle walks around talking nonsense, revealing his profound ignorance, and trying to keep everybody amused by his constant talk of his cattle and a barrel of »apple sarse» which he had lost.

The first performance of *The People's Lawyer* took place on July 3, 1865, and the piece ran until August 5.[4] The part of Solon Shingle was acted by John E. Owens, an American actor advertised as having performed the part for over 170 consecutive nights in New York to overcrowded houses.[5] Owens was the main attraction of the play; his name appeared in large letters on the playbills.[6]

The critic of *The Times* detected new traits in Shingle's Yankee character:

> Mr. John E. Owens, from the United States, who is now playing at the Adelphi, is perhaps one of the most elaborate artists ever seen upon any stage, that of Paris not excluded. He represents an old farmer from one of the Eastern States, probably New Jersey, who has his mouth filled with tobacco whenever he appears on the stage, and is evidently in a stage of semi-inebriety, which has become to him a second nature. With small features, and a forehead rendered abnormally large by artificial means; with a long ill-fitting surtout that looks as if it had been tossed upon him with a pitchfork; with a hat, in which the brim has lost its boundary-mark, and which is capable of falling into the most fantastic shapes, he presents a figure totally unlike anything that has hitherto been seen on this side of the Atlantic. His talk is as odd as his appearance; he does not indulge in that strange imagery which we have been accustomed to regard as one of the offshoots proper to New England and the regions adjoining, nor is his dialect that which we habitually pronounce to be Yankee. A new type is clearly before us. Whether it corresponds to anything in actual life or is a fantastic creation of the actor we are

---

[1] *Lord Chamberlain MSS 6/1865*. [2] *Ibid., 2/1856.*

[3] This part had been acted in America by both Yankee Hill and Josh Silsbee.

[4] Playbills in *Enthoven Collection*. [5] *Ibid.*

[6] John E. Owens died in 1886. For a biography, see L. E. Shipman, »John E. Owens,» in *A Group of Theatrical Caricatures*, Dunlap Society Publications, Ser. II, vol. 4 (New York, 1897).

unable to judge, but, whatever be the origin of the idea, it is carried out with a consistency of detail that is really marvellous. The rambling stories which the old man tells about his father, who »fit into the revolution,» and about a certain barrel of cider called »apple sass,» of which he has been robbed or defrauded, and the chuckle by which these narratives are accompanied, and which is often suddenly exchanged for a look of blank importance, seem to arise from a strange compound of senility, low cunning, and muddle, which it is extremely hard to analyze, but which most singularly manifests itself in the concrete. When this strange figure seats himself with great difficulty, carefully gathering up the tails of his unseemly coat, and uttering an indescribable squeak of triumph when he is fairly »settled down,» the effect upon the audience is most remarkable. So hearty a roar is seldom awakened by mere dumb-show.[1]

The Observer called the play itself »beneath contempt,» and concurred in the above opinion of Shingle's character not being »one with which we are familiar.» Owens's acting was commended.[2] *The Sunday Times* devoted much space to *The People's Lawyer*, and approved of Owens, but disliked the script. Here Solon Shingle was called a truthful picture of American character because of his self-conceit, shrewdness, business acumen, dry humour, self-centered philosophy, semi-logical absurdity, self-satisfaction, chewing of tobacco, curiosity, laughing, and similar features.[3] The critic of *The Era* recognized *The Two Apprentices*, performed in London thirty-six years previously, as a prototype of *The People's Lawyer*. He called Shingle »tolerably familiar to those who have become acquainted with the 'funny' literature of America.» Here Owens was said to be about 45; he had visited the Continent in 1852 and ascended Mont Blanc.[4] Other reviewers tended to praise Owens's acting but to condemn the play as worthless.[5] With the comment: »This is the sort of thing that we have to put up with when stern necessity requires that we should go to the theatre,» *Fun* parodied Shingle under the name of Draco Beach.[6]

Wilkie Collins's and Charles Fechter's comedy *Black and White*, a melodrama with several comic Negroes in a Trinidad setting in 1830, was printed in London in 1869.[7]

In addition to the better known activities of prominent men of the theatrical world like Boucicault, the Anglo-American contacts in the

[1] July 5, 1865, 7.
[2] July 9, 1865, 7. [3] July 9, 1865, 3. [4] July 9, 1865, 11.
[5] *Examiner*, July 29, 1865, 475; *Reader*, VI, 48 (July 8, 1865).
[6] I n.s., 102—3 (July 29, 1865).
[7] Printed by C. Whiting, Beaufort House, Strand. Available in *Lord Chamberlain MSS 2/1869*, licensed on March 18.

field of stage entertainment were extensive in the sixties. Thus, in 1861 Drury Lane arranged a stage recital of Longfellow's *Hiawatha* with musical accompaniment.[1] The American comedian John Sleeper Clarke visited London in October, 1867. He did not act in parts caricaturing transatlantic character.[2]

With the exception of a few comments on Solon Shingle's originality the plays containing caricatures of American character that were shown in England in the sixties show no new elements. They continue the traditions of the previous decades without innovations. In the sixties written American humour became extensively popular in Britain; now the English could get the genuine product for a few pence at any bookstall. Negro minstrelsy was still an important medium of light entertainment. Thus, although English interest in American life had been stimulated by the Civil War, the drama had lost in relative importance as a medium of American humour. The standards of the English theatre were gradually improving; reviewers were no longer ecstatic about slight farces, although they could appreciate good acting even where it was obviously exaggerated to the point of caricature. With his humorous lectures, Artemus Ward introduced the lecture platform as a vehicle of American humour in England in the sixties; his tradition was to be continued by Mark Twain. In short, the sixties were the last decade in which caricatures of American character retained their importance on the English stage. With the advent of Mark Twain in the early seventies, Britons could concentrate on a greater American humorist; and when American social comedies, *e.g.* those of Augustin Daly and Bronson Howard,[3] began arriving in Europe, crude caricatures of Americans had lost their novelty. Survivals of the early trend can be found well into the twentieth century, but they were relics rather than innovations. The golden age of the stock Yankee, frontiersman, immigrant, and Negro was disappearing; more up-to-date presentations of American character were to occupy their former positions on the English stage.

---

[1] *Athenaeum*, February 16, 1861, 235. This anticipated the later popularity of Coleridge-Taylor's version.

[2] Matthews and Hutton, *Op.cit.*, V. 103; *Athenaeum*, March 7, 1868, 365.

[3] The first play by Daly to be performed in England was the drama *Leah, the Jewish Maiden*, Adelphi, October 1, 1863. The first of Daly's comedies was *Garrick; or, Acting in Earnest*, which was presented at Edinburgh in 1874. Bronson Howard's burlesque *Ingomar the Idiotic* was first imported in 1871, and introduced the playwright to the British public. (*Nicoll*.)

CHAPTER X

SUMMARY AND CONCLUSIONS

1. Summary.

Charles Mathews the Elder brought the first important comic Americans to the English stage. His 1824 entertainment, produced after his return from the United States, included characterizations of a Yankee, a Kentucky Colonel, a Negro, an American Frenchman and an American-Dutch lady. Although the analysis of these parts had not yet crystallized into the patterns followed by later playwrights and actors, Mathews can be said to have brought a series of new stock characters to the English stage. He also sang the famous »Possum up a Gum Tree» which anticipated Negro minstrelsy.

Mathews' successes encouraged two English playwrights, Peake and Moncrieff, to write plays dealing with humorous Americans. Moncrieff's *Monsieur Mallet* of 1829 was an attempt to delineate the »National Manners and Peculiarities» of the United States, and is the first play, at least in England, to present the full range of transatlantic character by including a frontiersman among its dramatis personae. Jeremiah Kentuck may well be the first Westerner on the stage; traditionally Nimrod Wildfire of Paulding's *Lion of the West*, 1830, has been quoted in this connection.

In 1827 James H. Hackett, an American actor specializing in stage humour, American speech, and regional traits, visited the London stage. His early performances were failures, and the reviews condemned them because of the staleness of much of his material that was taken from Mathews, the vulgar language, and the unintelligibility of many of the jokes.

Washington Irving's *Rip Van Winkle* was repeatedly produced in dramatic form in England from 1832 onwards. The melodramatic elements were stressed, but the Dutch-American traits of Rip and his fellow-villagers also received due attention. The lazy, indolent, easy-going New-York Dutchman became one more representative of the United States on the English stage. Yankee characters were inserted into the dramatizations. *Rip Van Winkle* proved its popularity and was revived in 1865. Hackett and Joseph Jefferson both played Rip in England.

A version of Paulding's *Lion of the West* was performed in London in 1833 under the title of *The Kentuckian*. William Bayle Bernard, the author, probably limited his efforts to cutting down the three-act original into a minor farce. Hackett's acting of Nimrod Wildfire proved popular, but external reasons limited the run of the play. Reviewers were still struck by the oddity and novelty of Wildfire's character, and indicated that the part was at times difficult to appreciate.

George Handel Hill, the American actor better known as »Yankee Hill,» acted Yankee parts in England in 1836. Hiram Dodge of Bernard's *The Yankee Pedlar* was one of his impersonations. This play was the first to contrast Northern and Southern characters with one another on the English stage. The press was laudatory, and the audience now had little trouble in appreciating a Yankee part. Hill returned to England in 1838 and achieved a minor success with a farce entitled *New Notions*.

Several minor farces, among them Moncrieff's *Tarnation Strange*, profited from the vogue of humorous American characters in the thirties.

In 1836 Negro minstrelsy was introduced in England by Thomas Dartmouth Rice, the American blackface comedian. The new type of entertainment proved extremely popular and provided amusement for large British audiences up to and beyond 1870. It also provided the English stage with a new concept of the humorous American Negro. Negro minstrelsy was gradually divorced from the legitimate stage and formed an independent institution.

In the forties, the set types of the Yankee, the frontiersman, and the Negro can be found in many plays on the English stage. Edward Stirling's *Yankee Notes* contains samples of both Negro and Western character. Two one-act farces by Cornelius Ambrosius Logan, the American playwright, *Yankee Land* and *The Vermont Wool-Dealer* together with some other plays provided an opportunity for Dan Marble, another American actor specializing in the native humour of his country, to display his talents. The press praised his performances, and the critics had no difficulty in appreciating the humour. Marble entertained the Londoners for over a month, until the complete failure of his fourth play terminated his sojourn in England.

In 1850, *Fashion* by the American Mrs. Mowatt-Ritchie proved a minor success of more than twenty performances. Here Adam Trueman, an honest American farmer, was contrasted with the artificial snobs of transatlantic cities. *Fashion* can be said to be the first American social comedy to be presented in England.

Josh Silsbee, the American actor, visited England in the early fifties. He established his success in *The Forest Rose and the Yankee Ploughboy* by the American Samuel Woodworth, and played in several other farces. Silsbee was popular in Edinburgh and Manchester as well as in London. Several other plays presenting humorous Americans were produced in this decade. Two American actor couples, the Florences and the Williamses, visited Britain. The ladies specialized in acting the Yankee girl, while their husbands supported them mostly in Irish parts.

Numerous English dramatizers of *Uncle Tom's Cabin* inserted humorous Yankees, Negroes, and even an occasional frontiersman into their versions, and emphasized the humour of Mrs. Beecher Stowe's original to provide relief to the melodrama.

Tom Taylor's *Our American Cousin*, one of the great successes of the sixties in England, was originally based on the contrast between Asa Trenchard, a comic American, and Dundreary, the English snob. Although the latter was the main attraction of the play, reviews bear witness to the fact that Asa Trenchard also contributed to the success of the play in England.

In 1862 Drury Lane was visited by an American actress, Mrs. Hough, who impersonated a New Hampshire girl in *The Yankee Legacy*. Another American comedian, John E. Owens, performed Solon Shingle in *The People's Lawyer* at the Adelphi in 1865.

Numerous other plays of less importance contained caricatures of Americans.

The period from 1824 to 1870 is the golden age of caricatures of transatlantic men and women on the English stage. The drama was the first medium to introduce native American humour to England in large quantities; with the rise of the cheap book in the fifties and sixties it lost this privilege. The works of good American humorists became increasingly popular. In the last decades of the nineteenth century American social comedy arrived in England and eclipsed the early vogue of the Yankee, the frontiersman, and the Negro. Where they occur on the English stage after 1870 they should be considered survivals, not innovations.

2. Conclusions.

I.

In the light of this account of the history of caricatures of American character on the English stage, several facts merit further consideration.

The sheer bulk of material on American humour on the English stage is surprisingly large. The humorous Americans who trod the boards of English theatres between 1824 and 1870 can be expected to outnumber the comic representatives of any other nation with the possible exception of France. It is no exaggeration to say that the Yankee, the frontiersman, and the American Negro were among the prominent stock characters of the English nineteenth-century stage. Their vogue was not restricted to one or two specialized theatres; in spite of the system of favourite topics which was a typical feature of many English playhouses of the last century, transatlantic drollery was performed practically everywhere. Whether dressed in evening clothes and top hat, or in a well-worn Sunday suit; whether residing in Belgravia or Stepney; whether arriving to the theatre in a coach or a hansom in the company of a beauty in diamonds and furs, or on foot, pockets bulging with beer-bottles, the Briton of a hundred years ago had his chance of getting acquainted with American stage fun. The theatre has always been a sensitive indicator of popular taste: if Jonathan's presence was frequent, the public must have liked him. Even the reviewers, who often wished to assert their more catholic tastes by condemning plays with popular appeal, were swept into frequent admiration of plays portraying comic Americans. What, then, were the factors that caused this extraordinary interest in the humorous representatives of another, far-off nation?

First, the nineteenth-century Englishman was interested in America. The anti-American sentiments of the revolutionary period and of the War of 1812 had gradually given way to a profound curiosity. If the Americans were able to defend themselves against the greatest power on earth, their system of government and way of life must contain sound traits. On the other hand, would the Americans be able to establish a stable government and economic order at a time when this was difficult in England? It was in pursuit of answers to these and similar questions and sometimes in quest of money that the ceaseless flow of English visitors to the United States started. But travel was tedious and expensive, and the visitors were few; those who had to stay at home satisfied their curiosity by reading travel-books written by their more fortunate — or unfortunate — countrymen. The market for travel-books on America was insatiable. From de Tocqueville through Mrs. Trollope and Dickens to the more scholarly Lord Bryce, scores of authors, professional or amateurish, profited from the Englishman's thirst for facts about the growing Republic of the West. Charles Mathews' American entertainment came at a time when John Bull's information about Cousin Jonathan was still scanty. By bringing Jonathan alive to England Mathews gave a very concrete and detailed, albeit caricatured, idea of his character to John Bull. The latter was pleased and clamoured for more. This appeal was registered by cash-conscious theatre managers, who set out to provide the public with what it wanted. The English interest in American humour was built on a solid foundation: the English interest in America.

The close relations between the English and American stage made it possible for English theatre managers to profit from this interest. The more or less common language on both sides of the ocean had long prompted actors of either country to cross the ocean to gain experience and gold from the sister nation. Many, perhaps most of the great Anglo-Saxon actors of the nineteenth century played in both countries; many, perhaps most of the well-known playwrights had their plays produced on both sides of the Atlantic. This process was greatly aided by the lack of comprehensive copyright statutes between England and the United States. From our perspective Anglo-American dramatic contacts seem like a snowball: once set in motion it gathers momentum and grows. When prominent men of the theatrical world once got acquainted with conditions on the other side of the ocean, they always remembered the demands across the waters, and whenever opportunity arose, tried to profit from their knowledge. New York successes were taken to London, and vice versa. It is but a part of this process that American comedians specializing in their native humour, like Hackett, Hill, Marble, Silsbee, Jefferson, Owens, and the Florences displayed their talents in England. The English interest in American stage humour could rest on a second important cornerstone: the close relations between the English and American stage in the nineteenth century.

At this time the drama was a field where English cultural supremacy could not make itself felt. At hardly any time in the history of the English theatre have standards been so low as in the early and middle nineteenth century. If Britons felt justified in assuming haughty attitudes towards American civilization and the beginnings of American letters in their other manifestations, they really had little right to assert their superiority in the field of the drama. True, American standards were no better; they could be no worse. If most of the plays containing humorous Americans were trash, so were most of the other comedies and farces that were presented in England. The constant search for American originality had resulted in one discovery: American humour; the influence of the American short story was too subtle to be clearly felt at the time. The apparent freshness and vigour of American fun compensated for its lack of aesthetic value. Thus, a third circumstance making possible the vogue of caricatures of American character on the English stage was the low standard of the English theatre itself.

The fourth factor furthering the importation of American characters to the British stage consisted of the inherent nature of transatlantic humour. As soon as the initial difficulties of the twenties and thirties had been overcome and Jonathan had become a familiar figure, any normal adult or youngster could appreciate his antics. No subtle wit was involved, no Oxonian degrees were necessary for a full understanding of the taciturn shrewdness of the Yankee, the lusty exaggerations of the frontiersman, or the hearty hilarity of the Negro. Linguistic difficulties existed, but they were conquered: if American actors at first tended to emphasize the humour of language, a few initial failures cured them of the habit. Slight adaptations and a careful enunciation seem to have taken care of the rest, while the British public rapidly overcame its first distaste for the queer idiom. If a man, born within one mile from Bow Bells, could enjoy Yorkshire humour, no extensive re-education was necessary to enable him to laugh at Jonathan the Yankee. Nineteenth-century Britons were keenly aware of a difference between American stage humour and their own, but they enjoyed this difference. Critics repeatedly praised American characters because of their most American traits; they enjoyed Jonathan as he was, and if they sneered at his alien features on principle their sneer was not sufficiently venomous to kill their enjoyment. Whatever results may be derived from intellectual analyses of the differences between English and American humour, it remains a fact that nineteenth-century stage caricatures of transatlantic character had enough universal appeal to be appreciated in England. It is pleasant, but idle, to speculate about the »innate» humour of the Anglo-Saxon race; it should, however, be remembered that Elizabethan humour showed the tendency towards lusty exaggeration which in the nineteenth century was more often than not considered an American trait, and that American humour had its origins in an unbroken folk tradition, while English literary humour of the nineteenth century was mainly based on the traditions of an educated minority, and could hardly trace its ancestry in an unbroken line from the Elizabethans.

Thus, if Jonathan's popularity on the English stage of the last century could only be rivalled by that of Pierre, but not by those of Fritz or any others, there were tangible reasons for it. The great topical interest in things American, the close contact between the English and American theatre, the low state of British drama, and the nature of American humour all contributed to the effect that the theatre-going Londoner of a hundred years ago had some difficulty in escaping contact with comic stage Americans.

II.

A surprising aspect of the history of caricatures of American character on the English stage is the great difficulty in separating true American humour from pseudo-American, *i.e.* American-type humour written and acted by Englishmen in imitation of the genuine product. The only way in which a clear-cut dichotomy can be achieved is by external criteria. It would be easy, but meaningless, to distinguish between the products of English-born and American-born playwrights. It would be equally easy and equally meaningless to draw a line between plays that were first produced in America, and plays that were first produced in England. These facts are pertinent, and where known they have been included in the discussion at their proper places; decisive they are not. The same plays were performed on both sides of the Atlantic with identical or different casts; the same actors played in England and in the United States; the same playwrights wrote for both countries; and both audiences enjoyed the same jokes, possibly with slight alterations. Beyond folklore it does not often happen that one country takes over the humour of another country with such ease that external criteria have to be used as a basis of classification.

10 — *Soc. Scient. Fenn. Comm. Hum. Litt. XVIII. 1.*

It should be frankly admitted that one of the reasons for this difficulty of clear classification may be due to the limitations of method. The present-day investigator must needs limit himself to the perusal of dusty manuscripts; the best will in the world will not recall the actors of yore from their resting-places to repeat their performances for a critical scholar. A word-picture of a theatre performance remains but the second-best approach. Perhaps the American characters of an English playwright or actor would be different on the stage from those of an American; judging from the written records alone this was not the case. To a modern reader, the humorous Americans of English playwrights seem much the same as those of American ones. All of them remain types with gross, exaggerated characteristics; the lack of subtlety and detailed character delineation made imitation a comparatively easy task.

The reasons why humorous Americans became so popular on the English nineteenth-century stage also explain how English playwrights or actors came to know so much about transatlantic fun. The widespread interest in things American led newspapers to devote some space to American news. Moreover, many, perhaps most English periodicals and dailies, including the august *Times*, did not hesitate to print frequent, but sporadic American anecdotes, downright jokes, or amusing news items. As the critics duly remarked, some of the »Jonathans» they heard on the stage were old friends originating in various sources of this kind. Many of the travel-book authors also included passages in their books which provided material for stage treatment, including samples of American English. Charles Mathews had instigated a tradition in England, and many of the early playwrights resorted to his analyses whenever they wanted to round off their own conceptions. Further knowledge of American humour could be derived from printed books like Haliburton's *Sam Slick* series, which were equally popular on both sides of the Atlantic. And after Hackett, Hill, and Marble had entertained the British public with their authentic representations of comic Americans, there was little excuse for the English playwright who was incapable of dashing off a humorous American character at will. All these various sources were available to Bernard, Peake, Moncrieff, Stirling, and the other Britons who exerted their pens in depicting transatlantic peculiarities. Judging from the results, they knew how to apply their knowledge: however unoriginal, repetitive, monotonous, and eclectic, their characters show no significant differences from the corresponding creations of native American playwrights. Besides, an expert actor could be expected to iron out all improbabilities from their scripts.

The characters of early American humour were not always developed with verisimilitude. Thus Haliburton's Sam Slick displays a mixture of both Yankee shrewdness and frontier impetuosity; his creator was a Canadian, whose knowledge of the Yankee was not quite so profound as he led his readers to believe. The tendency to fuse different types of regional Americans into one single representative of the United States thus existed in the field of written American humour. If English playwrights or actors departed from clear-cut analyses of the Yankee and the frontiersman, and moulded the two together into one American, they had authoritative precedents to follow. Therefore even the criterion of accuracy in keeping apart the comic representatives of different regions of the United States proves inadequate for differentiation between true American and pseudo-American stage humour.

The language, perhaps at first sight the best criterion of the playwright's competence, also fails to provide any clear clues. The play manuscripts were carelessly written, and one who has spent months in perusing the licensing copies cannot help suspecting that they were often hastily copied out by people who took little interest in details like spelling. There are instances where the licensing copy shows attempts at indicating American pronunciation; such attempts were seldom consistent. Even if they were, the correlation between various spelling devices and their phonetic equivalents would remain a matter of conjecture. It is evident that many of the manuscripts merely told the actor what was to be said, not how it was to be pronounced; in the cases of experts like Hackett, Hill, Marble, and Silsbee, this procedure seems quite natural. As to the vocabulary, the Americanisms were often comparatively few and consisted mainly of stock words and phrases, many of them constantly recurring ever since Charles Mathews' 1824 show. Whenever an English playwright wanted to write »American,» he inserted a liberal supply of catchwords and phrases like »I guess,» »I calculate,» »tarnation cute,» »I reckon,» and allowed the actor to do the rest. Perhaps an English playwright would have tended to overdo his American English and exaggerate its salient features even more than his American counterpart did. A thorough and extensive word-count, a comparison of the results with the language of written

American humour, and a concomitant investigation of American usage, standard and dialectal, might yield some conclusions as to the authenticity of the American English of playwriting Britons; such an undertaking is beyond the scope of the present study. The substandard grammar would be even more difficult to deal with. In general, one may be sure that the »queer» pronunciations and idioms of the stage Americans enhanced the effect of their humour on an English public. However obnoxious American usage may have been to critical Britons of the nineteenth cenrury, the stage Americanisms were accepted as an integral part of the characterizations.[1]

It remains a tribute to the closeness of Anglo-American relations in the dramatic field that it is difficult to find any meaningful basis for differentiating between true American and pseudo-American humour on the English stage prior to 1870.

III.

When dealing with the problem of explaining what factors stimulate one nation's interest in another nation's fun it is convenient to accept a social rather than a psychological or physiological theory of humour. Bergson's basic concept of humour as a social corrective is one of the most famous attempts to deal with these difficult questions, and in spite of many endeavours to modify or elaborate his chains of thought the latter have well withstood the test of time.[2] If we start from Bergson's fundamental statement:

... si l'on trace un cercle autour des actions et dispositions qui compromettent la vie individuelle ou sociale et qui se châtient elles-mêmes par leurs conséquences naturelles, il reste en dehors de ce terrain d'émotion et de lutte, dans une zone neutre où l'homme se donne simplement en spectacle à l'homme, une certaine raideur du corps, de l'esprit et du caractère, que la société voudrait encore éliminer pour obtenir de ses membres la plus grande élasticité et la plus haute sociabilité possibles. Cette raideur est le comique, et le rire en est le châtiment ...[3]

---

[1] A very readable account of the attitudes of Britons towards American English is included in Henry L. Mencken's *The American Language* (New York, 1937), and *The American Language, Supplement I* (New York, 1948).

[2] A recent attempt is Alfred Stern, *Philosophie du rire et des pleurs* (Paris, 1949).

[3] *Le rire* (Paris, 1947), p. 16.

the problem reduces itself to the following questions: In what respect was American nineteenth-century humour a social corrective? To what extent could nineteenth-century Englishmen appreciate American fun, i.e., to what extent were they aware of the incongruities between humorous American characters and their society? Or did they perhaps juxtapose American characters with English society, and achieve an effect sufficient to produce laughter?

Early native American humour was based on folk and oral traditions. Seventeenth and eighteenth-century immigrants brought with them the humour of their home countries. Apparently the only non-English group that migrated during this period and preserved its own humorous tradition consisted of Germans, mostly from the Palatinate, who settled in Pennsylvania and are known as the »Pennsylvania Dutch.» Even today their folklore shows peculiarities attributable to its Germanic origins. However, Pennsylvania Dutch humour ought to be considered a thing apart; it has not played a prominent role in the shaping of American humour.

More important was the humorous tradition brought over the ocean by immigrants from England. The immigrants of the early seventeenth century were Elizabethans and Jacobeans in their humour and thought. The patterns of their culture did not prove conducive to the extensive written recording of humour. Thus, while showing the stylistic devices of their period, the works of Nathaniel Ward and Sarah Kemble Knight cannot be considered indicative of the emergence of anything like a native American type of fun.

This does not mean that the settlers lacked sense of humour. Many men, from early Merrymount to later frontier settlements, must have whiled away long evenings with stories and jests. Man's story-telling urge applied to American life on the basis of an English tradition — in those words we might define the qualities of the earliest American humour. And since humour is always influenced by the society in which it exists, and since American society from the very beginning had its own peculiarities, American humour must have gradually developed its own characteristics. The most important type of transatlantic society to be considered in this respect is the frontier rather than the old seaboard settlement. The latter conformed to more rigid patterns, and in them life was more dominated by cultural currents from Europe. The frontier again was a society typical of America alone; nowhere else did such conditions exist. And it was the humour of the frontier that proved the most important germ of native American humour in the nineteenth century.

It was in the nature of frontier society to place severe demands on the individual. When a small group of men were fighting for their existence under adverse conditions, great claims were made on everybody's willingness to tackle his share of the work. Shirking was not popular. Therefore even slight deviations from the standard may have called for punitive measures, which according to Bergson start with laughter: the man who fails to fit is made the butt of a joke.

When communications improved, growing numbers of outsiders and potential frontiersmen intruded upon the early settlers. They were often an economic menace, and their behaviour and way of life was often radically different from that of the backwoods population. This again called for punitive laughter. The Yankee, as exemplified by the peddler, became the laughing-stock of many areas, including Haliburton's Nova Scotia. The Negro had his difficulties of adjustment in an alien society and climate among people of an alien race who spoke a different language and took the attitude of masters. When he failed to fit the pattern he was laughed at. Conversely, many frontiersmen had dealings with people outside their immediate groups. When they entered alien settlements with their coonskin caps, odd clothes, appalling manners and self-sufficient ideals, they failed to fit; the result was a cycle of jokes at the expense of the Westerner. The foreign immigrant was not yet a social danger. In the eighteenth and early nineteenth century immigration had not yet risen to its peak; the days when one million human beings crossed the Atlantic every year were still to come; American society had not developed the intense social pressure towards Americanization which faced the immigrants of the twentieth century. Thus there were not enough foreigners around to warrant their being made stock victims of fun. Irving's New-York Dutchmen and the *ancien régime* French were essentially romanticized survivals of a past age; their careers can be traced to the literary works of Irving and the fun of Charles Mathews. It was not until much later that Hans Breitmann initiated a new vogue of humorous treatments of the recent immigrant.

These observations deal with broad trends and are necessarily oversimplified. It seems, however, that Bergson's theory can be used to account for the selection of the stock characters of American humour in the early nineteenth century. The Yankee, the frontiersman, and the Negro were the most important ones, and there are reasons why these very characters were selected to amuse the American population. When American humour began to find expression in literary media, which is usually said to have taken place around 1830, the ridicule of these characters immediately found its way into writing and to the stage. They were not invented overnight: they had grown out of a humorous tradition shaped by social forces. We may therefore answer our first question and say that the stage caricatures of American character of the early nineteenth century were part of a tendency to ridicule such character types that showed extreme qualities and »rigidity.»

The gradual development from caricature towards social comedy can be explained in similar terms. When American society crystallized into set patterns, when the geographical frontier vanished, and when communications improved, a new unity pervaded the United States. The most flagrant and extreme differences in ethical and moral codes and in manners began to disappear. There was a gradual standardization which ironed out striking individuality; ultimately the question of a crude frontiersman's behaviour in a city *salon* lost its topical interest. The individual's adjustment to society now became the most important problem. Therefore the crude, exaggerated caricatures of early American humour had to give way to more sophisticated, more real portrayals of the social adjustment of individual citizens of the United States.

When English audiences laughed at American stage humour they must have done so on different grounds from their American cousins. The most rigid representatives of the inhabitants of the United States would of course have failed to fit English society. The »mob rule» of the American system of government was considered a dangerous feature and a bad example for the English lower classes by conservative Victorians, who were not always confident that the social problems of England could be solved without violence. The British aristocrats tended to ridicule everybody who did not acquiesce in the narrow codes ruling their own lives. The middle classes, rising in position and wealth, tended to be optimistic and satisfied with a social order making this improvement possible, and to resent rigid attitudes deviating from their own. The lower classes of early nineteenth-century Britain showed a tendency to be intolerant to those who were different, who were not »reg'lar.» These general attitudes might have resulted in laughter at the expense of Cousin Jonathan. The stock representative of the United States stubbornly refused to admit English political and cultural supremacy, which was taken for granted by the majority of Britons; this obstinacy may also have called for condescending and punitive ridicule. It seems that all classes of the English nineteenth-century population had cause to laugh at the Yankee, the frontiersman, and the other stage Americans.

Numerous comments bear out that the English were very much aware of the alien qualities of American humour both on and off the stage. Perhaps they even exaggerated its strangeness. A modern reader of British nineteenth-century comments on the United States or on American literature cannot help feeling that the ideological differences between the United States and Britain were magnified by the writers. At a time when some Britons cast wistful glances at the less democratic past and when the menace of dictatorships was not acute it was easy to allow the formal difference between a kingdom and a republic completely to obscure the beginnings of parallel developments in the two countries. Even the most discerning travelbook authors found the task of emphasizing differences more rewarding than the listing of similarities; many of them contented themselves to stating that in certain regions they had found people who lived practically like their English counterparts. In spite of what the Englishman thought, it is plausible to think that a frontiersman was not much more strange to a Londoner than to a Bostonian.

We may conclude that if nineteenth-century Englishmen were unaware of the complex social forces that made Americans laugh at their stock stage comedians, they had compensating reasons to enjoy transatlantic fun. They could juxtapose American characters with English society, with the American society they had read about, or with that presented on the stage. With the advent of American social comedy, more of the differences between the United States and Britain were eliminated from the stage: there was little difference between the goings-on at Washington Square and Grosvenor Square. Yet the impact of the comic stage American had been great.[1]

---

[1] As late as 1891, when Henry James's *The American* was staged in England, Christopher Newman's clothes suggested the influence of a caricatured concept of transatlantic man. (Edel, *Complete Plays of Henry James*, p. 186.)

IV.

It has not proved feasible to formulate any true general statements about the differences between English and American stage humour prior to 1870.

The often heard dictum that American humour was based on overstatement, English humour on understatement, is too sweeping; numerous exceptions can be found. Even if many British commentators based their remarks on this criterion, they were limiting their opinions to specific instances. There was much English humour not dependent on understatement, and much transatlantic drollery that built on miosis rather than hyperbole. The Yankee character, shrewd and taciturn, did not always exaggerate. On the other hand, Dickens's characters are exaggerated to the point of caricature. This aspect does not yield any clear-cut differences between the humour of the United States and that of England.

As to the caricatured presentations of American character on the stage, the early tendency was to make the comedians funny by emphasizing their inherent »rigidity.» Their behaviour was more interesting than their adjustment to their surroundings. Much English eighteenth and nineteenth-century fun was founded on a different basis: twists in the social ladder. In Britain, where the segmentation of society into clear-cut strata was accepted as normal and natural, humour was often based on the incongruities that resulted when people were placed in strata not their own. This device is clearly observable *e.g.* in the works of Thackeray, notably *Vanity Fair;* in some of the *Bab Ballads;* and in the works of cartoonists like du Maurier. However, hard-and-fast generalizations will again result in absurdity. Thus, most of the *vers de société* type of humour does not stress this aspect, and the preoccupation with social problems of some humorists led them to treat their characters with much understanding: society, rather than the individual, could be made the villain, the laughing-stock. Yet the method of indicating a man's predestined place on the social ladder, moving him to another rung and laughing at the ensuing incongruity was more used in English than American humour prior to 1870.

Early American stage humour again built on exaggerated types, and the main interest was in character, not in social adjustment. There was no distinct social ladder acceptable to wide segments of the American population: the values of one American community could be vastly different from those of another. Thus the social considerations discussed in connection with Bergson's theory were not based on fixed, immutable concepts of the superiority of certain definable groups of people, but rather on the adjustable scales of values in different communities. In America during the frontier period the social ladder was not easily definable. As a consequence American humour prior to 1870 tended to stress regional contrasts rather than social ones.

Judging from the successes of presentations of humorous Americans on the English stage these two different approaches to humour were mutually compatible. The American's absolute refusal to adapt himself to the requirements of an alien environment may have furnished English audiences with the idea of rigidity that resulted in laughter. The Englishman was conditioned to a world of social levels, and if an American failed to fit this world, the consequences were humorous. The British public may have tried to identify American characters with some stratum of English society, and enjoyed the resulting incongruity. Thus the American technique of caricature could be converted into twists in the social ladder by a mind used to a world of clear social strata. The result was still humorous.

V.

It is impossible to form an accurate estimate of the number of Britons who saw the Yankee, the frontiersman, the Negro, or the immigrant presented on the English stage prior to 1870. Even excluding the minstrel shows the number of Londoners who saw such performances could be expected to be well in the hundreds of thousands. This audience came from different social strata and must have represented a more complete cross-section of the English population than did the readers of American books or travel-books on the United States, at least before the wholesale introduction of the cheap book. It was only the upper or middle-class Briton who could compare stage caricatures of American character with other sources of information, and be fully aware of the distorted and stereotyped nature of the stock American on the stage; as a rule these social classes refrained from patronizing the theatre until the latter half of the century. Even many reviewers believed in the essential verisimilitude of the stage Yankee or frontiersman. Therefore we may conclude that the stage presentations of American character were among the influences that shaped the nineteenth-century Englishman's concepts of his transatlantic cousins. This is particularly true since more profound stage analyses of individual American character were very rare before the rise of American drama in the last decades of the nineteenth century.

APPENDIX

A Chronological List of First Performances on the English Stage of Plays Containing Caricatures of Americans.

For information on the availability of these plays, see the notes of the present work; Allardyce Nicoll, *A History of Early Nineteenth Century Drama*, Vol. II (Cambridge, 1930); and Nicoll, *A History of Late Nineteenth Century Drama*, Vol. II (Cambridge, 1946). Some printed versions are listed in *The Player's Library: The Catalogue of the Library of the British Drama League* (London, 1950). The plays marked with + have not been found in Nicoll's play lists; those marked with an asterisk are there listed under »Unknown Authors.»

+ March 25, 1824. *Mathews in America*. English Opera House. Comic Entertainment.
   September 3, 1824. Richard Brinsley Peake, *Jonathan in England*. English Opera House. Operatic Farce.
+ April 5, 1827. *Sylvester Daggerwood*. Covent Garden. Farce.
+ April 5, 1827. James H. Hackett, *Yankee Stories*. Covent Garden. Comic Entertainment.
   January 22, 1829. William Thomas Moncrieff, *Monsieur Mallét; or, My Daughter's Letter*. Adelphi. Drama.
   December 26, 1829. Thomas Dibdin, *The Banks of the Hudson; or, the Congress Trooper*. Coburg. Melodrama.
   January 10, 1831. *Jonathan Dobson, the Congress Trooper*. Coburg. Melodrama.
   October 1, 1832. William Bayle Bernard, *Rip Van Winkle; or, the Helmsman of the Spirit Crew*. Adelphi. Burletta.
+ November 17, 1832. James H. Hackett, *Jonathan in England*. Drury Lane. Comedy.
* November 17, 1832. Samuel Beazley, *The Militia Muster*. Drury Lane. Comic Entertainment.
   March 9, 1833. William Bayle Bernard, *The Kentuckian; or, a Trip to New York*. Covent Garden. Farce.
   May 3, 1833. Charles Burke, *Rip Van Winkle; or, a Legend of the Kaatskill Mountains*. Haymarket. Romantic Drama.
* June 18, 1833. William Bayle Bernard, *The Long Finn; or, the Treasure-Seeker's Dream*. Adelphi. Melodrama.

July 9, 1836. Thomas Dartmouth Rice, *Bone Squash Diabolo*. Surrey. Comic Opera.

November 1, 1836. William Bayle Bernard, *The Yankee Pedlar; or, Old Times in Virginia*. Drury Lane. Burletta.

November 7, 1836. William Leman Rede, *A Flight to America; or, Twelve Hours in New York*. Adelphi. Burletta.

January 9, 1837. *Caspar Hauser; or, the Wild Boy of Bavaria*. Queen's. Drama.

January 26, 1837. *A Down East Bargain; or, Love in New York*. Queen's. Farce.

* July 21, 1838. William Bayle Bernard, *New Notions*. Haymarket. Farce.

* August 1, 1838. Richard Brinsley Peake, *Job Fox, the Yankee Valet*. English Opera House. Burletta.

August 3, 1838. William Thomas Moncrieff, *Tarnation Strange*. Strand. Farce.

+ August 3, 1838. Richard Brinsley Peake, *The Emigrant's Daughter*. English Opera House. Melodrama.

December 31, 1838. Thomas Proclus Taylor, *Jim Crow in His New Place*. Adelphi. Extravaganza.

* December 24, 1842. Edward Stirling, *Yankee Notes for English Circulation*. Adelphi. Farce.

* September 28, 1844. Cornelius Ambrosius Logan, *The Vermont Wool-Dealer*. Strand. Drama.

* October 7, 1844. Cornelius Ambrosius Logan, *Yankee Land; or the Foundling of the Apple-Orchard*. Strand. Farce.

November 4, 1844. *Sam Patch the Jumper*. Haymarket. Drama.

December 15, 1848. *Yankee Doodle upon His Little Pony*. Royal Amphitheatre. Pantomime.

December 26, 1848. Nelson Lee, *Harlequin and Yankee Doodle*. Royal Amphitheatre. Pantomime.

* February 26, 1849. J. Stirling Coyne, *Cocknies in California*. Adelphi. Farce.

January 9, 1850. Anna Cora Mowatt Ritchie, *Fashion; or, Life in New York*. Olympic. Comedy.

September 23, 1851. Samuel Woodworth, *The Forest Rose and the Yankee Ploughboy*. Adelphi. Comedy.

October 13, 1851. Charles A. Somerset, *The Bloomer Costume! or Brother Jonathan in England!* Grecian Saloon. Farce.

September 13, 1852. *Uncle Tom's Cabin; or the Negro Slave*. Standard. Drama.

* September 14, 1852. G. H. George, *A Colour'd Commotion*. Strand. Extravaganza.

September 20, 1852. Edward Fitzball, *Uncle Tom's Cabin; or, the Horrors of Slavery*. Olympic. Drama.

* September 20, 1852. Eliza Vincent, *Uncle Tom's Cabin; or, the Fugitive Slave*. Victoria. Drama.

* October 9, 1852. C. D. Pitt, *Uncle Tom's Cabin*. London Pavilion. Drama.

November 1, 1852. John Courtney, *Uncle Tom's Cabin*. Surrey. Drama.

November 3, 1852. *A Wife for a Day*. Standard. Farce.

November 8, 1852. *Paul; or, the Fortunate Slave*. Strand. Drama.

November 29, 1852. Tom Taylor and Mark Lemon, *Slave Life; or, Uncle Tom's Cabin.* Adelphi. Drama.
+ December, 1852. *Love and Larnin'.* Theatre Royal, Manchester. Farce.
December 27, 1852. Edward Fitzball, *Uncle Tom's Cabin.* Drury Lane. Melodrama.
* May 16, 1855. Edward Ranger, *The American in England.* Theatre Royal, Manchester. Comedy.
* April 28, 1856. William Jermyn Florence, *The Yankee Housekeeper.* Drury Lane. Farce.
May 12, 1856. *Mischievous Annie; or, a Lesson for Husbands.* Drury Lane. Farce.
May 26, 1856. Dion Boucicault, *The Young Actress.* Drury Lane. Musical Interlude.
June 30, 1856. *Customs of the Country.* Adelphi. Farce.
+ July 26, 1856. *Our Gal.* Adelphi. Farce.
August 12, 1856. Mrs. Barney Williams, *Irish Assurance and Yankee Modesty.* Adelphi. Farce.
September 25, 1856. *Lucifer Matches; or, the Yankee —!* Adelphi. Extravaganza.
February 15, 1858. *Yankee Courtship; or, Away Down East.* Adelphi. Farce.
+ February, 1858. *Latest from New York.* Adelphi.
October 22, 1860. *Pioneers; or, the Maid of the War Path.* Lyceum. Drama.
September 23, 1861. *Red John the Daring; or, Settlers' Perils.* Britannia. Drama.
October 19, 1861. John Brougham, *Pocahontas; or, the Gentle Savage.* Princess. Extravaganza.
November 11, 1861. Tom Taylor, *Our American Cousin.* Haymarket. Comic Drama.
March 10, 1862. *The Sons of Columbia: A Story of the American War.* Britannia. Drama.
April 17, 1862. *A Leap for Liberty.* Queen's. Drama.
September 1, 1862. *The Yankee Legacy.* Drury Lane. Farce.
September 8, 1862. John Oxenford, *Sam's Arrival.* Strand. Farce.
+ October, 1862. *A Southerner Just Arrived.* Olympic. Farce.
December 14, 1863. Henry J. Byron, *Lord Dundreary Married and Done For.* Prince of Wales Theatre, Liverpool. Farce.
August 4, 1864. *My American Aunt; or, Dundreary in Difficulties.* Princess Theatre, Edinburgh. Comedy.
July 3, 1865. J. S. Jones and Cornelius Ambrosius Logan, *The People's Lawyer.* Strand. Drama.
July 26, 1865. *The Confederate's Daughter; or, the Tyrant of New Orleans.* Britannia. Drama.
September 4, 1865. Dion Boucicault and Joseph Jefferson, *Rip Van Winkle.* Adelphi. Drama.
* March 5, 1866. W. W. Sidney and T. F. Phillips, *Rip Van Winkle.* Theatre Royal, Norwich. Drama.

* March 13, 1866. John Strachan and Henry Davis, *Rip Van Winkle; or, Somnambulistic Knickerbockers*. Theatre Royal, Newcastle. Burlesque.
  March 23, 1866. *Rip Van Winkle*. Theatre Royal, Oldham. Drama.
* July 18, 1867. R. H. Beverly, *The Last Slave*. New Adelphi Theatre, Liverpool. Drama.

BIBLIOGRAPHY

This Bibliography is restricted to works referred to in the text or notes of the present study. For more extensive bibliographical information on American and English drama and theatre, American humour, and the reception of American literature in England, the reader should consult the bibliographies and references in the works marked with an asterisk.

I. Newspapers and Periodicals.

The American Magazine
The Athenaeum
The Atlas
Blackwood's
The Critic
The Edinburgh Review
The Englishman
The Era
The European Magazine
The Evening Sun
The Examiner
Fun

The Illustrated London News
The Manchester Guardian
The Morning Herald
The Morning Post
The Observer
Punch
The Reader
The Spectator
The Sun
The Sunday Times
The Times

II. Series of Plays.

G. H. Davidson's *Minor Theatres*
Dicks' Standard Plays
Duncombe's British Theatre
French's Acting Edition
Lacy's Acting Edition of Plays
Webster's National Drama

III. Books and Scholarly Articles.

Adkins, Nelson F., »James K. Paulding's 'Lion of the West'.» *American Literature*, III, 249—258 (1931).
Allibone, S. Austin, *Critical Dictionary of English Literature*. 2 vols. Philadelphia, 1870.

Arnold, S. J., *Forgotten Facts in the Memoirs of Charles Mathews, Comedian.* London, 1839.
Baker, H. B., *History of the London Stage.* London, 1904.
— *The London Stage.* 2 vols. London, 1886.
Bayliss, Lilian, *The Old Vic.* London, 1925.
Beecher Stowe, Harriet, *Uncle Tom's Cabin.* London, 1852.
Behn, Aphra, *The Novels of Mrs. Aphra Behn.* London, 1913.
Bell's Life in London. London, 1836.
Bergson, Henri, *Le rire.* Paris, 1947.
Bernard, John, *Retrospections of America, 1797—1811.* New York, 1887.
Besant, Walter (ed.), *London in the Nineteenth Century.* London, 1909.
Blair, Walter, *Horse Sense in American Humor.* Chicago, 1942.
*— *Native American Humor.* New York, 1937.
— »The Popularity of Nineteenth-Century American Humorists.» *American Literature*, III, 175—194 (1931).
Brackenridge, Hugh Henry — see Newlin, Claude M.
Bradley, Phillips (ed.), *Democracy in America by Alexis de Tocqueville.* New York, 1945.
Brereton, Austin, *The Lyceum and Henry Irving.* London and New York, 1903.
Briggs, John, *The History of Jim Crow.* London, 1839.
Brook, Donald, *The Romance of the English Theatre.* London, 1945.
Bryce, James, *The American Commonwealth.* London and New York, 1889.
Cairns, William B., *British Criticisms of American Writings, 1783—1815.* Madison, Wis., 1918.
— *British Criticisms of American Writings, 1815—1833.* Madison, Wis., 1922.
Carson, William G. B., *The Theatre on the Frontier.* Chicago, 1932.
Clarence, Reginald, *The Stage Cyclopaedia.* London, 1909.
Coke, E. T., *A Subaltern's Furlough.* New York, 1833.
Conway, Moncure D., *Autobiography.* London, 1904.
The Darkey Drama, a Collection of Approved Farces, Interludes, Scenes, Etc. 12 vols. London and New York, n.d.
Dickens, Charles, *American Notes.* Leipzig, 1842.
Dickson, H. E., »A Note on Charles Mathews's Use of American Humor.» *American Literature*, XII, 78—83 (1940).
Disher, Maurice Willson, *Blood and Thunder.* London, 1949.
Eastman, May H., *Aunt Phillis's Cabin, or Southern Life as It Is.* London, 1852.
Edel, Leon (ed.), *The Complete Plays of Henry James.* Philadelphia and New York, 1949.
Fairchild, Hoxie Neale, *The Noble Savage.* New York, 1928.
Fields, Annie, *The Life and Letters of Harriet Beecher Stowe.* London, 1897.
Genest, John, *Some Account of the English Stage from the Restoration in 1660 to 1830.* 10 vols. Bath, 1832.
Gilbert, Douglas, *American Vaudeville.* New York and London, 1940.
Glover, Samuel, and Jeffreys, Charles, *The Uncle Tom Ballads.* London, 1852.
*Gohdes, Clarence, *American Literature in Nineteenth-Century England.* New York, 1944.
Gross, John, *Lincoln's Own Stories.* New York and London, 1912.

A Group of Theatrical Caricatures. Dunlap Society Publications, ser. II, vol. 4. New York, 1897.
Haliburton, Thomas Chandler (ed.), *Traits of American Humour.* 3 vols. London, 1852.
Hartman, John G., *The Development of American Social Comedy from 1787 to 1936.* Philadelphia, 1939.
* Hartnoll, Phyllis (ed.), *The Oxford Companion to the Theatre.* London, 1951.
Hill, George Handel, *Scenes from the Life of an Actor.* New York, 1853.
Hirn, Yrjö, *Goda vildar och ädla rövare.* Helsingfors, 1941.
Hodge, Francis, »Charles Mathews Reports on America.» *Quarterly Journal of Speech,* XXXVI, 429—499 (1950).
Hollingshead, John, *My Lifetime.* 2 vols. London, 1895.
Hutton, Laurence, *Curiosities of the American Stage.* New York, 1891.
James, Henry, *Notes of a Son and Brother.* London and New York, 1914.
— *A Small Boy and Others.* London and New York, 1913.
Jefferson, Joseph, *Autobiography.* London and New York, 1889.
Lacey, Alexander, *Pixérecourt and the French Romantic Drama.* Toronto, 1928.
Lewes, George Henry, *Dramatic Essays.* London, 1876.
Life at the South, or, Uncle Tom's Cabin as It Is. London, 1852.
The London Mathews. London, 1824.
Mackay, Charles, *Through the Long Day.* 2 vols. London, 1887.
MacMillan, Dougald (ed.), *Catalogue of the Larpent Plays in the Huntington Library.* San Marino, Calif., 1939.
Massett, Stephen C., *Drifting About.* New York, 1863.
Mathews, Mrs. A., *Memoirs of Charles Mathews, Comedian.* 3 vols. London, 1839.
Matthews, Brander, *Rip Van Winkle Goes to the Play, and Other Essays.* New York, 1926.
— »The Rise and Fall of Negro Minstrelsy.» *Scribner's,* LVII, 754—759 (1915).
— , and Hutton, Laurence, *Actors and Actresses of Great Britain and the United States.* 5 vols. New York, 1886.
Mayhew, Henry, *London Labour and the London Poor.* 4 vols. London, 1862.
Mencken, Henry L., *The American Language.* New York, 1937.
— *The American Language. Supplement I.* New York, 1948.
Mesick, Jane Louise, *The English Traveller in America, 1785—1835.* New York, 1922.
Mitford, Mary Russell (ed.), *Stories of American Life by American Writers.* 3 vols. London, 1830.
Morley, Henry, *Journal of a London Playgoer.* London, 1866.
Musser, Paul H., *James Nelson Barker, 1784—1858.* Philadelphia, 1929.
Newlin, Claude M. (ed.), *Modern Chivalry by Hugh Henry Brackenridge.* New York, 1937.
Nicoll, Allardyce, *British Drama.* London, 1949.
— *A History of Late Eighteenth Century Drama.* London, 1927.
— A History of Early Nineteenth Century Drama. 2 vols. Cambridge, 1930.
— A History of Late Nineteenth Century Drama. 2 vols. Cambridge, 1946.
Opinions of the British Press on the Performances of George H. Hill. New York, 1837.
The Origin of Jim Crow. London, 1837.
Paskman, Dailey, and Spaeth, Sigmund, *»Gentlemen, Be Seated!» A Parade of the Old-Time Minstrels.* Garden City, N.Y., 1928.

Paul, Howard (ed.), *The Book of American Songs.* London, 1857.
Pemberton, T. E., *A Memoir of E. A. Sothern.* London, 1890.
The Player's Library: The Catalogue of the Library of the British Drama League. London, 1950.
Playfair, Nigel, *The Lyric, Hammersmith.* London, 1925.
Pope, W. Macqueen, *Theatre Royal Drury Lane.* London, 1945.
Power, Tyrone, *Impressions of America during the Years 1833, 1834, and 1835.* 3 vols. London, 1836.
*Quinn, Arthur Hobson, *A History of American Drama from the Beginning to the Civil War.* New York, 1943.
* — *A History of American Drama from the Civil War to the Present Day.* New York, 1936.
— *Representative American Plays.* New York, 1917.
— (ed.), *The Literature of the American People.* New York, 1951.
Reed, Perley Isaac, *The Realistic Presentation of American Characters in Native American Plays prior to 1870.* Columbus, Ohio, 1918.
*Reynolds, Ernest, *Early Victorian Drama, 1830—1870.* Cambridge, 1936.
Reynolds, Harry, *Minstrel Memories — The Story of Burnt Cork Minstrelsy in Great Britain from 1836 to 1927.* London, 1928.
Rourke, Constance, *American Humor.* New York, 1931.
— *Davy Crockett.* New York, 1934.
Rusk, Ralph L., *The Literature of the Middle-Western Frontier.* 2 vols. New York, 1925.
Sadleir, Michael, *Yellow-Backs.* London, 1938.
Sala, George Augustus, *My Diary in America.* London, 1865.
Saxe-Wyndham, H., *The Annals of Covent Garden.* London, 1906.
Shawe-Taylor, Desmond, *Covent Garden.* London and New York, 1948.
Sherson, Errol, *London's Lost Theatres.* London, 1926.
Smalley, Donald (ed.), *Domestic Manners of the Americans by Frances Trollope.* New York, 1949.
*Spiller, Robert E.; Thorp, Willard; Johnson, Thomas H.; and Canby, Henry Seidel (eds.), *Literary History of the United States.* 3 vols. New York, 1948.
Stern, Alfred, *Philosophie du rire et des pleurs.* Paris, 1949.
Stowe, Charles E., *Life of Harriet Beecher Stowe.* Boston and New York, 1889.
Tandy, Jennette, *Cracker-Box Philosophers in American Humor and Satire.* New York, 1925.
de Tocqueville, Alexis — see Bradley, Phillips.
Tolles, Winton, *Tom Taylor and Victorian Drama.* New York, 1940.
Trent, William P.; Erskine, John; Sherman, Stuart P.; and Van Doren, Carl, *Cambridge History of American Literature.* 4 vols. New York, 1917—1921.
Trollope, Frances — see Smalley, Donald.
Uncle Tom in England; or a Proof that Black's White. London, 1852.
Wallack, Lester, *Memories of Fifty Years.* New York, 1889.
*Watson, Bradlee, *Sheridan to Robertson.* London, 1926.
Wiley, C. H., *Life in the South.* London, 1852.
Wittke, Carl F., *Tambo and Bones: A History of the American Minstrel Stage.* Chapel Hill, N. C., 1930.

INDEX OF PERSONS AND PLAY TITLES

Additional Scenes to Our American Cousin 129n
Alabama, The 135
Allen, Andrew Jackson 77
Alzine ou les Américains 111n
America 25
America; or, the Colonists 26
American Heroine, The 24
American in England, The 118—119
American Indian, The 25
American Indian; or, Virtues of Nature, The 24
American Notes 39, 94
American Slaves 24
Americans, The 26
André 25
Arnold, Samuel James 26, 28n, 30

Bacon, Jas. 24
Banks of the Hudson, The 48—49, 59, 75
Barber, J. H. 25, 99
Barker, James Nelson 25, 26
Barnett, Morris 68n
Basket Maker, The 27
Battle of Lake Champlain, The 14
Beazley, Samuel 50n
Beckett, Gilbert à 82
Beecher Stowe, Harriet 111—114, 117, 141
Behn, Aphra 22
Belle Sauvage, La 132
Bergson, Henri 148, 150, 154
Bernard, William Bayle 53, 55, 56, 56n, 57, 61, 66, 70, 72, 140, 146
Betty, H. 117

Beverly, H. R. 20n, 135
Bickerstaffe, Isaac 14n
Bird, Robert Montgomery 16n
Black and White 137
Black God of Love, The 79
Blacksmith of Ghent, The 15
Blockade, The 12
Blockade of Boston, The 24
Block-Heads, The 12
Bloomer, Mrs. Amelia Jenks 106
Bloomer Costume!, The 106—107
Bloomer Wives, The 106n
Bloomerism; or, Follies of the Day 106n
Bloomers, The 106n
Bone Squash Diabolo 78
Booth, John Wilkes 20
Boucicault, Dion 57—58, 120, 124, 124n, 134, 137
»Boz« — see Dickens, Charles
Brackenridge, Hugh Henry 31, 36
Braham, John 26
Breck, Charles 25
Breitmann, Hans 38, 150
British Captain, The 27
Brougham, John 132
Brown, Joe 88
Browne, Charles Farrar — see Ward, Artemus
Bryant, William Cullen 61n
Bryce, James 143
Bryant, Jerry 88
Buckley, James, Bishop, Swaine, and Fred 87
Buckstone, John Baldwin 19, 46, 55, 57, 128, 129, 131n

Bunkum Muller 130n
Burke, Charles 56, 57
Burgoyne, John 12, 24
Byron, George Gordon 28, 135n
Byron, Henry J. 130

Campbell's Minstrels 88
Carr, Mrs. 24
Caspar Hauser 69
Celeste, Mme. 108
Chatterton, F. B. 17n, 19
Christy Minstrels, The 89
Clarke, John Sleeper 138
Clemens, Samuel Langhorne — see Twain, Mark
Cockins, George 24
Cocknies in California 100
Coke, E. T. 63—64
Coleridge, Samuel Taylor 74
Coleridge-Taylor, Samuel 138
Colleen Bawn 57n, 134
Collins, Miss 116
Collins, Wilkie 137
Colman, George 20n, 24n, 43, 50, 62, 104
Colour'd Commotion, A 88
Confederate's Daughter, The 135
Congo Melodists, The 87
Conquest of Canada, The 24
Contrast, The 11, 12, 24, 63, 102, 107n
Cooke, T. P. 46
Cooper, James Fenimore 22, 49, 53n, 98, 111
Courtney, John 112n
Cowardy, Cowardy, Custard 80
Coyne, J. Stirling 100
Crockett, David 12, 13, 46, 61n, 68, 69
Crockett, Sally 14
Cruikshank, George 129
Customs of the Country 120

Daly, Augustin 138
Daly, Miss 74
Daniel Boone 16n
David Garrick 130n
Davidge, Mrs. 48
Davis, Bancroft 127n

Davis, Henry 59
Dibdin, Charles 24
Dibdin, Thomas John 23, 26, 48, 59, 75
Dickens, Charles 28, 39, 94, 98, 100, 143, 153
Dooley, Mr. 38
Down East Bargain, A 69
Downing, Jack 68, 69, 125
Dunlap, William 24, 25
Durivage, F. A. 134n
Dowton, W. 50

English Sailors in America, The 23
Emigrant's Daughter, The 59, 75
Ethiopian Serenaders, The 83, 87—88
Every Man in His Humour 70
Eyre, Edmund John 25

Fair American, The 24
Fashion 102—106, 140—141
Father; or, American Shandyism, The 24
Father of an Only Child, The 24
Fechter, Charles 137
Fink, Mike 13, 46
Fitzball, Edward 111n, 112n, 113n
Flaherty, Bernard 77
Flight to America, A 72, 79—80
Florence, Mr. and Mrs. William Jermyn 119—122, 141, 143
Foreign Prince, The 80
Forest Rose, The 107—109, 141
Forrest, Edwin 14, 77, 100
Fraud and Its Victims 124n
French Flogged, The 23

Garrick, David 27, 104
Garrick Club, The 65
Garrick; or, Acting in Earnest 138n
George, G. H. 88
Gillray, James 129
Gladstone, Charlotte B. 78
Gladstone, William Ewart 88
Godfrey, Thomas 9n
Goethe, Johann Wolfgang von 17n
Goldfinch 29
Graupner, Gottlieb 14, 77
Gunmaker of Moscow, The 15

Hackett, James H. 47n, 49—52, 56n, 57, 61, 63—65, 66, 71, 97, 100, 111, 122, 139, 140, 143, 146, 147
Hague, Sam 88
Hague's Georgia Minstrels 88
Haliburton, Thomas Chandler 134n, 146, 147, 150. See also Slick, Sam
Hall, Mr. 82
Halleck, Fitz-Greene 61n
Hammond, Mr. 74, 75
Harlequin and Yankee Doodle 100
Harper, Ned 80, 87
Hermann, Charles 113n
Hiawatha 138
Higgie, Thomas 95n
Hill, George Handel 66—71, 75, 97, 98, 99, 100, 108n, 109, 111, 122, 140, 143, 146, 147
Hollingshead, John 91
Holmes, Oliver Wendell 125
Honeymoon, The 105
Hood, Tom 59
Hoosier, The 16n
Horn, Eph 88
Hoskins, Mr. 116
Hough, Mrs. 134, 141
Howard, Bronson 138
Humphreys, David 43n
Hunter of the West, The 16n
Huzzah for the Boys of the West 16n

Idiot of Normandy, The 15
Incle and Jarico 24n
Indian Princess, The 26
Ingomar the Idiotic 138n
Irish Assurance 120—121, 122
Iroquois; or, the Canadian Basket-Maker 27
Irving, Washington 15, 52, 98, 139, 150

James, Henry 21n, 152n
Jarvis, John Wesley 31, 34, 36
Jefferson, Joseph 56, 57—58, 60, 78n, 127, 140, 143
Jim Crow in His New Place 80
Job Fox; or, the Yankee Valet 75—76
Jonathan in England 42—44, 47, 50—51

Jonathan; or, the Man of Two Masters 99
Jones, J. S. 136
Jonson, Ben 70

Keeley, Mrs. 116
Keene, Laura 127n
Kemble, John R. 89
Kentuckian, The 16n, 20, 61—65, 140
Kentucky Rifle, The 16n
Kerr, John 56n
King, M. P. 26
Knight and the Sprite, The 82
Knight, Sarah Kemble 149
Koningsmarke 72
Kotzebue, August von 17n

Lacy, Thomas Hailes 95n, 124n
Lady of Lyons, The 130n
Lantum Serenaders, The 88
Last Slave, The 20n, 135
Latest from New York 123
Leah, the Jewish Maiden 138n
Leap for Liberty, A 134
Lebatt, Miss 116
Lee, Nelson 100
Leicester 25
Leland, Charles Godfrey 125. See also Breitmann, Hans.
Leland, Oliver S. 102
Lemon, Mark 82, 112n
Leon, Francis 88
Leslie, John 111n
Lewes, George Henry 18, 103n
Life in America 60
Life in Cincinnati 16n
Life in London 22n
Lincoln, Abraham 20, 128n, 135
Lion of the West, The 13, 16n, 46, 60, 139, 140
Logan, Cornelius Ambrosius 95, 96, 136, 140
Long Finn, The 59, 72
Longfellow, Henry Wadsworth 138
Longstreet, Augustus Baldwin 35
Lord Dundreary Married and Done for 130

Lowell, James Russell 125
Lucifer Matches 120
Ludlow, Noah 12
Lutz, John 127n

Macaulay, Thomas Babington 28
Mackay, Charles 90
Macready, William 100
Magawisca 111
Main Street, Louisville 16n
Manfred 135n
Massett, Stephen 22n
Marble, Danforth 97—99, 100, 111, 122, 140, 143, 146, 147
Marryatt, Frederick 98
Martin Chuzzlewit 95
Mathews, Charles 5, 27—47, 50, 51, 65, 66, 68, 69, 72, 77—78, 100, 111, 139, 143, 146, 147, 150
Mathews, Charles James 128
Mathews in America 33—42
du Maurier, George 153
Mead, T. 116
Mephistopheles 79
Midsummer Night's Dream, A 127n
Militia Muster, The 35, 50, 51
Mischievous Annie 120
Mitchell, William 22n
Mitford, Mary Russell 46n
Moncrieff, William Thomas 22n, 26, 44—47, 52n, 60n, 72—73, 139—140, 146
Monsieur Mallét 36, 45—47, 52n, 59, 60n, 72, 75, 128, 139
Morley, Henry 129
Mowatt Ritchie, Anna Cora 102, 103, 104, 106, 140
Murdock, J. 14, 25
My American Aunt 130
Mysteries of an American City, The 89

Neal, John 10, 39n
Newcombe, Miss 116
New Notions 70—71, 140
New Way to Win Hearts, A 14
Nick of the Woods 16n
Noah, Mordecai 11
Noble Heart, The 103n

Norton, Wash 88
Nothing to Nurse 123

Obi; or, Three-Finger'd Jack 14
O'Keeffe, John 27
Oroonoko 14n, 25, 77
Othello 14n
Our American Cousin 57n, 125—131, 141
Our Gal 120
Owens, John E. 136—137, 141, 143
Oxenford, John 130

Padlock, The 14n
Patch, Sam 99n
Paul, Howard 90—91, 118
Paul Jones 23, 48
Paul; or, the Fortunate Slave 118
Paulding, James Kirke 13, 46, 60, 72, 139, 140
Peake, Richard Brinsley 43, 44, 50, 59, 75, 139, 146
Pedlar, The 16n
Peel, Robert 88
People's Lawyer, The 136—137, 141
Peters, William Cumming 78
Phillips, T. F. 59
Pilot, The 53n
Pioneers, The 49
Pioneers; or, the Maid of the War Path 131
Pitt, C. D. 112n, 115
Pixérecourt, Guilbert de 17n
Pocahontas; or, the Gentle Savage 132
Pocahontas; or, the Indian Princess 26
Poe, Edgar Allan 66n, 102n
Ponteach 23
Poor of Liverpool, The 124
Poor of New York, The 124n
Power, Tyrone 50, 64, 74
Prince of Parthia, The 9n
Prince, Oliver H. 35
Purse; or, the American Tar, The 15
Purse; or, the Benevolent Tar, The 15

Ranger, Edward 118—119
Raymor & Pierce's Christy Minstrels 88

Red John the Daring 132
Red Rover, The 111
Rede, William Leman 60, 72, 79
Relief of Lucknow, The 134
Rice, Thomas Dartmouth 14, 57n, 72, 78—82, 83 ff., 90, 94, 140
Rip Van Winkle 15, 52—60, 72, 139—140
Robinson Crusoe 14, 14n
Rogers, Robert 23
Royal Original Christy's Minstrels, The 89

Sala, George Augustus 77, 88, 91, 125
Sam Patch the Jumper 99
Sam's Arrival 130
Schiller, Friedrich von 17n
School for Scandal, The 105
Seamon and Somers, minstrels 89
Selby, Mr. 116
Sheridan, Richard Brinsley 104, 105
Shoemaker of Toulouse, The 15
Sidney, W. W. 59
Silsbee, Josh 106, 108—111, 122, 141, 143, 147
Simpson 27
Simpson, Alexander 66n
Slave, The 25
Slick, Sam 13, 38, 73n, 97, 98, 146, 147
Smiles and Tears; or, the Widow's Stratagem 26
Smith, James 39
Smith, Sol 14, 77
Somerset, C. A. 106
Sons of Columbia, The 134
Sothern, Edward Askew 127 ff., 130
Sotherne, Thomas 14n
Southerner Just Arrived, A 134—135
Spectre Bridegroom, The 52n
Speculation 70n
Spitfire, The 135
Stirling, Edward 80, 94, 140, 146
Stone, John A. 61n, 63
Strachan, John 59
Streets of London, The 124n
Strong, Paschal 29
Sutton, Charles 89

Sweatnam, Willis P. 89
Sweeney, Joe 80, 87
Sylvester Daggerwood 49

Tailor in Distress, The 14, 77
Talfourd, T. N. 100
Tarnation Strange 73—75, 140
Tayleure, Mrs. 57
Taylor, Tom 112n, 113, 114, 125, 127n, 141
Tears and Smiles 25
Thackeray, William Makepeace 91, 153
Tobin, John 105
Tocqueville, Alexis de 143
Tonson 29
Tree, Ellen 74
Trip to Paris, The 29
Triumphs of Love, The 14
Trollope, Mrs. Frances 21n, 62, 64n, 65, 98, 105, 143
Trust, The 25
Twain, Mark 5, 101, 138
Two Apprentices, The 137
Two Bloomers, The 106n
Tyler, Royall 11, 12, 24, 63, 102, 107n

Uncle Jonathan; or, Independence 47—48
Uncle Remus 38
Uncle Tom's Cabin 15, 22—23, 60, 88, 109, 111—117, 134, 141

Vermont Wool-Dealer, The 96—98, 140
Vestris, Mme. 19, 128
Victoria, Queen of England 17, 88, 89
Vincent, Eliza 112n
Vintagers, The 25
Virginia Minstrels, The 87
Virginian Mummy, The 79
Wags, The 25
Wallack, Lester 127n
War-Whoop, The 26
Ward, Artemus 11, 89, 124, 138
Ward, Nathaniel 149
Watkins, H. 132
Washington, George 77
Webb, Charles 95n

Webster, Benjamin 19, 57
Westmore, Alphonso 16n
White, John Blake 11
White, Charles 77
Who Wants a Guinea? 50
Wife for a Day, A 109
Wigwam, The 99
Wild, George 116
Wildfire, Nimrod — see *Kentuckian, The*
Williams, Mr. and Mrs. Barney 120, 122—123, 141
Wolcott, C. M. 123
Woodworth, Samuel 107, 141

Yankee Courtship 123
Yankee Doodle upon His Little Pony 100
Yankee Housekeeper, The 119—122
Yankee Land 95—96, 99, 140
Yankee Legacy, The 132—133, 141
Yankee Notes 80, 94—95, 140
Yankee Pedlar, The 66—69, 109, 140
Yankee Stories 49
Yankey in England, The 43
Yates, Frederick Henry 46, 55, 57, 72
Young, H. 112n
Young Actress, The 120